5679498
355.332.

BOND

The Victorian
Army and the
Staff College,
1854 - 1914

HERTFORDSHIRE COUNTY LIBRARY

This book is due for return on or before the date shown. You
may extend its loan by bringing the book to the library or,
of return,
e, and the

REN
INF
AT

CENTRAL RESOURCES
LIBRARY
01707-281530

L.32A

8/12

Please renew/return this item by the last date shown.

So that your telephone call is charged at local rate,
please call the numbers as set out below:

	From Area codes 01923 or 0208:	From the rest of Herts:
Renewals:	01923 471373	01438 737373
Enquiries:	01923 471333	01438 737333
Minicom:	01923 471599	01438 737599

L32b

2 4 NOV 1999

1 4 JUN 2002
2 5 NOV 2003

L 33

D1615025

THE
VICTORIAN ARMY
AND THE
STAFF COLLEGE
1854–1914

by the same author
VICTORIAN MILITARY CAMPAIGNS (ed.)

THE
VICTORIAN ARMY
AND THE
STAFF COLLEGE
1854–1914

Brian Bond

EYRE METHUEN
LONDON

First published 1972
by Eyre Methuen Ltd
11 New Fetter Lane, EC4P 4EE
© 1972 Brian Bond
Printed in Great Britain by
Cox & Wyman Ltd
Fakenham, Norfolk
SBN 413 27630 9

COUNTY
COPY

HERTFORDSHIRE
COUNTY LIBRARY

355.332

5679498

to the memory of my mother

OLIVE BESSIE SARTIN

Contents

Illustrations

TABLES

ACKNOWLEDGEMENTS FOR THE ILLUSTRATIONS

All the illustrations are reproduced by kind permission of Maj.-Gen. A. M. Taylor M.C., Commandant of the Staff College, except for the following: Capt. J. H. Lefroy (photograph in Royal Artillery Society Proceedings, January 1967, from a portrait by Berthon in Toronto); British infantry at Magersfontein and 'The Loss of the Convoy at Waterval Drift' (*With the Flag to Pretoria*); the Staff College, Quetta, and 'The First V.C. of the European War' (National Army Museum, the latter on loan to the Staff College). Photographs of Wavell as a G.S.O.3. in 1914 from J. Connell, *Wavell: Scholar and Soldier* (Collins), and of Capt. E. F. Calthrop from F. S. G. Piggott, *Broken Thread* (Gale & Polden). Cartoon, 'Our Future Staff' from *Punch*, 5 March 1859.

Acknowledgements

I should like first to acknowledge my indebtedness to John Shy, Neil Summerton, John Gooch and John Terraine for taking the trouble to read individual chapters in typescript and giving me the benefit of their expert knowledge. Special thanks are due to Doctors Gooch and Summerton for generously allowing me to draw extensively on their unpublished theses in my Chapters 7 and 8 respectively.

Among many people who kindly allowed me to borrow and quote from private papers in their possession I am particularly grateful to Mrs Evelyn Arthur (*Memoirs* of Sir John Burnett-Stuart); Viscount Esher (Esher *Journals* and *Correspondence*); Mrs A. M. B. Sandison (Edmonds *Papers*); and Maj. Cyril Wilson (*Diaries* of Sir Henry Wilson). Sir Bernard Fergusson lent me documents relating to Field-Marshal Earl Wavell's early days in the Army; and Mr J. A. P. Lefroy patiently answered my questions about the family history of Sir John Henry Lefroy.

Besides their general interest and encouragement, I am enormously indebted to the late Sir Basil and Lady Liddell Hart for allowing me to use Sir Basil's library as my own. Sir Basil's death in January 1970 deprived me of the benefit of his critical comments, which would doubtless have been voluminous.

I am glad of this opportunity to say thank you to the numerous archivists and librarians whose interest, courtesy and expert assistance have brightened and lightened many hours of painstaking research. My colleague Antony Grant of the Centre for Military Archives at King's College, London, has been unfailingly helpful during the past five years; his departure to a new post in the autumn of 1971 will be a great loss to the College, as well as to me personally.

For many years Mr D. W. King and his colleagues have made it a pleasure for me to work at the Old War Office (now Central and Army) Library. Although it is invidious to mention some individuals and not others I must beg the pardon of the latter in naming Mrs G. Davies, Mr C. A. Potts, Mr J. Woods, Mr D. Bradley and Mr N. B. Leslie, all of whom have been of tremendous assistance during the long gestation of this book.

Mr Robert Mackworth-Young, the Royal Librarian, granted me access to the Royal Archives at Windsor Castle, and Miss Jane Langton and her assistants went to a great deal of trouble in searching for relevant documents for me. I should like to acknowledge the gracious permission of Her Majesty Queen Elizabeth II to consult the Royal Archives and to quote from them certain passages in the text.

Lt-Col F. W. Young and Mr Kenneth White, successive Librarians at the Staff College, made my visits to Camberley enjoyable as well as academically rewarding. I should also like to express my thanks to the staff of the National Library of Scotland, the Scottish Records Office, the Public Record Office and all the other libraries and archives which I visited in the course of writing this book.

My publishers, and others mentioned above, have saved me from many factual errors, obscurities and inconsistencies, but I alone am responsible for those that remain.

Last, but far from least, I have depended entirely on my wife Madeleine for typing and re-typing my longhand drafts. She alone knows the full cost – in many senses – of bringing this book to the point of publication.

Medmenham, Bucks, June 1971   Brian Bond

I am grateful to the following publishers and literary agents for permission to quote from books whose copyright they hold:
Edward Arnold Ltd, for *Stray Recollections* by Charles Callwell. Cassell & Co Ltd, for *The Theory and Practice of War* by Michael Howard (ed); *The Education of an Army* by Jay Luvaas; and *At G.H.Q.* by J. Charteris. William Collins, Sons and Co, Ltd, for *Wavell: Scholar and Soldier* by J. Connell; and *The Memoirs* of Field-Marshal Viscount Montgomery. Constable & Co Ltd, for *The Staff and the Staff College* by A. R. Godwin-Austen. Harrap & Co Ltd, for *Allenby: a Study in Greatness* by Sir A. Wavell. Hutchinson & Co Ltd, for *The Fire of Life* by Sir G. Barrow; *Annals of an Active Life* by Sir N. Macready; and *Haig: the Educated Soldier* by John Terraine. M.I.T. Press for *The Development of Technical Education in France 1550–1850* by F. Artz. Frederick Muller Ltd, for *Soldier True* by V. Bonham-Carter. Oxford University Press for *The Politics of the Prussian Army* by G. A. Craig; and *The British Army: Civil-Military Relations, 1885–1905* by W. S. Hamer. A. P. Watt & Son for *Sir Henry Wilson* (Volume I) by C. Callwell. Weidenfeld & Nicolson Ltd, for *Professional Men* by W. J. Reader; and *The German Officer Corps* by K. Demeter. Acknowledgement of the many other publications, to a few of which I am only slightly less indebted than to some of those mentioned above, has been made in the footnotes.

ABBREVIATIONS

p.s.c.   passed Staff College (Camberley or Quetta)

D.S.-C.   on Directing Staff at Camberley

D.S.-Q.   on Directing Staff at Quetta

C.C.   Commandant Camberley

C.Q.   Commandant Quetta

B

THE
VICTORIAN ARMY
AND THE
STAFF COLLEGE
1854-1914

Introduction

It was Michael Howard who first aroused my interest in the
Victorian Army by directing my postgraduate research towards
a reconsideration of the effects of the Cardwell reforms. Over a
decade I published a number of articles on various aspects of
military reform and edited a book entitled *Victorian Military
Campaigns*, but I wanted ultimately to write a book to illuminate
the development – truly a transformation – which took place in
the character of the British Army between the notorious debacle
in the Crimea and the dispatch of the small but highly efficient
Expeditionary Force to France in 1914. This development,
though real enough, was difficult to pin down; and I was
perplexed by the immensity of the field – in which at first very
few scholars appeared to be interested. Yet the education and
training of officers presents an admirable mirror of the professional quality of the Army, and, furthermore, the history of
the Staff College provides a reliable guide to the state of officer
education. Indeed the crucial importance of the Staff College
before the First World War lay in the fact that it was the only
institution devoted to the instruction of the future leaders of the
Army after they had been commissioned: the Imperial Defence
College and the Joint Services Staff College were as yet unheard
of.

In the Crimea era it was still fashionable to deride the
necessity for special training for the Staff, but the contribution
of the Great General Staff under von Moltke to Prussia's
dazzling victories in the 1860s ushered in a new era. In the
nineteenth century, Britain possessed no General Staff in the
German sense: if there was a 'Brain of the Army' capable of
producing a 'School of Thought' it was to be found at Camberley in the Staff College, and nowhere else.

Moreover, working at a time when the performance of British generals in the First World War was once again the subject of bitter controversy, it seemed to me somewhat unrealistic to judge the generals entirely on their achievements *during* the war without taking into account the pre-war education and training that had already to a large extent moulded their professional personalities. Whatever their limitations – and they were certainly serious – it is essential to bear in mind that French, Haig, Robertson and their fellow-generals were regarded as the *élite* of their profession in 1914; they were the outstanding products of a *system*. If criticism was to be tempered by understanding, it was necessary to take that system into account. This leads directly to a close study of the Staff College – through which nearly all the leaders of 1914 had passed – and, later, of the General Staff.

Considering the enormous importance of efficient staff work in modern warfare, it remains a field that has been badly neglected by military historians. As regards the Staff College, Camberley, apart from a booklet to mark the centenary in 1958, the only full-length history is still Maj. A. R. Godwin-Austen's *The Staff and the Staff College*, published in 1927. This lively account was the work of a graduate of the College with a good mind, a sharp pen and a delightful sense of humour. In the almost total absence of Staff College manuscript material – presumed destroyed by 'friendly' action during the First World War – I have been glad to draw on Godwin-Austen's book as a vital quarry; indeed, without it this book could hardly have been written. Why, then, did I consider it worthwhile to do so?

First, Godwin-Austen was writing primarily as a regular officer for a potentially large readership of past, present and future students of the College. Naturally he devoted a good deal of space to such matters as the history of the buildings, sporting events and festive occasions. In a deliberate attempt to lighten the narrative he occasionally, as he admits, adopted a 'flippancy of tone' which erred in the direction of irreverence. This calculated risk succeeded in the all-important respect that his book remains immensely readable, but it had the drawback of making the tone appear at times to be frivolous and even anti-intellectual. The Drag, for example, though doubtless of great social significance, was a dubious criterion by which to evaluate the professional progress of the College.

Secondly, though Godwin-Austen does attempt to cover 'the Staff' as well as the College by interspersing his narrative with summaries of campaigns, reforms and organizational changes, he is not entirely successful in placing the history of the College within the broader context of the gradual transformation of the Army. This is perhaps a roundabout way of saying that he was not a professional historian. Thus, acutely aware of the problems and pitfalls, I offer no apology for devoting considerable space to such aspects as the Cardwell reforms, the South African War, the formation of the General Staff and the opening phase of the First World War.

Thirdly, our knowledge of British military history before 1914 has been considerably extended and deepened in recent years by the work of scholars such as Jay Luvaas, Albert V. Tucker, W. S. Hamer, John Gooch and Neil Summerton. Their researches, to which my references pay grateful acknowledgement, have – I hope – given this study an extra dimension. In addition I have drawn upon unpublished sources, such as the Edmonds and Haig Papers and the Wilson Diaries, which were either not available to Godwin-Austen, or which at any rate he did not use.

Lastly, there is the matter of scholarly apparatus. Godwin-Austen largely dispensed with footnotes and included only a summary of the principal authorities used in each chapter. On the whole, in quoting and paraphrasing, he handled his sources with scrupulous care, but he has left a tedious task for anyone who wishes to check a particular reference or to pursue the subject further. In the hope that a few readers will be stimulated to extend their reading – as well as to make plain my indebtedness to others – I have given my sources in full.

CHAPTER ONE

The development of military professionalism and the rise of General Staffs in the nineteenth century

The increased interest in military education in the eighteenth century. The French Revolution underlines the importance of educated and thoroughly trained officers. How potential officers were educated in Prussia, France and Britain. Problems posed by the narrow social sector from which officers were traditionally drawn. The development of a 'professional' structure and spirit in the British Army compared with the growing civil professions. The origins and significance of the Continental General Staff system and why Britain lagged behind.

The military profession is a recent creation of modern society. 'Prior to 1800,' in the opinion of Samuel P. Huntington, 'there was no such thing as a professional officer corps. In 1900 such bodies existed in virtually all major countries.' The nineteenth century had indeed witnessed remarkable developments putting the officer's career structure on a definite basis, both as regards obtaining a commission and subsequent advancement. These developments tended to place a greater premium than hitherto on professional zeal, qualifications and length of service as against privilege stemming from aristocratic birth, influential connections or wealth. Huntington seems to assume, however, that officer corps dominated by mercenaries or aristocrats, and existing in a political context where 'interest' and privilege were enormous assets, were incapable of taking a serious (or professional) attitude to military science, education and training. There is overwhelming evidence on the contrary, to show that a passionate concern with these matters existed – particularly in France – from the earliest days of standing armies in the sixteenth century. In short, the Napoleonic era marked an important new phase, but not the origin of the concept of the army officer as a professional man.[1]

Perhaps the most important aspect of this development, which only achieved recognition in the course of the nineteenth century, was that would-be officers needed to be specially educated in military or semi-military institutions *before* obtaining a commission, whereas previously a haphazard system of apprenticeship *after* commissioning had been preferred. This radical departure from tradition (which persisted much longer in most navies) in turn raised the controversial question as to whether advanced professional education and training were desirable to qualify officers for positions in the higher command or on the staff.

Before the Napoleonic Wars armies and navies can scarcely be said to have been led by professionals as that term came to be understood in the nineteenth century. Officers were for the most part mercenaries or aristocrats: the former tended to view war as a business, the latter as a hobby. 'In place of the professional goal of expert service, the former pursued profit, the latter honour and adventure.'[2] After the Thirty Years War (1618–48), the military role of the aristocracy had increased while that of the mercenary captain declined. This was but one symptom of the consolidation of nation states whose monarchs felt the need for permanent military forces. Given the comparative poverty of national treasuries and the dreadful nature of the military trade, it was not surprising that the rank and file tended to consist of long-term 'volunteers' from the dregs of society drawn into service – and servitude – by a mixture of bribery and coercion. For their officers the monarchs relied heavily upon the feudal nobility to whom they offered social and political privileges in return for onerous and financially unremunerative service in arms.

Thus the military forces became the property of the Crown rather than of more or less independent individuals. The officers obtained a permanent employer and – more important as a precondition of professionalism – a permanent focus of loyalty. In the course of the eighteenth century, excepting in the 'scientific corps' of artillery and engineers, the aristocracy, and more especially the lesser and often impoverished nobility, attained a near monopoly of the officer ranks in the European armies.[3] 'The *noblesse* wanted a rewarding life in the open air consonant with their conceptions of honour; the king wanted a loyal officer corps. The *bourgeoisie* generally was more keen on the ring of coin than the roar of cannon.'[4] It is of course dangerous to generalize about the attitude of the *bourgeoisie* since there were national variations in the status of commissioned service. In Austria, for example, being an army officer in the eighteenth century – at least in the lower ranks – carried lower status than in England.

The social composition of the eighteenth-century officer corps to some extent militated against the development of professionalism. In the first place aristocratic birth was virtually a *sine qua non* to obtain entry to all but technical arms. Thus in Prussia Frederick William I compelled the nobility to serve in the Army, while his son Frederick the Great, after having been obliged to admit middle-class officers during the intensive warfare between 1740 and 1763, proceeded to purge the officer corps in the firm belief that only the aristocracy possessed to the full the military virtues of honour, loyalty and courage.

This domination of the Army by the upper classes was reinforced and perpetuated by offering them a near monopoly of places at the cadet academies, several of which were founded in the mid eighteenth century. The French École Militaire, for example, was founded in 1751 expressly to serve the needs of sons of officers and the poorer nobility.

'The regulations organizing the new institution provided for the education of 500 nobles, preference being given to those without fortunes; the purposes of the school were charitable as well as educational. Boys might enter between the ages of eight and thirteen and might stay on until the age of twenty. Besides having to prove their nobility for four generations on the father's side, applicants had only to know how to read and write.'[5]

The French Government blatantly used military commissions as outdoor relief for the aristocracy, with the result that
by 1775 there were nominally 60,000 officers – only about one
in six actually serving – as against 180,000 other ranks. On the
eve of the French Revolution, despite drastic reductions, there
were still about 6,333 nobles and only 1,845 commoners and
1,100 soldiers of fortune.[6] In the Prussian service before the
catastrophic defeat at Jena in 1806 there were only 700 non-
nobles in an officer corps of over 7,000.[7]

Not surprisingly, wealth, birth and interest played a major
part in determining advancement to high rank. Except in the
artillery and engineers, the British Army retained the system of
purchasing commissions up to and including the rank of
lieutenant-colonel until 1871. A less institutionalized system of
purchase also existed in the Austrian Army up to 1857.[8] Purchase was ended in France before the French Revolution
chiefly because it handicapped the poorer country nobles
rather than because it prevented recognition of professional
merit. Indeed, the purchase system tended to discriminate
against poor nobility in favour of affluent *bourgeoisie*. Derisory
standards of pay and the absence of regularized pension schemes
also severely restricted the social sector from which officers
could be drawn.

Although military academies began to spring up in the
eighteenth century, the level of professional education was low,
and they seldom fulfilled the hopes of their founders. This was
so largely because in their administration, governments were
attempting to combine two conflicting ideas: that of educating
a large number of poor nobles and that of advancing technical
education. As to the former motive, a French historian has
bluntly described Louis XV's École Militaire as '*une fondation
d'intérêt philanthropique plus encore que d'intérêt militaire* . . .'[9] A
further obstacle to the development of the academies lay in the
fact that there were other and easier ways to obtain military
commissions and advancement. This was true of Prussia, where
Frederick the Great founded the Ritter Akademie (significantly
also known as the Académie des Nobles) in 1765 to provide an
education for the diplomatic service as well as the Army.

Although the King himself supervised instruction and regarded the school as a proving ground for promising young officers, it was handicapped by the fact that commissions could be obtained at the age of twelve or thirteen. In France and Britain too it was quite common for young boys – and even occasionally females – to obtain commissions by purchase.[10]

An additional complication was that the new military schools tended to be more concerned with instilling certain values and behaviour in very young boys than with military instruction as such. Hence there arose a chronic debate as to what, beyond regimental drill, military education ought to be. The French, from 1751 onwards, laid heavy stress on mathematics, beyond any practical needs of future infantry officers, for its effect in developing and sharpening the intellect. Scharnhorst, the outstanding member of the Prussian military reform movement from 1806 till his death in 1813, shared this view which was to exert widespread and long-lasting effects on military education. For example, higher mathematics played a disproportionately large part in the syllabus of the British Staff College until well into the second half of the nineteenth century.[11]

Quite separate schools existed to train technically proficient officers for the artillery and engineers. Since what military science there was related chiefly to these arms, it was in the engineering schools that the most strictly professional education could be obtained. The French founded an artillery school at Douai as early as 1679, and an engineering school at Mézières in 1749. Prussia's engineering school dated from 1706. The Royal Military Academy at Woolwich – significantly known as 'The Shop' – was founded in 1741 to provide a gentlemanly and technical education for both engineers and artillery. Although the instruction provided was better than nothing, neither the cadets' military knowledge nor their discipline achieved a high standard in the Academy's first sixty years. Even the passing-out examination instituted in 1764 was dropped on the outbreak of war in 1793.[12]

If the term is employed loosely, 'military staffs' can be traced back to the earliest recorded warfare. Indeed 'when some unknown warrior chief asked help or advice from one of his co-belligerents, military history saw the first functioning of the military staff'.[13] However, until the advent of more complex warfare in the late eighteenth century, specialist staff training and organization were of permanent importance only in logistics. Consequently the key figure in the early staffs was the Quartermaster General – a title which would later appear anomalous when revived by Germany for its operational chief of staff. With few exceptions, then, the pre-French Revolutionary Staff had little to do with military operations and consequently occupied a lowly status in the eyes of commanding generals. France was exceptional in possessing a truly modern general staff, organized by Lt-Gen. Pierre Bourcet between 1766 and 1771 and revived after 1783.[14] Britain was more typical in having no specialist training and no permanent staff organization before the Napoleonic wars. She was highly exceptional in delaying the creation of a regular general staff until 1906.

The French Revolution and the Napoleonic wars, indeed, brought to a head a number of factors which, already before 1789, had begun to put a premium on greater professionalism in the leadership of armed forces in peace and war. In the first place, standing armies were becoming larger so that the individual commander, however brilliant, was unable any longer to maintain personal control in battle: greater responsibility and initiative devolved upon junior commanders. Moreover, even before the injection of ideology and mass enthusiasm in the French Revolutionary wars, improvements in communications and the destructive power of weapons were making warfare more intensive and potentially decisive as an instrument of policy. Above all, armies and navies were becoming sophisticated organizations requiring a multiplicity of experts, as exemplified in the combatant arms by the differentiation of the cavalry into heavy and light regiments, dragoons and hussars, and in the infantry by the emergence of specially trained skirmishers and light infantry units.[15] It became increasingly difficult for the officer to remain competent in all branches of war; moreover the politician and the policeman were beginning to be regarded as specialists in the control of violence by means quite different from the soldier.

Clearly, the growth of nation states also provided a strong impetus to military professionalism. National treasuries provided the necessary wealth to maintain large standing armies while political events, such as the dismemberment of Poland, provided irrefutable evidence of the likely fate of nations which could not defend themselves. The rate of advance of military professionalism was closely related in each country to the degree to which national security was felt to be threatened. Even so it was usually only after a disastrous defeat that governments were prepared to initiate drastic military reforms. Thus, for example, Prussia's emergence as the greatest military power in Europe owed its origins to the reforms following defeat and humiliation in 1806. The quality of the French Revolutionary armies owed a great deal to the extensive military reforms after 1763. France again overhauled her military institutions after 1815 and 1870, Britain after 1856 and 1902, and Austria after 1866.

The modern nation-states system also stimulated professionalism in another way. A professional officer corps must be imbued with a sense of service to the nation. It is a great advantage if the officer's loyalty can focus on a single authority, most obviously a sovereign ruler. 'Where there are competing authorities, or competing ideas as to what ought to be the authority, professionalism becomes difficult if not impossible to achieve.'[16] Here lay one great advantage for Prussia (and later the German Empire) over France between 1815 and 1914.

Huntington has suggested a close link between the introduction of mass conscription and the growth of professionalism. In his view amateur officer corps had been feasible in the eighteenth century only because the rank and file were long-service professionals who knew their trade. After 1815 the continued practice – with varying degrees of thoroughness – of relying upon 'civilians in uniform' demanded greater professional competence on the part of the officers. Certainly the connection appears to hold good for Prussia, which retained the most rigorous system of universal conscription and also developed the most professional officer corps in the second half of the nineteenth century. Gen. Sir John Hackett has pointed out, however, that the thesis is far harder to sustain from a study of the military history of Britain and the United States. Recent experience of national service also underlines Gen. Hackett's point that in some respects conscription may exert an unfavourable influence on a professional officer corps. In part the disagreement may lie in the interpretation of the term 'professionalism' – Huntington himself is critical of writers who exaggerate the importance of 'the armed horde' – but until further research has been done, it seems safer to suggest that Prussia's early development of a highly proficient officer corps owed more to her total strategic and political environment than to the particular demands of her recruitment policy.[17]

Though civilians frequently pay lip-service to military expertise, it is difficult to grasp imaginatively that the management of violence ideally requires the officer's dedicated attention throughout his career. Not only has the officer to master the art of warfare which is constantly evolving; he is also dealing continuously with people. Above all, broad and deep general knowledge is not just a bonus useful for a top-level commander; it is an integral professional qualification since the organization and application of armed force is closely related to the whole cultural pattern of society. There was, however, great uncertainty about the *nature* of military expertise and how it was best acquired: in the other emergent professions the body of expert knowledge to be mastered was more easily identified.

The development of professionalism, embracing expertise, a sense of responsibility and a corporate spirit,[18] is most clearly observed in the conditions of entry to, and initial education for, commissioned rank, in the systems of promotion and advancement, and in the higher education of officers. How do these aspects of the officers' career structure compare in the experience of Prussia, France and Britain?

Three main stages are discernible in the struggle to secure professional standards at the initial entry to commissioned rank. The first problem was to break the monopoly of wealth, birth

and interest and eventually remove such non-professional considerations altogether. Secondly, to impose certain basic tests of
professional competence and training. Thirdly, to require a
liberal or gentlemanly education which should be acquired in
civil academies *before* undertaking specifically professional education.

Prussia evolved a complicated procedure which managed to
combine rigorous educational standards with the preservation
of aristocratic – or at least gentlemanly – traditions. The first
task of the would-be officer was to gain a nomination by
the colonel of a regiment. Next, provided he had achieved the
appropriate school-leaving certificate, he would serve in the
ranks for at least six months. After this basic military training
he could become a 'Sword Knot ensign' (*Portepeefähnrich*), in
which rank he would undergo about nine months of professional
training at one of the divisional War Schools before taking
a special qualifying examination in military subjects. Even
this was not the last hurdle, for it was necessary for the
young ensign to be formally approved by the officers of the
regiment. Thus it remained possible to exclude undesirable
officers, however well qualified, and there can be no doubt that
this safeguard was exercised in the more glamorous regiments.

Since few of the poorer nobility who provided the backbone
of the Prussian officer corps could afford to send their sons to
the public *gymnasien* (or grammar schools), the War Ministry
maintained special cadet schools which combined military discipline with an inferior education in liberal arts subjects. As the
standard of the preliminary examination in general knowledge
was steadily raised, the cadet schools began to lose headway to
the *gymnasien*. Between 1856 and 1870 the numbers who had
passed through the *gymnasien* increased fourfold (of course the
Army as a whole also expanded considerably after 1866), but
significantly a large proportion of these went into the scientific
corps.[19] By 1856, when the War Schools (or divisional schools)
began to be reorganized and expanded, the entry system had
developed to the point when a good general education could be
assumed for all officer candidates. The War Schools were

henceforth able to concentrate on practical professional instruction, omitting even mathematics and foreign languages from their courses. British observers were deeply impressed with the lack of emphasis on competition compared with France: 'the object seems to be, not to establish an accurate *comparison* of the educational attainments of a number of individuals, but to form a *general estimate* of the abilities, character, and military capacity of each ... But the most remarkable feature ... is the care bestowed upon the higher objects of education, upon forming and disciplining the mind and encouraging habits of reflection.'[20]

In France, the Revolution swept away the aristocracy's virtual monopoly of entry to the officer corps and – despite strong pressure for a reversal of policy at the Restoration – it was not restored. Even more than in Prussia, French officers were expected to have gone through a normal secondary education in civil schools before commencing their professional instruction. Only the Prytanée Militaire, founded in 1800 and since 1808 situated at La Flèche, continued to exist as a preparatory military school for officers' sons. France differed sharply from both Prussia and Britain in that, as a consequence of legislation by War Minister Marshal Gouvion Saint-Cyr, in 1817–18, some two-thirds of the officers of the artillery and engineers were recruited from pupils of the École Polytechnique (founded in 1794), while in the Line about two-thirds were promoted from the ranks and only one-third had gone through St Cyr (founded in 1803). Very few of the ex-rankers rose above the rank of captain.[21]

Competition was the keynote at all levels of French military education, and this was especially true for entry into and graduation from the Polytechnique and St Cyr. The former in particular was recognized as the world's outstanding technical school and was imitated in many countries including Russia and the United States. Its students were mostly middle-class young men struggling to obtain a coveted position in the public services. Every successful candidate was entitled to partial or entire support by the State depending on his means. In 1857 not less than a third of the students at each was still financed by the State. An official British study group of 1857 carried away the impression that each year the thirty or forty ablest graduates from the Polytechnique invariably opted for the Civil Service, so that although military education was comparatively democratic, the Army did not succeed in getting the best brains of the country. They also regarded as a defect 'the exclusively mathematical spirit' encouraged at the Polytechnique. On the other hand, an American, Henry Barnard, writing about the Polytechnique early in the Second Empire, placed the State services selected by the students in the following order: roads, bridges and mines; then munitions, naval architecture, army engineering, artillery, general staff, hydrological corps, tobacco administration, telegraph, general navy; and last, naval artillery.[22]

In Britain, with the exception of the Ordnance Corps, wealth and influence continued to play an important part in securing a commission until 1871, when the system of purchase was eventually abolished. Before that the first major inroad into aristocratic privilege had come with the foundation of the Royal Military College in 1802, since free commissions were in principle available for successful graduates who wished to enter the infantry or cavalry.[23] Nevertheless purchase remained the usual method of entry into the officer corps; for example, of 4,003 first appointments to the Army between 1860 and 1867, 3,167 were by purchase and only 836 without.[24] The Duke of Cambridge was merely echoing the Duke of Wellington and a wide spectrum of conservative military and political opinion when he insisted that, in contrast to Prussia, 'the British officer should be a gentleman first and an officer second'. By the 1800s, then, Britain possessed adequate institutions for preliminary professional education for commissioned service in both the Army and the Navy.[25] But the majority of young men continued to enter directly into their Army commissions, while the Navy – despite the existence of the Naval Academy – continued to 'catch 'em young', enlisting future officers between the ages of twelve and fourteen. Moreover, down to the Crimean War, the education provided at Sandhurst, and to a slightly lesser degree at Woolwich, resembled that at a second-rate public school, and was far inferior to, say, St Cyr.[26]

The first half of the nineteenth century also witnessed, in France and Prussia, the acceptance of a more professional system of advancement *within* the officer corps. In Prussia the system of promotion only after examination, introduced by Scharnhorst among the military reforms following defeat in 1806, was not swept away in the reaction after 1815. Seniority was the chief criterion in promotion up to captain, though qualification for the General Staff often provided for a more rapid advance. Selection was used for a rigorous weeding-out among majors qualified for advancement to lieutenant-colonels, and officers passed over were expected to resign. In France the law enacted by Gouvion Saint-Cyr in 1818 sought to put advancement on a professional basis. Seniority would determine two-thirds of all promotions up to lieutenant-colonel but thereafter all appointments would be by selection.[27] Favouritism and excessively slow advancement in the lower ranks were recognized as the chief defects, and the entire system was overhauled in 1832. Officers were then guaranteed in their ranks subject only to being found guilty of some serious misdemeanour by court-martial. In 1851 a comprehensive scheme of retirement pensions was introduced.

In Britain, however, a really professional system of advancement was incompatible with the existence of the purchase system which of course affected the majority of first commissions offered for the infantry and cavalry, and of promotions up to the rank of lieutenant-colonel.[28] At the time of the Crimean War a captaincy might cost £2,400 and a lieutenant-colonelcy £7,000 – in 'smart' regiments it would be much more. As mess expenses, social activities – in particular hunting – could cost several hundred pounds per annum and the rate of pay remained nominal, it was abundantly clear that – except in India – officers could not serve without substantial independent means. Against these material factors, buttressed by a great weight of military opinion, including that of the Duke of Wellington, attempts to introduce professional qualifications into the system of promotion made little headway. A test case was the attempt to make successful completion of the Staff College course obligatory for appointment to staff posts in peacetime. In the protracted debate over the proposal to abolish purchase in 1871, Edward Cardwell still found it necessary to emphasize the advantages of a professional officer corps:

> ... if there is one lesson which we have learned from the history of the late campaign [the Franco-German War], it is this – that the secret of Prussian success has been more owing to the professional education of the officers than to any other cause to which it can be ascribed. Neither gallantry nor heroism will avail without professional training.[29]

'The history of military education to the present time,' Correlli Barnett has written, reflecting a widely-shared view, 'has been a tug-of-war between these two qualities: between the conception of a soldier as a fighting-man and the new conception of him, born of the industrial age, as a military manager; between a traditional *élite* and the social changes that have gradually swamped it.'[30] Further reflection, however, suggests that there were actually *three* opposed viewpoints rather than two. These may be summarized as follows: first, soldiers are 'born' whether one is using the concept of genius or of aristocracy; second, military leaders are *moulded* from an early age by institutions that influence every aspect of their personalities – a prison-like regimen plus massive doses of classroom instruction, usually with an emphasis on mathematics; finally, there is the view that officers should be trained, *after* acquiring a basic civilian education, by a programme of realistic practical instruction. The second and third positions are opposed to each other as bitterly as either is to the first: there are even some visible links between the first and third viewpoints in their emphasis on 'natural' education as opposed to 'artificial' classroom indoctrination. The confusion caused by the existence of *three* positions helps to explain some of the prolonged agonizing about whether military 'education' is necessary or beneficial.[31]

The Prussian military reformers after Jena regarded the narrow class basis and inflexible attitudes of the senior officers as the greatest obstacle to a national regeneration. Thus the eloquent Grolman proclaimed that 'In order to fight it is not necessary to belong to a special class', and in an order of 1808 he stipulated as a general principle for officer selection that 'A claim to the position of officer shall from now on be warranted, in peacetime by knowledge and education, in time of war by exceptional bravery and quickness of perception'.[32] Reservations speedily modified these high ideals. Frederick William III insisted on his right to select regimental commanding officers, and senior commanders were heard to mutter (not for the last time) that staff education, by developing a field marshal's talents in junior officers, would merely encourage insubordination.[33] Indeed traditional, or what Correlli Barnett has termed 'neo-feudalist' attitudes remained formidable on the Continent down to Prussia's astounding military victories in the 1860s.

In Britain, officers with advanced views on military education and training, such as Colonel Le Marchant, Sir John Moore and their successors after 1815, had to contend with even more deeply entrenched attitudes because the British Army had never been infected with revolutionary ideas and in addition had emerged victorious from the Peninsular War and from Waterloo.[34] Not merely the traditional officer class but even military reformers such as Sidney Herbert continued to rate the qualities of a gentleman above those of a professional officer.[35] Lord Wolseley, writing in 1887 of the British officer of fifty years earlier, remarked that 'The very prejudices of the English gentleman only serve to make him all the more popular with his soldiers . . . the officer demanded from his men an implicit obedience, *not only because he was their officer* [my italics], but also their social superior and, as he believed, their natural born leader . . . The relations between the officer and private with us have always partaken very much of the patriarchal and feudal character.' But at that time (1837), Wolseley continued, the officer 'was entirely wanting in military knowledge. Neither he nor even the generals under whom he served recognized its necessity. Had not Marlborough and Wellington won great victories and placed England on a pinnacle of military glory with a previous race of English gentlemen as officers, to whom the science of war was as little known as it was to them? They knew how to lead their men as straight under the heaviest fire as their fathers and grandfathers had done before them, and what more was necessary or should be required of them? . . . the reputation of being a really good officer was then by common assent accorded to the man who brought the manly "all round" qualities of the English gentleman, of the English sportsman, to bear upon a sound knowledge of drill and a quick aptitude for its practice in the field.' Finally, 'the English general of that day seemed to think that all military excellence consisted in moving a few hundred soldiers about in a small barrack-yard without crowding or confusion'.[36]

Wolseley's mention of that particular brand of courage, assisted by an inherited sense of duty, needed to lead men straight under the heaviest fire, must cause us to remember the fearfully close quarters at which battles were fought into the Crimean era, and to reflect that, up to a point, the 'neo-feudalists' had a strong case. The fact that officers derived from a similar social background strengthened their *esprit de corps*. If the class from which they came also put a high value on courage, boldness, physical fitness and leadership, it imbued the officer corps with ready-made military virtues. The point at which these 'natural' qualities proved insufficient was partly determined by the sheer progress of the practice of war. The participants in the Crimean War were not particularly well educated or professional in their approach but their shortcomings were none the less apparent. Within a few years the appearance of a genuinely professional and well organized officer corps in Prussia was to expose the inadequacy of the traditional military virtues, valiantly though these were displayed by Austria and France.

When studied by foreign observers in the course of her rise to military dominance in Europe, Prussia's military education programme represented a striking success story. Viewed, however, in the broader context of Germany's social and constitutional development during the nineteenth century, the process is less edifying; it comprised one sector of the struggle of the *bourgeoisie* for emancipation from the forces of autocracy and feudalism. When, as Karl Demeter has written, even in Prussia more and more officers were being recruited from the *bourgeoisie*, 'the question of officers' social origins could not be more closely bound up with the question of their technical education and training. The first lies at the heart of the second'.[37]

Scharnhorst had laid down in 1808 the basis of military education which was to serve Germany throughout the nineteenth century. His experience in cadet school and in the service of Hanover had convinced him – years before Jena – of the inherent dangers in the Prussian generals' excessive deference to blue blood and their contempt for education. When his system, based on education as well as professional merit, had to stand the severe test of application in peacetime there soon appeared a great gulf between theory and practice. In 1825, for example, a Commission under Prince William discovered that the divisional schools were failing in their purpose. Cadets were entering them at eighteen or nineteen years of age with such a poor general education that their progress was slow and they tended to show a spirit of resistance to study and morality alike. The Commission proposed that the courses in the divisional schools be reduced from three years to one, and that in every province several hundred places should be created in the *gymnasien* where the sons of necessitous officers could be given a cheap general education between the ages of thirteen and seventeen. This, according to Demeter, was designed to bar the way to commissions via the divisional schools for the uneducated working classes. 'There is hardly a line [in the Report] that does not breathe an ill-concealed distaste for the "competition" of the "uneducated working-classes" who want to enter the State-financed divisional schools: "mediocrity and lack of culture are to be curbed" – yet only in respect of "undesirable officer material".'[38]

The scheme of special bursaries for officers' sons was rejected on grounds of cost, and when the duration of the divisional schools' courses was reduced in 1828, the poor nobility and officers were hard put to educate their sons to the minimum standard. Although they mobilized a powerful political lobby, their claims to special privileges were opposed in 1835 by the Crown Prince (later Frederick William IV), who had consulted Hermann von Boyen, one of the leading reformers during

the Napoleonic era and War Minister 1814–19. The latter
pointed out that all citizens paid taxes to maintain an army
and all were liable to service: the officer corps must be recruited
from the ablest candidates whose qualifications must include a
good general education. These ideas found expression in
Frederick William IV's Ordinance of 1844. The Prince of
Prussia (later William I) expressed the anxiety and resentment
of the traditional officer class in asking 'how are the sons of the
needier nobility, of impecunious officers, to be given the education that is now required? Where are they to find the money
for getting their sons as far as the Prima [the highest class of a
secondary school].'

The German historian Meinecke commented that 'the corps
of officers turned the intellectual achievements of the day to
account, but it did not take them into its heart, it adopted the
practical lessons to be drawn from them rather than the ideal
they represented'.[39]

The fiercest phase in the struggle for raising the level of
education for the first commission took place in the 1860s as
the result of an Ordinance of 31 October 1861 which laid it
down that candidates must produce a certificate of fitness
(*Primareifezeugnis*) before they could even enter the War Schools
(attendance at which was now compulsory to obtain a commission). The opposition, led by General Manteuffel, the chief of
the Military Cabinet, persuaded William I to delay the application of the Ordinance to 1865 and to announce that 'special
zeal for the service and a recommendation from the appropriate corps of officers would fully compensate for deficiency
in scientific education'. William I continued to grant numerous
dispensations to the certificates of education required to enter
the War Schools, mainly in the interests of shielding the old
Prussian nobility; his grandson was obliged to follow the practice down to 1900 by the sheer shortage of officers.

As Demeter points out, the Military Cabinet and the War
Ministry, though apparently bitterly at odds over the detailed
educational requirements for a commission, were fundamentally
at one in wishing to attract the kind of men who would make
good brother officers and leaders. While there can be no denying

the strength of the rearguard action described in detail by Demeter, it surely remains the case that the German Army was unrivalled in the late nineteenth century in the all-round quality of its officer corps.[40]

Indeed, the German Army vividly exemplifies the ability of nineteenth-century officer corps to adjust to new demands for professionalism without opening their ranks to tradesmen or lower classes. The paradox has often been noted that the junkers modernized themselves professionally without changing their traditional outlook and values. In Correlli Barnett's words 'They remained spiritually true pre-industrial neo-feudalist warriors.' Moreover they succeeded to a remarkable extent in transmitting their values to the mass of bourgeois officers who had to be accepted as the Army expanded between 1870 and 1914. It is indeed little exaggeration to say that by 1914 their values had become dominant in German politics and society.[41]

Though the British Army was less dominated by its equivalent of the junker class and existed in a very different political environment, it too succeeded in preserving down to 1914 the values and attitudes of the landed gentry. But, unlike the Prussian Army, it was reluctant to adopt professional standards so that, compared with the leading Continental armies, it remained 'amateur' at least until the South African War.

Clearly a major explanation of this lagging behind was the feeling that Britain could afford to maintain a small and unprogressive army since geography, the Royal Navy and industrial and commercial primacy together afforded her both power and security. It is hard to realize, in these days of national decline, that for a large part of the nineteenth century the Royal Navy was not merely superior to any individual rival, but was more than a match for any possible *combination* of enemies. Despite recurrent invasion scares the English Channel remained an almost insuperable obstacle to the sea-borne invader. Whether Britain could afford to remain neutral in 'splendid isolation' while a hostile land power achieved a Continental hegemony was quite another matter. Although Britain found herself powerless to dispatch an expeditionary force either in 1864 (in defence of the Danish Duchies against

Prussia and Austria) or in 1870 (had Prussia infringed Belgian neutrality), Prussia's rapid rise to military dominance raised the awful possibility that one day she might need to employ her Army to defend her vital interest in the security of the Low Countries. As Huntington succinctly commented on the belated abolition of purchase in 1871: 'with reluctance Parliament conceded that Moltke might be a greater threat than Cromwell.'[42]

How did the development of the civil professions in nineteenth-century England affect the officers of the Regular Army?

'The professions as we know them are very much a Victorian creation, brought into being to serve the needs of an industrial society.'[43] The 'learned' professions – medicine, law and the Church – were acceptable occupations for gentlemen essentially because of their close connection with the established order in the State. They were distinguished from the 'mechanical' professions by the fact that they required a liberal education – i.e., the education of a gentleman – consisting largely of Greek and Latin literature and mathematics. The Army, though hardly learned in any other sense, also expected its officers to have the education of a gentleman. Indeed, fighting, particularly on land, was considered, next to government service, the most gentlemanly occupation of all. 'The trouble with the Army, in time of peace, was that it was less likely to provide a competence than to tempt a young man to squander his way into debt.'[44] Hence the advantage, almost the necessity, for landed property which broke the direct connection between work and income and enabled the Army officer – like the country gentleman – to enjoy his 'independence'.

It comes as something of a shock to discover that qualification by written examination, today virtually a *sine qua non* for entry to a profession, was enforced in not a single one until the early nineteenth century. The Royal College of Physicians, for example, admitted only graduates of Oxford or Cambridge – where, ironically, virtually no medical education was available. The examination for a fellowship was entirely oral and in Latin. No serious qualifying examinations were held for any branch of the legal profession until 1836, while not until 1872 did the

Inns of Court make examination compulsory. However, the portent of things to come was manifest in the Apothecaries Act of 1815 which for the first time set up a Court of Examiners and made detailed regulations for a course of professional education.

In the first half of the nineteenth century the new middle classes were waging two struggles simultaneously: to achieve respectability for trades and new professions, and to raise the lower branches of established professions (i.e. the law and medicine) to equal status with higher branches. The latter conflict particularly had brought out by the 1850s the contrasting attitudes between the old professional man and the new. The latter believed in systematized qualification based on a properly organized professional education rigorously tested; the former preferred to rely on the traditional tests of a liberal education and personal contacts to gain admission and the acquisition of professional competence afterwards.[45]

In none of the professions was the traditional attitude more entrenched than the Army. Although the profession of arms was often bracketed with the learned professions, the value of a specialized training was held at even more of a discount.

> The qualities valued in an officer were the qualities valued by the country gentry: courage, physical toughness, a determination to stand up for one's rights, a touchy sense of honour. Almost the only aquired skill highly regarded was horsemanship, and that was taken for granted. The notion that an officer should be a professional soldier, qualified by technical as well as by the traditional virtues of a gentleman, was derided and looked down upon, except in the engineers and artillery, two corps which were only rather doubtfully fit for gentlemen to serve in.[46]

In the context of these assumptions it is not difficult to see why the purchase system flourished. It ensured that officers were gentlemen (that is, men of independent means and possessing liberal education), so that the constitution consequently had nothing to fear from self-seeking mercenaries, while the officers were not dependent on political favour for their livelihood. In purely financial terms, then, commissioned service was certainly not an attractive proposition. Infantry commissions cost approximately £450–£500 and a cavalry commission more than £800. An ensign needed a private income to support an expensive way of life on 5s 3d a day and a lieutenant on 6s 6d. But, of course, purchase was chiefly an investment in social status, hence its attraction for the younger or less intellectually promising sons of the well-to-do and socially ambitious upper middle classes – merchants, physicians, lawyers, clergymen and country gentlemen.

Even before the Crimean War, however, the early Victorian concern for efficiency and a minimum level of competence in the civil professions began to make minor inroads into the amateurism of the military service. The purchase system was criticized by individuals in Parliament and by commissions of inquiry and, more specifically, after 1849 no one was allowed to purchase a commission without first passing an elementary oral examination in half a dozen subjects. In practice 'the education of a gentleman' was frequently accepted as an adequate qualification from those who contrived to fail the examination, and the test remained a nominal one until more stringent regulations were laid down by the Council of Military Education, appointed in 1857. In parenthesis it may be noted that the Navy received far less critical attention, even though 'interest' continued to be essential to obtain a commission throughout the nineteenth century. The Navy possessed more prestige in the country, but on the other hand far fewer families desired a naval career for their sons; also naval commissions were not purchasable and the early age of officer recruitment appeared to guarantee rigorous professional training in the Service.

The Civil Service was probably even more of a butt for political criticism than the Army, and its reform further opened the door to the cold winds of competition for military commissions. In 1853 the principle of competitive entry to the India Civil Service was adopted under the Government of India Act, and two years later a Commission was set up, by Order-in-Council, to examine candidates for the home Civil Service. In the 1850s it was still a revolutionary notion that positions in

Government Service ought to depend on the results of competitive examinations rather than on the patronage of influential men.

The brilliant group who devised the qualifications for the
Civil Service, including Sir Stafford Northcote, Sir Charles
Trevelyan, T. B. Macaulay and Benjamin Jowett, were all
products of the 'gentlemanly' classical education of Oxford and
Cambridge, where there was a strong antipathy to specialized
or utilitarian training. For half a century or so such men as
these had risen to the top in the public service on the foundation
of scholastic successes at university. Why not apply the same
standards to applicants for the higher Civil Service, the Army
and other important posts in the service of the State?

By 1870 open competition was the sole means of entry to
nearly all the branches of the Civil Service, and nominations
to screen the candidates were gradually abandoned. The
Foreign Office, however, remained the great exception by
maintaining a system of 'limited competition' for many years.
'Diplomacy remained a profession of immense prestige and
dignity, but not a way to earn your living.'[47] From the 1850s
it was the India Civil Service examination that set the standard
and this had been devised with the revolutionary aim of discovering intellectual merit irrespective of class or religion.
Thus mastery of English was stressed rather than the classics,
and needless to say this constituted a dramatic challenge to the
public schools, where the emphasis was overwhelmingly on the
classics.[48]

A significant proportion of the middle classes welcomed the
adoption of competitive examinations as a shattering blow to
aristocratic privilege and closed systems of patronage. The
public schools found themselves under increasing pressure to
introduce 'modern studies', though they continued to lag
behind Continental countries due to British snobbery towards
science and technical knowledge.

To apply competitive examinations to the Civil Service was
one thing; to apply it to the Army quite another. Among the
numerous objections the two most important were: that skill in
passing examinations offered no guarantee that the young man

would be a fighter – or a gentleman; and that the examination requirements would ruin the educational system by leading to 'cramming'. These misgivings were not entirely without foundation. The public schools' inability or unwillingness to provide adequate preparation for the Army entrance examination did lead to a proliferation of cramming establishments: 'six months at a crammer became an accepted if not very dignified episode in the education of a Victorian gentleman'.[49]

Unlike the Church, the Army did to a great extent follow the form if not so much the spirit of the Civil Service entry system. By 1863 entrance to the Royal Military Academy at Woolwich had become purely competitive, though the emphasis was on mathematics rather than English. After several years of utter confusion, the Royal Military College at Sandhurst became, in 1874, the sole avenue to a commission in the infantry or cavalry. The only way of avoiding the competitive examination for entry to Sandhurst was to obtain a nomination after serving in the Militia.

Yet the abolition of purchase in 1871 and the adoption of competitive examination as the normal means of entry to all arms of the service had a less disturbing effect on the class of young men who entered the officer corps, or on the regimental way of life, than many had feared. Some ten per cent of entrants to the India Civil Service came from modest backgrounds, being the sons of butchers, bakers, tailors, etc. Though precise figures cannot be given, there were probably far fewer tradesmen's sons among the officers in the Army. Except in India it remained almost impossible to live on an officer's pay; regiments with social prestige or strong local connections remained exclusive; and 'the cavalry's magnificence remained, on the whole, undimmed by brains'.[50] In short, allowing for the many differences, the British officer corps was following a similar path to the German. Bowing to civil pressures and recognizing – up to a point – the changing nature of warfare – the British Army in the second half of the nineteenth century reduced the influence of wealth and social position and substituted objective educational tests for entry and a regularized system for professional advancement. At the same time it succeeded to a

remarkable degree in preserving an essentially eighteenth-
century mode of life and in excluding all but a handful of
officers from the lower-middle and working classes. The Staff
College, as will be shown, played the major role in propagating
the urgent need for military professionalism, but a large
number of officers – perhaps even the majority – remained
unconvinced right up to 1914.

The historian of the Military Staff finds the origins of the
modern general staff system in the organization of the Swedish
Army in the time of Gustavus Adolphus. But several important
ingredients were lacking; commanders, for example, were still
participants rather than directors of their forces in battle, and
the distinction between the operational, logistical and administrative functions of the staff remained blurred.[51]

The term 'general staff', according to Dallas D. Irvine, has
been employed in seven senses, as follows:

1 The headquarters staff of an independent or unit army or
   of a similar force.
2 The body of general officers in a country's army as a
   whole.
3 The officers belonging to special auxiliary corps and
   administrative departments rather than to the traditional
   combatant branches of the military service.
4 The last two groups together.
5 A special corps or establishment of officers which provides
   staffs to assist various commanders of combined arms in
   exercising the functions of command and administrative
   control, as distinct from the functions of administrative
   management within established administrative departments.
6 A particular staff so provided.
7 A central military organ assisting the supreme military
   authority of the state in the same manner, and particularly
   in determining and implementing intellectually the higher
   directives which are to govern military activity.[52]

Our immediate concern is with the seventh meaning – the

central military organ or 'capital staff', and later chiefly with this and the fifth.

On the basis of loose definitions, the origin of the 'capital staff' can be traced back through antiquity. In its two distinguishing characteristics, however, the capital staff does not antedate the middle of the eighteenth century. These are: (1) 'the systematic and extensive collection in time of peace of specific information which may be important to the future conduct of operations', and (2) 'intellectual preparation for the future conduct of operations either through systematic development of skill for the handling of contingently anticipated situations or through the elaboration of specific plans for war, or both'.[53] France owed the creation of such a capital staff in 1766 to the genius of Lt-Gen. Pierre Bourcet. It was suppressed in 1771, reconstituted in 1783 and suppressed again early in the French Revolution. Bourcet was not only the principal author of the system of grand tactics with which Napoleon conquered most of Europe; as a peacetime chief of staff he anticipated most of the features of von Moltke's great general staff – except, of course, the use of railways. The omni-competent military genius of Napoleon was not favourable to the development of a new capital staff; indeed his influence lay 'like a dead hand' on the French attitude to the general staff for half a century after his death. As a result it was in Prussia that a modern capital staff evolved well in advance of France.[54]

The Prussian Great General Staff was derived from the quartermaster-general's staff of the seventeenth and eighteenth centuries. Its most important functions were the location, laying-out and fortification of the Army's camp, the supervision of field fortification, and the maintenance of fortresses. It was, in short, primarily a corps of engineers, a role which was underlined in 1796 when it was assigned the task of preparing a military map of Prussia.

Chief credit for refining and expanding the duties of the general staff belongs, not so much to Scharnhorst, as to Col. Christian von Massenbach who, as quartermaster-lieutenant, reformed the Prussian staff organization in the half-dozen years *before* Jena. The fundamental change which he effected was to

c

direct the staff's attentions to the general investigation of matters which would affect the conduct of future operations (as distinct from merely gathering information), and to the study of directives for these operations.[55] Scharnhorst revised Massenbach's system after Jena, in particular by making the capital staff one of the sections of the new war ministry. His distinctive contribution to staff development was to institute the 'general staff with troops' in senses 5 and 6 as given earlier.

Clearly the development of the modern general staff system was closely connected with changes in the nature of warfare. Only in Prussia did the general staff develop largely in peacetime in anticipation of future operational needs rather than as a belated response to adverse experience in war. The first factor which may indirectly have influenced the development of general staffs was the extensive and intensive road building and improving of the later eighteenth century. This accelerated the movement of troops, contributed to the break-up of armies as a single unwieldy mass, and facilitated supply. The second, and more direct, influence was the rapid progress of the cartographical science and technique which lay at the centre of the capital staffs' activities. The third and by far the most important factor was the gradual transformation in tactics which resulted from the introduction of the flintlock musket and the socket bayonet in the late seventeenth century; and great improvements in artillery in the second half of the eighteenth century. Briefly, these changes increased firepower and gave the infantry greater security against cavalry. Firepower afforded the infantry greater scope for manœuvre, and with the development of skirmishers the battle would open at greater distances and extend over a greater area. In sum, instead of a single massed army, directly under its general's eye and command, an army became a group of miniature armies (divisions and – under Napoleon – army corps) dispersed over vast areas and seldom brought physically together except on the field of a great battle. The art of war became, in a far more precise way than formerly, an art to be pursued upon the map and offering an infinitely greater number of problems and possibilities than ever before.

The need for a specialist group of men to assist the commanding general was apparent, all the more so as under monarchical regimes high commands were a virtual monopoly of royal princes and the higher nobility who could safely be relied upon neither to evince outstanding ability nor earnest devotion to professional studies. Staff officers would literally provide 'the staff' upon which such commanders could lean for advice. Often the staff officer's functions extended to participation in command, most strikingly exemplified in Prussia in the dual command system that evolved after 1806. Adequate maps must be provided, information about the terrain and the enemy's dispositions systematically gathered and sifted and, not least, written orders would increasingly replace oral ones. The next logical step would be the foundation of institutions to train such specialist staff officers in peacetime.

Needless to say 'the habit-bound military mind' did not grasp the full implications of these changes in warfare all at once. The initial emphasis on peacetime staff work tended to be upon the accumulation of geographical information. War archives were founded in France in 1688, Austria in 1711, Sweden in 1805 and Prussia in 1816.[56]

In Britain, where less urgent need was felt for military information about terrain, scientific attainments were confined largely to the artillery and engineers. The national survey, begun in 1784, was significantly entrusted to the Board of Ordnance. Consequently the quartermaster-general's department failed to acquire this additional function and remained a service of supply. Thus the British quartermaster-general's staff did not develop more comprehensive duties and retained its name long after its European counterparts had been transformed into, or replaced by, general staffs.

In time, the geographical branch in European armies was sub-divided into sections and new branches were formed for the study of military history and military statistics, that is data on the resources and organization of various foreign countries. With this expansion of functions in peacetime the need was seen for staff schools to provide education and training for staff service. Frederick the Great's Académie des Nobles, founded in

1765 to train young noblemen for the military and diplomatic services, has been called 'a vital landmark' in staff history and the 'forerunner of . . . the more famous Kriegsakademie'. A year earlier Bourcet had been appointed director of a French Staff College at Grenoble.[57] Britain established a staff school as the senior department of the Royal Military College in 1801, the Kriegsakademie followed in 1810 and the French École d'Application in 1818. Russia had no staff school until 1832, Austria until 1852.

Thus, by the middle of the nineteenth century there were usually four component parts of the capital staff system: a large cartographical unit, a small historical unit, a military statistics unit and a subsidiary staff school providing scientific education for cartographical work, an elementary training in staff duties and some knowledge of the higher conduct of war. Only with the advent of railways did the preparation of specific plans for war become a vital – perhaps the most vital – function of capital staffs. 'So far as capital staffs are concerned, it may be said that the first *fully developed* capital staff came into existence between 1857, when Moltke became chief of staff, and began to take railways into large consideration in his war plans, and 1867 when a quite distinct railway section was set up in the Great General Staff.'[58]

By 1806, then, Prussia possessed the essentials of a general staff system, yet for a time the new institution's precise responsibilities and powers remained uncertain. Theoretically it was inferior in status to the Ober-Kriegs-Kollegium under the aged Field-Marshal von Mollendorf. But a more influential rival was the Adjutant-General's department. The latter was functioning as 'a secret military cabinet and a kind of personal staff to the sovereign', and its chief, according to Stein, was interested in nothing but cards, port and tobacco.[59]

The new Ministry of War, established in March 1809, went far to resolve these institutional conflicts and to establish a definite role for the General Staff. The Ministry comprised two departments: a General Department of War and a Military Economy Department. The former, headed initially by Scharnhorst, possessed three divisions. The first – taking over the functions of the old military cabinet and the Adjutant-General's department – dealt with all questions of personnel; the second with training, education, war plans and mobilization (i.e. largely the General Staff); and the third with ordnance matters.[60]

The Prussian military institutions were subjected to further changes in 1821 initially on a personal issue of rank. Lt-Gen. von Müffling, formerly Blücher's quartermaster-general and lately commander of the Prussian army of occupation in France, a conservative, a martinet and a confidant of the King, found himself senior in rank, on taking over the General Staff, to the head of the department, Maj.-Gen. von Lilienstern. Müffling settled the matter by securing the independence of the Chief of the General Staff from subordination to the War Minister. Henceforth he would be treated as the latter's adviser, but with no right of access to the King except through the War Minister. Shortly afterwards, however, the Military Cabinet was revived and the old triangular conflict between Military Cabinet, War Ministry and General Staff broke out anew. In short, the Chief of the General Staff was still far from being the authoritative adviser of the Supreme War Lord (the King); indeed, during the long years of peace he was rarely summoned to the royal council or consulted. Moreover, his relationship with the commanding generals of the Army was ill-defined, and it was by no means clear whether he would be permitted to give them directives in time of war or whether he would even be invited to appear at field headquarters. In short he was little more than the director of a planning office. The constitutional crisis of 1848 revealed that in military matters the King was prepared to issue orders, in consultation with his personal advisers, in total disregard of the Minister for War.[61]

'The transformation of the General Staff into the agency charged with jurisdiction over all questions of command and the recognition of its chief as the highest adviser of the King in matters of warfare was the achievement of Helmuth von Moltke.' Von Moltke became Chief of the General Staff in 1857 and two years later received a small increase in status when he was allowed to report directly to the War Minister rather than through the General War Department, of which the General Staff comprised a division. In the great controversy over military reorganization in the early 1860s von Moltke was completely overshadowed by the new War Minister – Albrecht von Roon. When the war with Denmark began in 1864, von Moltke had little influence. 'Operational directives were sent directly to the field command from the War Ministry; and Moltke seems to have had no authority over, or contact with either Wrangel, or that commander's chief of staff, Vogel von Falckenstein.' The latter's incompetence provided von Moltke's opportunity; by the end of the campaign he had not only established himself as a most able chief of staff, but had also enhanced the reputation of the General Staff in the eyes of William I. The latter's admiration for von Moltke was made manifest in the royal cabinet order of 2 June 1866 which stated that henceforth commands of the General Staff would be communicated directly to the troops and no longer via the War Ministry. Outstanding successes in the field rendered this arrangement permanent.[62]

The superiority of Prussia's general staff organization undoubtedly gave her a decisive advantage over Austria in 1866 and France in 1870. What, then, were its distinguishing attributes? First, its semi-independence of the War Ministry from 1821, and the further enhancement of the institution's prestige and authority under von Moltke's direction from 1857. Closely connected was the fact that the Chief of the General Staff's appointment was, unlike most staff appointments in most armies, of unlimited duration. Von Moltke held the post for almost thirty-one years, and there were only seven occupants between 1821 and 1914.[63] This made possible a continuity of direction rarely attainable in countries with more democratic forms of government.

However efficient the organization of the General Staff, it could not have flourished without a steady supply of very able staff officers. Here the crucial role was played by the Kriegsakademie or War College, from the graduates of which the General Staff was largely, though never exclusively, recruited. Rather surprisingly the War Academy was not placed under the direct control of the General Staff until 1872, but from its foundation in 1810 it was in fact the nursery of that institution.

Foreign observers were profoundly impressed by the scholarly yet businesslike atmosphere and high intellectual level at the War Academy. Baron Stoffel, the perceptive French military attaché, extolled its virtues in the 1860s, writing: *'C'est une école d'enseignement militaire supérieur, sans égale en Europe, tant par le mérite des professeurs que par la nature et l'étendue des études . . . L'Ecole Polytechnique, celles de Metz et de Saint Cyr, ne sont que des écoles spéciales, comparées à l'Académie de guerre avec son programme si vaste.'* He warned his government that *'La composition de l'état-major prussien constituerait dans une guerre prochaine le plus sérieux élément de supériorité en faveur de l'armée prussienne,'* and emphatically ended his report *'méfions-nous de l'état-major prussien!'*

The British Military Education Commission of 1870 described the Academy as resembling 'a military university'. 'The general object,' according to the Commission, 'is to raise the scientific spirit of the army; its special object is to give such an education to the most talented officers of all arms, after they have proved themselves possessed of the practical qualifications of good regimental officers, as will fit them not only for appointments on the staff but for all responsible positions of high rank, for the command of regiments, for employment as instructors at the military schools, and for all duties which require scientific attainments . . .'[64]

By 1870 the annual intake for the three-year course was approximately fifty-five officers. The entrance by competitive examination was open to officers of upwards of three years' commissioned service, but personal distinctions and recommendations were also taken into account. The British Commissioners were greatly impressed by the virtual absence of competition at the Academy in contrast to France. Instead of a final examination at the end of the third year, several long essays – 'much like prize essays at the universities' – prepared in the course of the year, were submitted. These were assessed less on their factual accuracy than on the 'power of reflection and judgement, cultivation of the reasoning faculties and intellectual ability' displayed. Students were not arranged in order of merit on graduation and only very exceptional men were reported to the King and the Chief of the General Staff. All returned to regimental duty and only the best dozen or so were recalled to probationary staff appointments. Graduates were classified according to their special abilities and recommended for appropriate branches of the service: 'the great object . . . is not to demand a uniform standard of attainments from all alike, but to encourage individuals to aim at excellence in those subjects for which they have a natural taste'. Officers were not obliged to study under supervision as in France, nor submitted to frequent competitive examination as in the Staff College at Camberley. Although by 1870 the large number of non-military subjects open to choice at the Academy was coming under criticism from the Army, staff students until then had enjoyed an attractive range of subjects including: mathematics, higher geodesy, general history, history of literature, history of philosophy, universal geography, physical geography, chemistry, physical science, French and Russian. The British Report concluded that 'in the great majority of cases the candidates admitted are the most intellectual men in the service and . . . the ability of the army is well represented'. While there was no rule that the most distinguished generals should be products of the Academy, it seemed 'that at least a majority of the officers at present holding high commands have been at the Academy and served upon the Staff'.[65]

The preparatory foundations laid at the War Academy – including historical studies, staff rides, autumn manœuvres and war games (on the map) – were completed by the admirable system developed by von Moltke for advancement into and within the general staff. This sifting process began with the selection of some fifty officers from about 150 candidates for the Academy. About a year after graduation between twelve and twenty of the best were recalled from regimental duty and attached from one to two years to the Great General Staff at Berlin where they were trained in various sections under von Moltke's supervision. All were then again returned to regimental duty whence those who had impressed most were appointed to the general staff and promoted captain well ahead of their time: this was the main incentive which enabled such an exacting and avowedly *élitist* system to work. After about two years of staff service, usually with a corps or division head-quarters, these captains were again returned to regimental duty with a loss of general staff status. After a further two years, however, those who had fulfilled expectations were re-appointed to the general staff as majors, some seven or eight years ahead of officers commissioned at the same time. Before receiving each later promotion, general staff officers, with very few exceptions, were required to return to the command of troops for at least a year.

The virtues of this system were, first, that prospects of rapid advancement and the eventual achievement of high rank pro-vided the necessary incentive to the most able officers. Second, the general staff was selected from the best officers in the whole Army and not (as in France) exclusively from the War Academy. Third, the periodic return of staff officers to service with troops both ensured that they kept in touch with realities and also allowed for dead wood to be painlessly pruned; fourth, the discarded staff officers could yet provide an intellectual leaven for the whole Army; and, finally, the higher ranks of the staff were filled with comparatively young and vigorous men from whom chiefs of staff and generals could be selected in war. 'In combination with the Prussian practice of reposing great power in the hands of younger chiefs of staff, the system was far superior to any other that has ever been devised for the mobiliza-tion of military brain power.'[66]

If this conclusion was only to find widespread acceptance *after* the German triumph over France in 1870, the superiority of the German General Staff had been appreciated by a few individuals before that date, most notably by Baron Stoffel, the French military attaché in Berlin.[67] Unfortunately, the French awoke too late to the force of Stoffel's eloquent warnings and also failed to learn from the misfortunes of others.

In the first half of the nineteenth century the government of Austria displayed an almost suicidal tendency to scorn the advice – and even to reject the services – of its ablest generals.[68]

Acts of individual bravery rather than collective efficiency were encouraged by the highest prestige being attached to the award of the Cross of Maria Theresa. Unlike in Prussia, the Austrian Army did not slough off the eighteenth-century scorn for 'ink-splashers' and 'pedants'. After 1848 the Emperor made no concealment of his distrust of educated officers, noting on one proposed reform that 'the strength of the army lies not so much in educated officers as in loyal and gallant ones'. In this atmosphere it was hardly surprising that, although a general staff organization was created, it lacked the prestige, competence and spirit of its German neighbour. As far as prestige was concerned, the Austrian chief of the general staff was handicapped by a relatively modest position in the military hierarchy such that he could not hold his own with the departmental chiefs in the Supreme War Council. After 1849 the Chief of the Quartermaster-General Staff was by-passed and publicly humiliated by the Adjutant Corps. Moreover financial stringency so hampered the growth of the staff that when revolutions threatened to shatter the empire in 1848 only eleven trained staff officers were available for duty with the Army in Italy. It is significant that the Staff School in Vienna was established only in 1852 as a result of experience in the war against Hungary. One of the early students (and later Chief of General Staff), Beck, reported that the War College had speedily adapted itself to the prevailing values of the Army: the emphasis was on rote learning, and horsemanship featured excessively in the curriculum.[69]

The urgent need for a thorough overhaul of military education and general staff organization should have been made apparent by the Austrian Army's performance in the Italian campaign in 1859. 'The Austrian army marched into Italy without an adequate supply system, or accurate intelligence of enemy strength and capabilities, or even reliable maps to guide its movements . . . There was no clear chain of command, and unit commanders were constantly receiving contradictory orders from two or more higher officers and continually having to recall their troops from one pointless mission in order to despatch them on another equally so.'[70]

The opportunity was not seized. Neither of the two soldiers with the prestige to encourage military education and staff training, Benedek and the Archduke Albert, was sufficiently interested. Benedek, himself a member of the Order of Maria Theresa, believed that wars were won by courage, discipline and *élan*: war games and staff studies bored him. According to Chief of Staff Beck's biographer he was 'an opponent of every kind of staff work done at the green table and, above all, of every kind of scholarly activity by soldiers'.[71]

In conclusion, it was painfully obvious that the Austrian General Staff possessed none of the advantages of the Prussian when the test came against Prussia in 1866. It lacked prestige in the eyes of the combatant arms; its chief had been downgraded since 1849 as a definite policy of the Emperor's Military Chancery; and (until 1869) it remained a closed corps whose members were not selected primarily for outstanding merit and who lacked the benefit of frequent service with troops. In Bohemia the Austrians displayed the traditional military virtues to a magnificent degree but these were no longer sufficient to earn victory. As Benedek is said to have remarked after his eclipse, 'How could we have prevailed against the Prussians. We have learned so little, and they are such a studious people.'[72]

'The primary cause of the French military collapse in 1870 was previous reliance upon a vicious system for the education, promotion, and assignment of officers . . . it was almost completely effective in excluding the army's brain power from the staff and high command. To the resulting lack of intelligence at the top can be ascribed all the inexcusable defects of French military policy.'[73]

The French staff and command system, unrivalled since the Seven Years War, began to lose its superiority in the Revolutionary Wars. The ruthless practice then adopted of rapid promotion by merit brought its short-term rewards but also provided some pitfalls as a permanent system. Brilliant young officers who rose to high command were generally those who were able to get along without efficient staffs; trained staff officers were few and many of these were needed for command.

Commanders came to rely on their own innate ability rather than upon conscious and systematic method. The brilliant achievements of the French Army under Napoleon I added to the myth that generalship was an inborn, unteachable gift. Consequently the need for a careful division of the functions of command was scarcely felt in France, and staffs amounted to little more than the personal assistants of the general. The shortcomings of this individualistic command structure were not exposed in the numerous small-scale colonial wars undertaken by France between 1815 and 1870.

A determined attempt to rid the staff of mediocre officers and incompetent favourites was made by Marshal Gouvion Saint-Cyr who became minister of war in 1817. His solution was to create a completely distinct staff corps (*corps d'état-major*) in 1818, and to set up a staff school (École d'application d'état-major) in Paris as the sole means of entry to the staff. This reform greatly reduced favouritism but it was not a good system for discovering, and making full use of, the best brains in the Army. Between 1826 and 1833 staff and regimental service were again made to alternate, but from the latter year graduates of the staff school were directly appointed to permanent staff service. By the end of the 1830s the staff corps had become totally isolated from the other arms since even exchanges were forbidden.

The disadvantages of this system compared with Prussia's are obvious. The twenty-five annual places at the staff school were filled by competition between three graduates from the Polytechnique and the thirty best students of St Cyr. An equal number of second-lieutenants from the Army was allowed to compete but few in fact did so. Thus the staff corps (which contained 580 officers in peacetime) was open to the following criticisms: it recruited young men aged about twenty-one with no regimental experience and without proven ability in staff duties; as an exclusive corps it earned much jealousy in the combatant arms; and promotion was very slow.[74]

The course at the staff school was far inferior to that at the Kriegsakademie. It lasted only two years and lacked the university atmosphere – or the broad syllabus – of the latter. In the rigorous discipline of a school the young men were trained for the practical and routine duties of the staff corps rather than prepared for the exercise of all the higher intellectual functions of command. From 1831 the staff corps was heavily committed to assisting in preparing the great map of France, begun in 1803, so not surprisingly draughtsmanship received a disproportionate emphasis at the staff school. Military history was not studied at all, and in 1857 the Director admitted that the course on Military art and tactics was defective because it was difficult to find a teacher for the subject. In the Army generally the study of military history was discouraged since nothing could be published without being first submitted to rigorous censorship by the Ministry of War. Finally, neither in the staff school nor the staff corps were officers given theoretical and practical training for war by means of war games, staff rides or large-scale manœuvres with troops.[75]

The legend of French military superiority fostered under the Second Empire delayed realization that the staff system was desperately in need of reform. When the defeat of Austria and Baron Stoffel's reports at last made an impact, too little time remained for reforms to take effect. Under Marshal Niel as Minister of War an Imperial Decree of 19 July 1869 went some way to breaking open the closed shop of the staff corps. More lieutenants from the Army were to be admitted to the staff school than were required on the permanent staff. Those not selected would serve two years attached to another arm before returning to their regiments with the designation *adjoints d'état-major*. This reform brought three improvements: staff officers were permitted to exchange with the *adjoints*; the latter would provide a reserve of trained staff officers in war; and would raise the intellectual level of the Army in peace. Niel's successor, however, speedily negatived even this modest reform by reducing the number of admissions to the staff school to less than what it had been before.[76] Marshal Niel had more lasting success with his measures to convert the Dépôt de la Guerre into a genuine staff but this took a decade to achieve and resulted largely from the catastrophe of 1870.[77]

• • •

In the mid nineteenth century Britain lagged far behind Prussia and France as regards general staff organization. Indeed, as General Bronsart von Schellendorff noted in his monumental compilation, *The Duties of the General Staff*, 'There is really no such thing at all in the English Army as a "General Staff" regarded as a special body of officers. The "Staff" in the English Army is looked upon as consisting of the General Officers holding commands and the staffs attached to them in peace or war.'[78] In fact the duties of the British staff were far more extensive than those of European armies since they covered most aspects of military administration, whereas the function of a 'capital staff' or 'brain of the Army' at Head-quarters was scarcely understood and certainly not provided for.

By the War Office Act of 1870 the offices of the Commander-in-Chief and the Secretary of State for War were physically united and the latter was given direct control over the entire management of military affairs.[79] In practice, however, the War Minister seldom interfered in the detailed business of the Military Department which covered virtually all the branches included in Continental War Ministries. Von Schellendorff was astonished to find the duties of the Prussian Great General Staff performed in Britain by twelve general staff officers and four officers specially attached for duty in the Intelligence Department, which was only created in 1873. Apart from the staff of the Military Department there were the staffs of the District Commands; the staffs of the Viceroy and Army in India; the staffs in the Australian Colonies and the staffs of the other Colonies and of Egypt. After the Crimean War no officer was allowed to hold a staff appointment for more than five years, but this rule was not applied to the Duke of Cambridge, who was Commander-in-Chief for thirty-nine years, nor to Wolseley who was Adjutant-General for eight years.

The British Army before the South African War was not permanently organized into divisions or Army corps. It was, in short, little more than an aggregation of regiments. The only military district with some semblance of permanent organization for war was Aldershot where there was a division consisting of three infantry brigades, a cavalry brigade and detachments of engineers and artillery. Thus at the outbreak of war the whole of the staffs would have to be newly formed as well as the divisions. Von Schellendorff also noted the British addiction to very large staffs in the field – no less than 154 staff officers were appointed to a force of about 12,000 men for the Abyssinian campaign of 1867–8.[80]

The growth of professionalism in civil occupations and the transformation of the art of warfare from the late eighteenth century provided impetus for the development of military education in general and the formation of general staffs in particular. Prussia had led the way in evolving a general staff system which far excelled its rivals and played a major role in the great victories of 1866 and 1870. These achievements posed a dilemma for the other major military powers. They could not afford to ignore the Prussian example, but nor could they adopt it *in toto*. Britain had been among the pioneers of staff education during the Napoleonic wars but she had created no general staff, and after 1815 strategic security and the low priority of military efficiency among domestic political issues had contributed to the decline of military education at all levels.

The foundation of the Staff College after the Crimean War testified to a re-awakening of interest in military education and professional competence, but half a century was to pass before the College was complemented by the creation of a General Staff. The aim of this study is to throw new light on the development of military professionalism in Britain up to the First World War by focusing attention upon the work of the Staff College and its graduates in peace and war.

CHAPTER I. NOTES

1 Samuel P. Huntington, *The Soldier and the State* (Cambridge, Mass., 1957), p. 19. For a different approach to military professionalism which underlines the considerable progress in military education and science before 1800 see Frederick B. Artz, *The Development of Technical Education in France 1500–1850* (London, 1966).

2 Huntington, *op. cit.*, p. 20.

3 For example, in 1739 all 34 Prussian general officers were noblemen and so were 200 out of the 211 field officers. Until the Seven Years War the Apenburg Dragoons had not had a single bourgeois officer. See Karl Demeter, *The German Officer-Corps in Society and State, 1650–1945* (London,1965) pp. 5–7.

4 Correlli Barnett, 'The Education of Military Elites', *Journal of Contemporary History*, Vol. 2, Number 3 (July 1967), p. 16.

5 Robert Laulan, *L'Ecole Militaire* (Paris n.d.), pp. 14–19. See also Artz, *op. cit.*, pp. 89–90.

6 John W. Shy points out that the figures I have quoted for the social class of French Army officers in 1789 are largely guesswork based on a rough estimate of non-noble officers during the Seven Years War. In his opinion the proportion of noble officers in 1789 was considerably higher.

7 Demeter, *op. cit.*, p. 7.

8 'Report of the Committee on the Training of Officers for the Scientific Corps', 1857, p. 159 (hereafter referred to as Report, 1857).

9 L. Tutey, *Les officiers sous l'ancien régime* (Paris, 1908), cited by Huntington, *op. cit.*, p. 25 and Artz, *op. cit.*, p. 95.

10 For abuses of the British purchase system see Richard Glover *Peninsular Preparation: the Reform of the British Army 1795–1809* (Cambridge, 1963), pp. 148–9. Sir R. Biddulph, *Lord Cardwell at the War Office* (London, 1904), pp. 75–6.

11 David D. Bien, 'Military Education in 18th Century France', Proceedings of the Third Military History Symposium USAF Academy 1969, pp. 51–84. See also Artz, *op. cit.*, p. 240.

12 R. Glover, *op. cit.*, pp. 187–93. Sir John Smyth, *Sandhurst* (London, 1961), pp. 27–40.

13 J. D. Hittle, *The Military Staff: its history and development* (Harrisburg, Penn., 1944), p. 3.

14 *Ibid.*, pp. 79–80. Dallas D. Irvine 'The Origin of Capital Staffs', *Journal of Modern History*, Vol. X, Number 2 (June 1938), pp. 161–79. See especially pp. 167–8.

15 Peter Paret, *Yorck and the Era of Prussian Reform 1807–1815* (Princeton, 1966), *passim*, and 'Colonial Experience and European Military

Reform at the End of the Eighteenth Century', *Bulletin of the Institute of Historical Research*, Vol. XXXVII (May 1964), pp. 47-59.
16 Huntington, *op. cit.*, p. 35.
17 *Ibid.*, pp. 34, 37-9. Sir John Hackett, *The Profession of Arms* (The 1962 Lees Knowles Lectures) (London), pp. 61-3. For a comparative review of developments in the German, French, British and Russian Armies in the nineteenth century see G. Ritter, *The Sword and the Scepter* (Trans Heinz Norden) (Florida, 1970), Vol. 2, especially pp. 7-117.
18 Huntington, *op. cit.*, pp. 13-18.
19 Military Education Commission. 'Accounts of the System of Military Education in France, Prussia, Austria, Bavaria and the United States'. c47, 1870 (hereafter referred to as Report, 1870), pp. 327-8.
20 *Ibid.*, pp. 332-3.
21 Report, 1857, France, p. 3. The Prytanée Militaire was 'commonly considered a charitable institution, intended to give a free or partly free education to the sons of officers and non-commissioned officers'. By 1859 there were 400 pupils of whom three-quarters were educated entirely at the expense of the State. They ranged in age from ten to nineteen, the majority being under fifteen years of age on entrance. The course differed little from that given in the lycées, and the only strictly military aspects were drill and the drawing of maps and fortifications. Artz, *op. cit.*, p. 255.
22 Report, 1857, pp. viii-xii. Artz, *op. cit.*, pp. 230-43, provides an admirable account of the Polytechnique and its influence in the first half of the nineteenth century. The statistics he quotes for the careers chosen by Polytechnicians for the period 1795-1836 show that the vast majority entered either the artillery (nearly 1,700) or the military engineers (917); the third most popular choice was the corps of mines (196).
23 Cadets who satisfied the Board of Commissioners received a certificate entitling them to a commission without purchase. But since in most years more cadets graduated than there were vacant commissions for, many had to purchase. In 1854, for example, only 11 out of 95 purchased, but this compared favourably with an average of 46 in previous years. See Sir John Smyth, *op. cit.*, pp. 58-60.
24 Roy Lewis and Angus Maude, *Professional People* (London, 1952), p. 31, cited by Huntington, *op. cit.*, p. 43 n.
25 A Naval Academy had been established at Portsmouth as early as 1729. In 1773 it became The *Royal* Naval Academy and in 1806 The Royal Naval College.
26 Le Marchant's original plans of 1798-1800 for a Royal Military College envisaged three departments. The first (or Senior department) would instruct experienced officers in the duties of the staff, especially of the Quartermaster-General's staff in the field. The second (or Intermediate department) would teach the rudiments of military science to officers who had entered the service without previous military instruction, and would ensure that all officers had had a

minimum of six months' training. The third (or Junior department) would consist of a military school 'for those intended for the military profession from an early age'. The Intermediate department however was eliminated in the revisions that occurred before the Junior department opened at Great Marlow in 1802. Several drafts of the constitution of the Royal Military College are contained in W.O. 1/943. See also R. H. Thoumine, *Scientific Soldier: a Life of General Le Marchant* (London, 1968), p. 64. For an excellent study of the naval profession see Michael Lewis, *England's Sea Officers* (London, 1939).

27 Report, 1857, France, p. 3.

28 Apart from graduating from Sandhurst, the chief way to obtain a commission in the infantry or cavalry without purchase was by outstanding bravery in the field, for which one could also be rewarded with brevet rank (i.e. a higher rank in the Army than that held in the regiment). The main opportunity for *promotion* without purchase was by the death of a senior officer in the regiment, hence the macabre toast to 'a bloody war and a sickly climate'.

29 Sir Robert Biddulph, *op. cit.*, p. 117.

30 Barnett, *op. cit.*, p. 17.

31 I am grateful to John W. Shy for this suggestion.

32 Gordon A. Craig, *The Politics of the Prussian Army, 1640–1945* (New York, 1964), pp. 42–3.

33 *Ibid.*, p. 31.

34 Paret, *op. cit.*, pp. 204–8. Michael Howard, 'Wellington and the British Army', Michael Howard (ed.), *Wellingtonian Studies* (Aldershot, 1959), p. 78. Reprinted in *Studies in War and Peace* (London, 1970).

35 Sidney Herbert agreed with Sir Charles Napier that 'there was no officer in the world like the English gentleman', i.e. 'a man of liberal education who possesses the advantages that result from such an education. In this sense, looking to the constitution of the English Army, I think gentlemen will always make the best officers.' 'Hansard's Parliamentary Debates', Third Series, Vol. 147, cols 595–7 (28 July 1857). For Wellington's similar views see Michael Howard, *op. cit.*, p. 82.

36 General Viscount Wolseley, 'The Army'; Thomas Humphry Ward (ed.), *The Reign of Queen Victoria: a Survey of Fifty Years of Progress* (London, 1887), Vol. I, pp. 155–225. See especially pp. 167–9.

37 Demeter, *op. cit.*, p. 72.

38 *Ibid.*, p. 74.

39 Cited by Demeter, *op. cit.*, p. 76.

40 *Ibid.*, chapters 10 and 11 and Appendices 1, 5–10.

41 *Ibid.*, pp. 246–7. Barnett, *op. cit.*, p. 21. On the militarization of Wilhelmine Germany despite impressive social democratic opposition see M. Kitchen, *The German Officer Corps 1890–1914* (Oxford, 1968).

42 Huntington, *op. cit.*, p. 47.

43 W. J. Reader, *Professional Men: The Rise of the Professional Classes in Nineteenth-Century England* (London, 1966), p. 2; I have drawn heavily

on this admirable survey in the following pages. I am also indebted to
Rupert Wilkinson, *The Prefects* (London, 1964) and C. B. Otley 'The
Origins and Recruitment of the British Army Elite, 1870–1959' (Unpublished doctoral dissertation, University of Hull, 1965).
44 Reader, *op. cit.*, p. 8.
45 *Ibid.*, pp. 9–11, 16–19, 50–2, 54–7.
46 *Ibid.*, p. 74.
47 *Ibid.*, p. 96.
48 *Ibid.*, pp. 100–8.
49 *Ibid.*, p. 109.
50 *Ibid.*, pp. 97–8.
51 Hittle, *op. cit.*, pp. 38–40. See also General Bronsart von Schellendorff,
    The Duties of the General Staff, 3rd edn corrected and revised by
    Colonel Meckel (London, 1895).
52 Dallas D. Irvine, 'The Origin of Capital Staffs', *op. cit.*, p. 162.
    Irvine's meticulous scholarship and penetrating comments merit the
    admiration of all students of nineteenth-century military thought.
53 *Ibid.*, p. 165.
54 *Ibid.*, pp. 166–8.
55 *Ibid.*, p. 170. See also von Schellendorff, *op. cit.*, pp. 17–23, and
    Walter Görlitz, *The German General Staff* (London, 1953), pp. 20–2.
56 Irvine, *op. cit.*, p. 175.
57 Hittle, *op. cit.*, pp. 51–2, 79–80.
58 Irvine, *op. cit.*, p. 178.
59 Görlitz, *op. cit.*, p. 23.
60 *Ibid.*, p. 35. Craig, *op. cit.*, p. 51.
61 Görlitz, *op. cit.*, pp. 57–8. Craig, *op. cit.*, pp. 78–9, 108–9, 193.
62 Craig, *op. cit.*, pp. 193–5. F. E. Whitton, *Moltke* (London, 1921), pp.
    69–76.
63 Baron Stoffel, *Rapports Militaires écrits de Berlin 1866–1870*, 3rd edn
    (Paris, 1871), pp. 39–44. Von Schellendorff, *op. cit.*, pp. 27–8. Dallas
    D. Irvine, 'The French and Prussian Staff Systems before 1870',
    Journal of the American Military History Foundation, II (Winter 1938),
    pp. 192–203.
64 Stoffel, *op. cit.*, pp. 116, 131. Report, 1870, p. 301.
65 Report, 1870, pp. 305–26. See also 'General Remarks on Prussian
    Military Education', pp. 327–8.
66 Irvine, 'The French and Prussian Staff Systems before 1870', p. 196.
67 Stoffel, *op. cit.*, pp. 111–31 *passim*.
68 Gordon A. Craig, 'Command and Staff Problems in the Austrian
    Army, 1740–1866', Michael Howard (ed.), *The Theory and Practice
    of War* (London, 1965), pp. 45–52. See also Günther E. Rothenberg,
    'The Austrian Army in the Age of Metternich', *Journal of Modern
    History* (June 1968), pp. 155–65.
69 Craig, 'Command and Staff Problems in the Austrian Army', pp.
    53–7. Report, 1857, p. 180.
70 *Ibid.*, p. 60.
71 Cited by Craig, *ibid.*, p. 63.

72 *Ibid.*, p. 64. Report, 1870, 'The System of Military Education in Austria', pp. 354–5. For Austrian reforms in staff education and training after 1870 see von Schellendorff, *op. cit.*, pp. 66–74.
73 Irvine, 'The French and Prussian Staff Systems before 1870', p. 192.
74 Report, 1857, p. 65. Report, 1870, pp. 119–25.
75 Report, 1857, pp. 65–68. Irvine, *op. cit.*, pp. 201–2.
76 Report, 1870, Appendix G, pp. 520–8. Irvine, *op. cit.*, pp. 202–3.
77 *Ibid.* For a brilliant analysis of French military thought after 1870 see the same author's article, 'The French Discovery of Clausewitz and Napoleon' *Journal of the American Military History Institute*, IV (1941), pp. 143–161. See also von Schellendorff *op. cit.*, pp. 83–9, and *L' Enseignement Militaire Supérieur* (Paris, 1955), pp. 10–11, 13–15.
78 Von Schellendorff, *op. cit.*, pp. 97–108. The British Army's 'Staff' embraces senses 1, 2 and 3 given earlier and included: general officers actively employed, officers of the Adjutant-General's and Quarter-master-General's departments, other officers attached to the 'general staff' at the War Office, military secretaries, aides-de-camp, brigade-majors and officers on the staffs of district commands.
79 Von Schellendorff, *op. cit.*, pp. 97–100. The Military Department was divided into the following branches: the Military Secretary, Adjutant-General's and Quartermaster-General's departments, Inspector-General of Fortifications and Engineers, Inspector-General of Cavalry, Director of Artillery, Intelligence department, Military Education department, Medical and Veterinary departments. (See Table I, p. 118.)
80 *Ibid.*, pp. 106–9.

CHAPTER TWO

The decline of the Senior Department and the foundation of the Staff College 1815–1858

In a country so little dominated by military affairs as Britain it is not surprising that far-reaching army reforms have invariably been achieved only as a consequence of bitter experience in war. This was particularly true of the education of officers, which tended to be regarded by politicians as a costly luxury, and by senior officers as a dangerous tampering with the gentleman's inborn qualities of leadership. Thus not a single trained staff officer was available on the outbreak of war with revolutionary France in 1793. Indeed, there was no professional training at all for any but Ordnance Corps officers (i.e. gunners and sappers), until 1799, and right up to the Crimean War the Ordnance Corps remained virtually a separate army, wearing a distinctive uniform, taking no part in the affairs of the Royal Military College and providing no officers for the Staff.[1]

The low level of competence displayed by British officers in the Continental campaigns of the 1790s prompted the first serious attempt to provide professional instruction for infantry and cavalry subalterns and, beyond that, to produce officers trained in staff duties. Under the inspiration of Col. (later Maj.-Gen.) John Gaspard Le Marchant, a Guernsey-born cavalryman, supported by the Commander-in-Chief, the Duke of York, a Royal Military College was founded in 1799.[2] The College comprised a junior or cadet department at Marlow in Buckinghamshire, and a senior or staff department a few miles away at High Wycombe. The junior department moved to Sandhurst in 1812, and the senior department, after a few years at Farnham in Surrey, joined it in the same building in 1820.

Although Le Marchant had to contend with a great deal of opposition and obscurantism, the senior department quickly achieved a high reputation, mainly due to the steady flow of excellent officers it provided for Wellington's staff in the Peninsula. These included Sir George Murray, Sir John Hope, Lord Hardinge, General Wetherall and Sir William Napier. Indeed, Sidney Herbert exaggerated only slightly when he remarked in 1856, 'During the last five years of the Peninsular War I believe there was but one officer on the staff of the Quartermaster General who had not passed through our staff school at High Wycombe'.[3] So remarkable was the senior department's progress that whereas in 1799 the Horse Guards had been delighted to acquire the services of a Frenchman, General Jarry, as Commandant, after 1815 France looked to High Wycombe for a model in establishing her École d'Application.[4]

The term 'General Staff' at this time referred to all extra-regimental officers, civilian as well as military, and embraced three distinct types of staff officer: the General's personal staff, the staff of the civilian departments, and of the Adjutant General's and Quartermaster-General's departments. Thus only the third type were staff officers in the modern sense, and even then the Adjutant-General's department was largely confined to matters of routine, offering little scope for staff work proper.[5] In the Quartermaster-General's department, however, there was a genuine outlet for staff officers for the crucially important duties of surveying, sketching, map-making, the gathering and sifting of intelligence, and the movement and quartering of the Army.[6]

As for responsibilities, it is entirely appropriate to speak in personal terms of 'Wellington's staff'. He never so much as contemplated adopting the Prussian system in which the Chief of Staff enjoyed considerable authority *vis-a-vis* the Army commander; nor did he allow his Quartermaster-General to become an *éminence grise*. Sir George Murray he trusted and consulted but allowed him virtually no scope to take decisions. In particular, Wellington acted as his own Director of Military

Intelligence. Under less dominating personalities than Wellington, Major S. G. P. Ward has suggested, both the Adjutant-
General and Quartermaster-General tended to look for guidance or approval to their superiors at the Horse Guards.[7]

The High Wycombe course for future staff officers, though
not without a pedantic element, was on the whole extremely
practical, placing great emphasis, for example, on surveying
and sketching.[8] It can hardly be doubted that such alumni as
Murray and Napier were of great value to the Army after 1809,
but there were also a few pedants who created a bad impression
of the College in the minds of senior officers less convinced of
its importance than the Duke of York, Craufurd, Brownrigg
and Dundas. Wellington himself had never been an enthusiast
for the products of the Royal Military College, and if he had
had greater authority to select his own officers he would have
preferred more officers of 'family, fortune and influence'.[9]

After 1815 the senior department (as well as the junior),
steadily declined from every point of view: practical military
instruction virtually disappeared, Government financial support dwindled and then ceased altogether and, most discourag-
ing of all, its graduates were rarely given staff appointments.

Lt-Col Charles Napier, who graduated from the Senior
Department at Farnham in 1817, was highly critical both of
the incompetence of the instructors and examiners and of the
impractical nature of the course. He appended the following
scathing comments to the Collegiate Board's memorandum
which stated that the progress of the Senior Department was
'perfectly satisfactory':

Superb College Humbug. We did pass a decent examination;
but the whole course was *contemptible* and of no use to a military man beyond this, that a man studying mathematics,
fortification and drawing for two years must learn something.
But the style of the M.[ilitary] C.[ollege] was better calculated
to make *ten* ignorant and most conceited fools than *one* officer.
Sir Howard Douglas is perfectly ignorant of military affairs
and anything but 'able' and could not *teach* what he did not
know. Officers left Farnham with a smattering of mathematics,

of drawing, of fortifications – and a *thorough* conviction of their
vast military acquirements . . .

He proceeded to criticize each course in detail, remarking, for
example, of fortification that 'though all could *draw* and name
the lines on paper, I was the only man there (Sir H. Douglas
included) who could *throw up a field work* and I knew how to do
it *before I went there* or I should have never known. Sir Howard
is *quite ignorant* of fortification and no staff duties were taught!
What *stuff* then is here talked by five general officers and two
colonels [i.e. the examining board] and what ignorance of their
work!' Not content with destructive criticism, Col. Napier then
outlined his own idea of a practical examination for staff
officers: it consisted of a three-day field exercise in which a
series of related hypothetical problems would be presented to
the students, solutions to be worked out on the ground involving
the reconnaissance, planning and construction of a defensive
position. This, he concluded, was the sort of test that should
have been set 'had these muddleheads known how to examine'.[9b]
   To some extent this decline was the inevitable corollary of
the return to peace, and to a long period when there seemed to
be no need for a large standing army. With the disappearance
of permanent units larger than the regiment there went also the
appointments of brigade majors and divisional staffs – the Light
Division in 1813, for example, had employed seven staff officers.
Furthermore, the Quartermaster-General's department shrunk
under peacetime economies and, according to Ward, its last
product in the way of military science was probably Wyld's
Atlas in 1841.[10]
   Also, though the work of the senior department found a few
prominent champions, such as Gen. Sir Howard Douglas, the
concept of a General Staff on the Prussian model had never
established roots in Britain. Consequently between 1815 and
1854 the Army lost sight of the need for a nucleus of staff officers
with a mainly practical training, including a mastery of military
organization, horsemanship, foreign languages, facility in
sketching, experience in drafting and transmitting orders, and
in all the intricate problems involved in moving a large army

and bringing it into battle. This is to say nothing of intelligence work on foreign countries and armies or the study of Britain's strategic problems, since these aspects had never as yet been taught at the College or encouraged at the Horse Guards.

What came to prevail instead as the ideal of staff training was the 'scientific officer' closely resembling the specialists of the Ordnance Corps and distinguished chiefly by knowledge of higher mathematics. This trend was naturally emphasized by the disappearance of all the military instructors from the senior department. John Narrien, an eminent mathematician and astronomer, and his diminishing band of civilian colleagues, naturally tended to give academic courses, and even when pressed into teaching military subjects (such as fortification) the results were almost entirely theoretical.

In the period 1815–54 the senior department, then, though not without faults of its own, was largely a victim to the shortcomings of Britain's military system. Engineer and artillery officers received their training at the Royal Military Academy, Woolwich, while in the infantry and cavalry the purchase system put a premium on wealth and interest rather than professional qualifications, to secure a commission and for promotion up to the rank of lieutenant-colonel. The evils of the purchase and sale of commissions were clearly described by a Committee of Inquiry in 1857:

> This system . . . produces ill effects upon the constitution of the army and impairs its efficiency, by giving an undue preeminence to wealth, by discouraging exertion and by depressing merit. Under such regulations there is little inducement for officers to acquire proficiency in the science of war, or to study the military progress of other nations. An officer who performs his routine duties and who keeps a sum of money available to purchase his promotion . . . may look forward with confidence to the attainment of high military rank.[10b]

Moreover there was general acceptance of the Wellingtonian conviction that in war the combination of personal courage and the qualities of the English gentleman were all-sufficient. Thus Lt-Col W. H. Adams, Professor of Military Science at the Royal

Military College, bluntly told the Select Committee on Sandhurst in 1855:

> military education is but little valued by the greater part of
> the high military authorities. They consider after all, whether
> a man is professionally educated or not, it will make not the
> slightest difference with regard to his qualities as an officer;
> that is the opinion in this country, but it is not the opinion in
> other countries. If the matter is discussed in the House of
> Commons they immediately say, Such a person is a very
> distinguished officer; he has been engaged so and so; why
> not put him on the staff? . . . They [brave officers] consider
> from having gained all their honours merely by being dis-
> tinguished, that they can look down upon education more
> than another man would do. A staff officer is in France
> simply this: he is the cleverest man of the body. Of course
> being a man of the greatest attainments does not prevent his
> being equally brave as an uneducated man . . .[11]

These opinions, and especially that contested by Adams in
the final sentence, were still widely held by senior officers after
the Crimean War: before the war proponents of staff training
had little hope of a sympathetic hearing.

There were, however, some stirrings of schemes for the general
improvement of the military education of officers before the outbreak of the Crimean War. In 1849, the Duke of Wellington,
despite his general hostility to military education, laid down
two important principles: first, that no one should receive a
commission unless he should prove on examination to be
possessed of good average abilities, and to have received the
education of a gentleman; second, that no ensign or cornet
should be promoted to a lieutenancy, nor lieutenant to a captaincy, until he had satisfied a competent tribunal of his
professional and general acquirements and fitness. The first
principle did at least introduce the notion of an educational
requirement, though it also led to an increase in 'cramming';
the second remained a dead letter.

More than any other public figure it was Sidney Herbert
who struggled to secure a better all-round system of military

education in the unpropitious decade preceding the Crimean War.[12] As Secretary at War (1844–6) he had concentrated chiefly on improving army schools, and had appointed the Chaplain-General and well-known military biographer, the Rev. G. R. Gleig, Inspector-General of Military Schools. On returning to the War Office in 1853 Herbert turned his attention to Wellington's second principle. In a letter dated January 1854 to the Commander-in-Chief, Viscount Hardinge, Herbert proposed that a military instructor be appointed at the headquarters of every general's command to prepare junior officers for promotion. A board of examiners (unconnected with Sandhurst) might also be set up to conduct not only the examination for promotion, but also the examination for first commissions. 'Great inducements might be held out by reserving appointments on the staff to those who distinguished themselves [in the promotion examination]: none else should be admitted to the senior department at Sandhurst, which might thus become what the École d'État Major is in France.'[13]

Sidney Herbert believed, over-optimistically as events were to show, that it was no longer necessary to prove the need for and benefits of professional education in the Army. Lord Hardinge and the Cabinet approved Sidney Herbert's three-part scheme embracing the appointment of a Board of Examiners, the establishment of garrison instructors in every military district and the reform of the senior department. A sum was voted to these ends in the Army estimates for 1854–5.[14] The outbreak of war, followed by Herbert's resignation in February 1855, probably explains why nothing was done.

The suffering of the Army before Sebastopol in the winter of 1854–5 was the natural consequence of the country's general military unpreparedness. Given the lack of organization for supplies, transport and auxiliary services, the bureaucratic entanglement of War Office administration, and the incompetence of many of the senior commanders, much of the confusion and wastage that occurred was unavoidable. Nevertheless, it was widely agreed that the absence of a body of efficiently trained staff officers exacerbated the difficulties. Lord Raglan had no alternative but to rely on personal selection for his headquarters staff; and, as Major Godwin-Austen commented, 'it is hardly an exaggeration to say that no soldier existed with a conception of the requirements of an overseas campaign on a large scale. None had any idea of the functions of the Staff.'[15] Lord Panmure, who became Secretary of State for War in February 1855, wrote that 'The system by which an army should be provisioned, moved, brought to act in the field and the trenches, taught to attack or defend, is non-existent ... We have no means of making general officers or of forming an efficient staff.' Regiments in the Crimea were combed for officers possessing a Military College Certificate, and the Governor of the Royal Military College was given *carte blanche* to dispatch all suitable officers from the instructing staff and the senior department. Unfortunately these proved little better equipped for staff duties than officers with no qualifications at all.

Long before the war ended many thoughtful soldiers and civilians had grasped the propositions that a trained staff was essential for efficient military operations, and that such a body of experts could not be improvised from gallant but poorly-educated regimental officers. In January 1855, for example, the Prince Consort drafted a memorandum stressing the need for a staff of competent general officers and a staff corps to train subordinate officers for duties in the field. In his written comments on this memorandum, and in subsequent speeches in the House of Commons, Sidney Herbert pointed out that there were two related problems. The first was the lack of any large military organization in peacetime: 'Certainly no regimental officer except in India or the Cape has seen a Division.' The second was the need to reorganize and expand the senior department and make it the sole means of entry to the Staff. He had asked Lord Hardinge to appoint Maj. P. L. MacDougall to Sandhurst with this in view, but the latter was more urgently needed in the Crimea.[16]

It is some indication of the urgency with which Sidney Herbert and his successor at the War Office, Lord Panmure,[17] regarded the need to reform military education that the Select Committee on the Royal Military College, Sandhurst, presented its report on 18 June 1855 – in the middle of the war. This inquiry investigated the original objectives, history and present condition of the College in great detail and it constitutes an important landmark in the establishment of the Staff College.

The senior department was still regulated by the Royal Warrant of 1808 which stated that its function was 'to instruct officers in the scientific part of their profession, with the view of enabling them better to discharge their duty when acting in command of regiments . . . and at the same time of qualifying themselves to be employed in the Quartermaster-General and Adjutant-General's departments'. Except for the artillery and engineers it was the only institution in which officers could obtain instruction in the more scientific branch of their profession.

The inquiry revealed a lamentable state of affairs at this once distinguished institution. The Parliamentary grant had ceased completely in 1832, and the number of students had fallen to fifteen (in practice often fewer), each of whom paid a fee of £30 a year. This contribution by no means covered the cost of the department, so the iniquitous practice had arisen of making the cadets in the junior department subsidize their seniors. Only two professors were now exclusively attached to the senior department and to one of these John Narrien – now aged and nearly blind – the Committee paid a gracious tribute for in effect carrying on the department almost single-handed for many years. Although an eminent mathematician and astronomer (his book on the *Origin and Progress of Astronomy* was published in 1853), he had been obliged to turn his hand to fortification, gunnery, tactics and castrametation, leaving his colleague to teach military surveying. The poverty of the senior department's resources is evident from the fact that there was no book in English on staff duties, and no work on tactics recognized by the Horse Guards.

Also, though not stated in the Report, in the years before the Crimean War very few officers had come forward to be considered for entry, and some of these had less admirable motives than the advancement of their professional studies. This was only to be expected when so little store was placed on the Military College Certificate by the Horse Guards. As Col. Adams remarked: 'if I was told that such a person was on the staff, I should think that he had very good interest, but I should never say therefore that he was a very superior young man' (as would, he believed, be most likely the case in the French or Prussian Armies).[18]

The Committee performed an excellent task in exposing the inadequacy of officer education at the Royal Military College, yet its recommendations were remarkably timid. The Report suggested that a sub-committee of the Board of Commissioners should examine and report on the course of study and that the revised course should form the basis for a Parliamentary financial vote. One military instructor might be transferred from the staff of the junior to the senior department. The fee paid by officers at the senior department should not be increased, but nor should it be abolished. Officers who successfully completed the course at the senior department should have the opportunity to attend further courses at Chatham and Woolwich, and then be attached temporarily to regiments of other arms 'so that they may become acquainted with all branches of the profession'. The Committee emphatically opposed the formation of an independent corps of staff officers such as existed in France. On the vital issue of the employment of senior department graduates, it was recommended that 'officers so educated, if otherwise fit, should not be neglected in appointments to the staff'. This exposed the rock on which many well-intentioned but superficial reforms had already foundered: the Military College Certificate had come to be widely regarded as a handicap rather than an aid to staff employment. According to Gen. Sir Howard Douglas, 216 officers had received certificates since a new system of classification had been introduced in 1836, but only approximately 20 had ever been employed on the staff. In 1852 there were only 7 in staff appointments, and in May 1854 – two months after the outbreak of war – only 15 out of 291. Of the few Crimean generals who had obtained certificates, several, such as Sir William Eyre, Sir James Fergusson and Sir George Brown, had passed through in the Peninsular days when the department was still at High Wycombe.[19] A

Parliamentary Paper, called for on 1 May 1855, listed 42 officers who had received certificates at the senior department and had not been subsequently employed on the staff during the past twenty years. These included Lt-Col P. L. MacDougall (Canadian Rifles), then on half pay and shortly to become the first Commandant of the Staff College.[20]

All that can be said in favour of this Report is that it substantiated with a mass of evidence the deplorable condition of the senior department and established that the European nations took staff training far more seriously. This was true not only of major military powers like France and Prussia but also of Belgium, where future staff officers studied in all for six years. 'The officers of the Belgian Army,' an expert witness stated, 'are of a different class to ours, because they continue at all times to study amongst themselves, as their promotion depends upon it; and when our young gentlemen here are talking of breaking looking-glasses and furniture, the Belgian officers are talking over military matters and studying them.'[21]

Even had the Committee's recommendations been promptly implemented they were too modest to achieve any significant improvement. Since several of the eleven members were MPs who supported Sidney Herbert in his Parliamentary campaign for the reform of military education, it may be that the Report was deliberately toned down to proposals that had some hope of acceptance. For, of course, Parliament had not spent a farthing on the senior department since 1832 and improvements were bound to be costly. Lord Panmure's correspondence with the Duke of Cambridge reveals that Parliamentary radicals were particularly strident in their criticisms of the military staff.[22]

A characteristic shortcoming of many such investigations is illustrated by the proceedings of the Select Committee on the Royal Military College. It is that unless such a body has a dominating personality, or a precise notion of what it is looking for (as was notably the case with the three-man 'Esher' Committee on War Office Reconstitution of 1903), it is apt to blur the picture by ill-directed questioning of witnesses, and then to be confused by the weight of contradictory expert evidence.

Perhaps the most valuable testimony was that of Gen. Sir
Howard Douglas, whose experience of the senior department
stretched back to 1804 when he had been assigned to High
Wycombe to assist the ageing French Commandant, Gen. Jarry.
Gen. Douglas, in contrast with another famous Peninsular
veteran, Gen. Sir John Burgoyne, strongly defended the potential value of a resuscitated staff school. He stressed that the
department must be physically separated from the cadets, to
improve the atmosphere for serious study as well as to secure
ample quarters. The annual intake should be increased at once
from 15 to 30. Gen. Douglas put his finger on the present
course's greatest weakness in calling for more emphasis on practical field work and the study of military history – at that time
completely neglected. Like several other witnesses who knew the
senior department well, he insisted that no one should be employed on the general staff in preference to an officer who had
successfully passed through the senior department. When asked
by Col. Dunne MP, 'Have not a great many of those men who
have gone out [to the Crimea] without any previous knowledge
of fortification, acquired practical knowledge under fire in the
trenches?' the General replied crushingly, 'Yes, and many
lives have been lost in consequence.'[23] This exchange epito-
mized the contrast between those who continued to trust in
improvisation and 'muddling through', and others who believed
that a properly trained staff would greatly diminish such
blunders.

The Professor of Military Science at the Royal Military
College, Lt-Col W. H. Adams, after pointing out how unfavourably the British military education system compared with those
of Continental countries, gave the clearest general account of
the role of the staff officer in war:

A man may be a good general though he cannot read or
write, but he cannot be an efficient staff officer under such
circumstances; the good but [educationally] ignorant general
requires, more than another, well-educated staff officers; the
natural genius of the general originates a certain operation,
he calls upon his quartermaster-general's staff to make all the

OUR FUTURE STAFF.

A rather Heavy Dragoon (who has some idea of going in for a Staff Examination, rides over to the College to make inquiries). *"Well, how are you getting on?' What sort of things do they give you to do?"*

Gifted Member of Staff College. *"Oh, pretty well—been up Three Nights reading for last Examination. Knocked off dead and living languages, campaigns, trigonometry, analytical geometry, perspective, differential and integral calculus, rectification, quadrature and curvature of curves, theory of equation, contact and osculation, statics, dynamics, hydrostatics, castrametation (the Cavalry finds himself rising in his stirrups), equilibrium of arches, method of tangent, vanishing fractions, pneum—"* * * * *

[PLUNGER rides furiously back to Camp.

D

calculations and surveys etc., requisite to carry into execution his conception.[24]

With the ending of the Crimean War in 1856 the atmosphere in Parliament and the Press briefly appeared to be very favourable for far-reaching military reforms. Improvement in military education had influential supporters in the Prince Consort and the Duke of Cambridge – who became Commander-in-Chief in July 1856; while in the House of Commons Sidney Herbert and Gen. Sir George de Lacy Evans in particular kept the subject alive.

In January 1856 Lord Panmure set up a three-man Committee to report on the best means of re-organizing the system of training for officers of the scientific corps (that is, the Royal Artillery and Royal Engineers) who received their commissions from the Royal Military Academy, Woolwich. The Committee, whose members were Lt-Col W. Yolland R.E., Lt-Col W. J. Smythe R.A., and W. C. Lake M.A. (Fellow of Balliol College, Oxford), visited the military institutions of France, Austria, Prussia and Sardinia. Fortunately for the future Staff College the Committee exceeded its terms of reference and compared the senior department (unfavourably) with its foreign equivalents. Their report was published in January 1857 and reinforced the criticisms of the Sandhurst Committee just at a time when the impetus towards the reform of the senior department appeared to be weakening.

On the state of the senior department this Committee was even more outspoken than its predecessor:

> This Institution does not seem ... to have been regarded as a Staff School in the sense in which Schools bearing the same name in France, Prussia, Austria, and Sardinia, educate for the Staff Corps; since in these countries it is necessary that all officers on the General Staff should have frequented for some years the Staff School, whilst it appears that out of 216 officers who have received certificates at the senior department since 1836, only 15 were employed on the staff in May 1854. Nor can it be doubted that both the importance and the education of the senior department ... have greatly

diminished of late years; since latterly there has been an attendance of only nine or ten officers; whilst the whole instruction has been in the hands of two, indeed it may almost be said of one professor. The significance of this last fact may be estimated when we mention that for the Staff School in France there are thirteen military and five civil professors.

On military education as a whole they calculated that Britain spent less than one-twentieth of the amount spent by Prussia, one-thirty-seventh that of France and one-hundredth that of Austria. For the cost of Staff education the figures were France £5,814 per annum, Prussia £3,234, Austria £4,300 and Britain nil. 'If Military Education is a subject of importance,' the Committee added sharply, 'it is surely worth supporting with the same care with which other great nations direct it; if, on the other hand, it is unimportant, it would be best . . . to throw it aside entirely, and trust only to the education of Public Schools.' The annual expenditure at the time of £1,300 on officers' education upon no uniform system was 'indefensible upon any theory'. The Committee reiterated the opinion of the previous report that the essential thing was to give 'every conceivable premium and encouragement to such military requirements as the service of the Staff is thought to require'. 'It seems needless to urge that a College of this kind, opening the door to advancement and frequented when the mind is in its full vigour, would possess every inducement to call forth the energies of young officers of talent. But a senior department, offering a bare opportunity for military study with no ulterior results, stands in a wholly different position.'[25]

Schemes for the reform of Military Education and the establishment of a Staff School

Lord Hardinge, the Commander-in-Chief, was preparing a memorandum on military education in July 1856, but he suffered a stroke when attending on the Queen at Aldershot and was obliged to resign. As regards the senior department he saw the first step must be to obtain the best men. 'It is far from being the case at present,' he wrote, 'that the most promising officers go to the senior department, and the candidates latterly have been so few in number, that almost any officer, of ever so little attainment or promise, could enter the department.' Like the two committees of inquiry, he concluded that the answer lay in creating a feeling of certainty among the officers that merit would be rewarded. He proposed to confine entry to the Quartermaster-General's department to graduates of the senior department.[26]

A month earlier, on 5 June 1856, Sidney Herbert, speaking from the back benches, had initiated a very important debate in the House of Commons on the whole question of the education of officers. He took the conciliatory line that the officers in the Crimea deserved praise for adapting themselves so quickly, seeing that they had been given no opportunity to learn the higher branches of their profession in peacetime. In complete contrast with 1816, the Army was now extremely popular and there had never existed a keener desire to see it made efficient. Yet his scheme of 1854 – for a Board of Examiners and garrison instructors – though approved by the House, the Horse Guards and the Treasury, was now being dropped from the estimates. Most officers' education was assumed to end, he pointed out, when they were about sixteen, so not surprisingly 'ignorance of military matters has become a sort of badge of gentility'. Like another caustic critic of the prevailing standard of military education, Lt-Col Adams, Sidney Herbert accepted the purchase system and took the view that 'it is just because we have purchase that we the more require examination'. He proposed that the senior department be moved back to Farnham and the course made far more practical and military. After passing through the staff school he would allow officers three years to get to know the different branches of the service. Among Herbert's supporters in the debate were Edward Ellice, George de Lacy Evans, Colonel Dunne, Mr Rich and Viscount Goderich. The official reply was non-committal.[27] If Mr Punch may be taken as an accurate barometer of public opinion there existed a great deal of prejudice against improving officer education, and indeed much astonishment that such a thing should even be contemplated.[28]

How influential this debate was is unclear, but certainly the second half of 1856 witnessed almost hectic activity at the Horse Guards and the War Office in the drafting and discussion of schemes for a thorough re-organization of military education. Unfortunately the two offices did not work in close harmony; consequently there was some duplication of effort and conflict over personalities.

Though the Duke of Cambridge's biographer exaggerates somewhat in calling him 'a pioneer of exceptional originality in the realms of military education',[29] this was certainly one aspect of military affairs in which the Duke initially was clearly in favour of reform. In the autumn of 1856 he drew on the experience of the Rev. G. R. Gleig, Maj.-Gen. Duncan Cameron, late of the 42nd regiment, and a number of other officers. Simultaneously, Lord Panmure was working independently on the same problem, advised chiefly by a brilliant young artillery officer, John Henry Lefroy,[30] who had come to the War Minister's attention in 1854 as confidential adviser on artillery matters to the Duke of Newcastle.

Through no fault of his own Lefroy was not destined to become a second Le Marchant in the field of officer education, but in 1856 his clear thinking and confidence in the potential capacity of the British regimental officer to benefit from professional education played an important part in bringing about the foundation of the Staff College. In October 1855, Lord Panmure sent Lefroy to examine the medical facilities at Constantinople and Scutari. Undeterred by senior officers and scornful of 'red tape', he became an enthusiastic supporter of Florence Nightingale. On his return, though only a lieutenant-colonel, and occupying the anomalous post of chief clerk at the War Office, Lefroy threw himself into drafting a scheme for the complete re-organization of military education. The section on the Staff School does not adequately reflect the breadth of Lefroy's vision, but it contains some calculations and propolass which were to be adopted by the Staff College.

Lefroy estimated that 124 staff appointments were available, including 40 aides-de-camp but excluding the military secretary at headquarters. He assumed that most staff appointments would have a maximum tenure of five years, and that therefore about 25 vacancies would occur annually. Allowing for a few of these to be filled by officers who had gained distinction in the field, he thought the establishment of the Staff School should be 50 students: more in fact than there had ever been in the past or would be for many years.[31]

Allowing for eighteen months spent in attachments to the other arms, Lefroy calculated that the future staff officer would be absent from regimental duty for three and a half years. How could so long an absence be reconciled with the purchase system, under which seniority in the regiment gave the right of first opportunity to purchase to the next rank when a vacancy occurred? Lefroy recommended that full-pay officers should be borne as supernumeraries on the strength of their regiments, so the regiment would not be short of officers, nor the officer's interests suffer.

Many of Lefroy's detailed ideas for the improvement of staff education foundered on the assumption that the Staff School would be established in London. In view of a more recent but similarly unavailing proposal to transfer the cadet colleges to the capital (in the modern instance to the Royal Naval College at Greenwich), it is interesting to note Lefroy's reasons for favouring London in 1856:

1 The ablest instruction in the kingdom would be at command.
2 The invaluable resources of the Government School of Mines in Jermyn Street would be available.
3 The Topographical and Statistical Establishment of the War Office would be accessible at all times.
4 Several great libraries would be available.
5 Students would be able to acquaint themselves with our whole system of military administration.
6 London is nearly equidistant from Chatham and Aldershot, and close to Woolwich.

7 It would be under the eye of the Secretary of State for War, and of the Commander-in-Chief.

Apart from the positive attractions which were soon to be advanced for the Camberley site, two considerations probably tipped the scales against London: the cost of buying land and raising entirely new premises; and the distractions of the capital's social life for mature men unaccustomed to a rigorous course of study.

Lefroy's influence is most directly evident in the emphasis on competition, grading, and special distinctions for merit that characterized the early history of the Staff College. Considerations of cost presumably ruled out his suggestion that gold medals be awarded every year or two years and a limited number of Fellowships founded – 'analogous to those at the Universities, which should entitle the holder to a small annual payment (from £50 to £100) until attaining the substantive rank of lieutenant-colonel'. However, a system of honouring distinctions in various subjects was adopted; and success at the Staff College was soon to be recognized in the Army List, though Lefroy did not originate the now famous abbreviation 'p.s.c.'[32]

Lord Panmure had intimated confidentially[33] that Lefroy would be invited to implement his own comprehensive scheme as the first Director-General of Military Education; an undertaking in which he would probably have excelled despite his specialist background and lack of campaigning experience. Unfortunately this appointment was entangled in the much larger question of the ultimate responsibility for the control of military education. The Queen insisted that military education must be under the direct control of the Horse Guards, not the War Office. Lefroy's appointment was opposed on the grounds both of his junior rank and his position as Lord Panmure's adviser. 'We want a Director-General of Education very much,' the Queen wrote to the Prime Minister, Lord Palmerston, 'but he ought to be immediately under the Commander-in-Chief, if possible a general officer of weight, assisted by a Board of Officers of the different arms.' The Queen's fear was that if

Lefroy were appointed and made directly responsible to the War Office then the officers' mental advancement would be separated from their executive qualifications. The solution adopted was that the Department of Military Education was placed under the Commander-in-Chief but subject to the general control of the Secretary of State for War.[34] To avoid any embarrassment in dealing with senior officers, such as Maj.-Gen. Sir Harry Jones, Governor of the Royal Military College, the Duke of Cambridge became President of the new Council of Military Education, while most of the work was in fact performed by the Vice-President, Maj.-Gen. Duncan Cameron. Lefroy had to be content with the post of Inspector-General of Army Schools. Two years later, in 1859, the post was transferred to the Council of Military Education and Lefroy's services were lost to military education.[35] Later he wrote with some bitterness,

> It would have required much higher ability, rank and influence than I possessed to carry so big a thing through [the complete overhaul of military education] in the teeth of the Horse Guards, the opposition of many of the highest opinions in the service, . . . the Treasury, and the critics who were bound to find fault. The thing fell through. The Government laid out about £100,000 on a Staff College at Sandhurst; everything else remained much as before.[36]

Though Lefroy had apparently drawn up his memorandum unaware that similar plans were being worked out at the Horse Guards, the Duke of Cambridge had the benefit of the former's work and criticisms in preparing his own memorandum, the final version of which was dated 12 December 1856. Much of this document found its way into the Staff College regulations for it contained some admirable sentiments, such as deploring the professional soldier's narrowness of mind which, in the commander of an army, 'is incapable of taking a comprehensive view of the political, as well as military posture of things before it'; yet concluded on a cautious note, stressing the difficulties which a Staff School would encounter, rather than the improvements it would bring.[37]

The main product of these memoranda and discussions was the establishment, in April 1857, of a Council of Military Education, the duties of which were to select examiners and prepare examination papers for entry to the Army and the Staff School, as well as promotion; and to recommend professors and instructors for the Staff School, the Royal Military College (Sandhurst) and the Royal Military Academy (Woolwich).

Pending the establishment of the Staff College, the Duke of Cambridge, on 9 April 1857, issued instructions setting forth the qualifications to be demanded of all staff officers from 1 January 1858.[38] All staff officers were expected to be able to ride well, and 'to write a distinct and legible hand, and compose English correctly'. The latter requirement was inserted on the insistence of the Prime Minister, Lord Palmerston, who had commented on the draft order, 'I am sorry to say that the officers of the Army are apt, in general, to write like kitchenmaids'.[39] That the standard aimed at by the Commander-in-Chief was high, and for the most part sensibly practical, may be gathered from the accomplishments required of deputy assistants in the adjutant-general's and quartermaster-general's departments. These comprised: practical sketching – including 'flying sketching' from horseback – practical trigonometry and geometry with knowledge of logarithms; to read, write and speak at least one foreign language, to judge of ground and its proper occupation by all arms, to have perfect knowledge of castrametation and the principles of permanent fortification; and to be thoroughly acquainted with military geography and military history, especially as related to the campaigns of ancient and modern commanders.

The Duke of Cambridge also informed the Council of Military Education, in a minute dated 6 April 1857, that he favoured the immediate doubling of the students and staff of the senior department (that is, from 15 to 30 and 2 to 4 respectively). The Council, however, concentrated first on the examination of candidates for a direct commission, and as the summer wore on it began to appear that the creation of a Staff College had again been shelved. This suspicion caused Sir George de Lacy Evans and Sidney Herbert to initiate another important Parliamentary debate on military education on 28 July, when the House of Commons resolved that 'a higher standard of professional instruction ought to be established for the commissioned ranks of the Army, but especially for the Staff; and that this will best be promoted by recourse to competitive examination of officers desiring to qualify themselves for the Staff, and by assured encouragements for proficiency and general fitness for advancement'.[40] The following month the report of the Royal Commission on the Purchase System underlined these aspirations.[41]

By October 1857 the Council of Military Education had drafted a syllabus for the entrance examination and course of study at the Staff College. This was laid before the Queen and she invited the Prince Consort's comments. In general the latter approved, but took strong exception to what he justifiably regarded as an excessive emphasis on pure mathematics. His memorandum concluded:

> What is to be gained by making the officers of the army, and Staff in particular, *abstract mathematicians* instead of scientific soldiers? . . . The most exaggerated supporters of the mathematical system of Cambridge have never maintained that abstract mathematics had any value in themselves for the student, but assert that they are the *best* means for training the mind to take up afterwards any practical study in life, an assertion however which is doubted by many and denied by the whole University of Oxford. The military profession is a distinct profession like the law [etc], and mathematics once gone through at school have, with the exception of the case of the Artillery and Engineers, no value for it, except in their application to geodesy, topography, mechanics and physical philosophy. If we are to make our Staff officers theoretical mathematicians we should inflict the greatest injury upon the Queen's Service . . .[42]

The Queen therefore returned the papers unsigned, and the Duke of Cambridge wrote to Lord Panmure, 'There is a good deal of truth in what the Prince states as to Mathematical studies. I have shown these observations to Cameron and he is rather disposed himself to think that we have gone too far in requiring four books of Euclid . . .'[43] The Council nevertheless proved reluctant to modify its high mathematical requirements, and in self-defence quoted at length the opinions of headmasters of the great public schools who had actually suggested much higher qualifications.[44] It is probably significant that Cameron's two colleagues on the Council of Military Education were both from the Ordnance Corps; namely Col. J. E. Portlock R.E. and Lt-Col J. E. Addison R.A. This exchange of views perfectly illustrates the pronounced tendency in the early years of the Staff College to identify the trained staff officer too closely with the scientific specialists of the Ordnance Corps, whose education and duties related only very indirectly to the movement of large bodies of the troops in the field.

In its memorandum dated 25 November 1857, the Council of Military Education also rejected the suggestions of Sidney Herbert, Lefroy and others that the new Staff College should be removed from Sandhurst. The qualities of ground in the neighbourhood, it was argued, were very favourable for instruction in sketching; and the quiet, retired situation was ideal for study. Constitutionally, too, the Staff College was not as yet to escape from its subordinate role in the Royal Military College: the Commandant was required to report to the Governor of the College in matters of discipline, and even on educational questions letters to the Council of Military Education had to be first submitted to the Governor.

The revised General Order and Regulations embodying the work of the Council of Military Education were at last published on 17 December 1857, and the Staff College received its present title after 'fifty-eight years of chequered existence' as the Senior Department. The new title was of great significance, as the Council itself testified, 'since it recognized the real object of the institution' and left no doubt that an officer, by passing through with credit, would secure a staff appointment, 'no other channel of admission to the Staff being open after 1 January 1860, excepting in the case of officers either of the rank of lieutenant-colonel at that particular date or who have proved in the field their fitness for staff appointments'.[45]

The main features of the Staff College constitution were as follows.[46] The College was to be open to all arms of the service whether stationed at home or overseas, and its establishment of 30 students would be made up of 25 from the Line, Cavalry and Guards and 5 from the two branches of the Ordnance Corps – 'should any officers of those corps desire to compete for admission'.[47] Admission was to be by competitive examination, to qualify for which an officer needed at least three years' service, and a certificate on his all-round suitability for future staff employment from his commanding officer. If still a subaltern he must have passed his promotion examination to command a troop or company. The two-year course would open on 1 February each year and consist of four terms. Officers who successfully completed the course and passed the final examination would be graded in three classes according to merit, and those who particularly distinguished themselves would receive special commendation. After graduation, staff officers would be attached for six months each to the two arms other than their own, and the commanding officers of the units would report on them to the Adjutant-General. The instructing staff would be increased to nine, four of them to be serving officers designated 'professors in military subjects'. The Duke of Cambridge's unwillingness to make full attendance at the Staff College course a *sine qua non* for staff employment was patent in a curious regulation: officers who satisfied the conditions of entry but who did not wish to undergo the whole course could, with the Commander-in-Chief's permission, either simply sit the final examination or, provided a vacancy existed, take the examination set for the Junior Division at the end of the First year and attend for the second year. As Lefroy hinted, the Staff College course could hardly be said to provide indispensable training if officers could secure the qualification without coming to Sandhurst at all.[48]

The establishment of the Staff College was one of the more spectacular of the military reforms which were achieved in the later 1850s on the declining wave of popular interest created by the debacle in the Crimea. Four committees of inquiry, several Parliamentary debates and a flood of correspondence and memoranda testify that the concern for an improvement in military education – particularly of the Staff – on the part of politicians and soldiers was both deep and widespread. As was only to be expected, however, the recommended cures fell considerably short of the hopes of the most ambitious reformers such as Sidney Herbert and Lefroy. Nevertheless – on paper – the Staff College regulations could be welcomed with guarded optimism: much would depend on the spirit in which they were operated.

Though the Staff College eventually emerged from the deliberations of a Council, several individuals deserve recognition for their advocacy and ideas between 1854 and 1858. Sidney Herbert was the first and throughout the most eloquent advocate of a radical improvement over the whole field of military education, and he played an important part, along with Sir George de Lacy Evans and a handful of others, in keeping the issue alive in Parliament, though out of office himself between February 1855 and June 1859. Lord Panmure does not have the reputation of being a keen military reformer but, while his papers do not permit this verdict to be reversed, they do at least demonstrate his active interest in the reform of military education, and his willingness to put forward Lefroy's ideas. The latter may be considered unlucky in being pushed aside in favour of the Council of Military Education. Quite apart from his evident academic distinction and the thoroughness of his research, there emanates from his papers a spirit of confidence in the latent abilities of regimental officers to rise to the great educational challenge which, he hoped, would be symbolized by the founding of a Staff College. It is possible, however, that Lefroy was too much of a brilliant scientific individualist to have excelled as Director-General of Military Education or Commandant of the Staff College. The Prince Consort also, though necessarily much of his influence was behind the scenes and cannot be documented, was certainly deeply interested in the reform of military education. His memoranda on the subject show him to have had an admirably clear vision of the essentially practical training necessary for the improvement of staff work. The Duke of Cambridge, too, emerges with considerable credit from his first few years at the head of the Army. In this period he was far from being a reactionary on all aspects of military reform. He took a great interest in the development of schemes for the improvement of military education, and his own memorandum of December 1857 laid the foundation for the creation of the Staff College. Though he retained certain reservations about the degree to which promotion and key appointments should depend purely on merit as displayed in study and examinations, without his cautious encouragement the Staff College would scarcely have been established in 1858.

The ambitious academic standards set by the entrance examination and syllabus of the Staff College were in striking contrast to the resolutely anti-intellectual tradition fostered in the majority of regiments that comprised the mid-Victorian Army; a tradition reinforced since 1815 by Wellington's ill-concealed hostility towards 'army schoolmasters'. As Maj. Godwin-Austen, writing in the 1920s, aptly commented, the appetite of the typical regimental officer for education was then 'extremely delicate'. He thought it 'damned rot'.[49] Could the Horse Guards succeed in attracting the best brains in the infantry and cavalry for staff training without creating an *élite* group – a notion which was then highly suspect, particularly in military circles?

In drawing up the Staff College syllabus and regulations it is all too clear that the future staff officer was to be moulded in the image of the scientific specialists of the Ordnance Corps. Reconnaissance, military drawing, fortification and law were all of importance, but where was the emphasis on war? Apart from the military history course there was little scope for study-ing the practical problems of military operations. A largely theoretical course would tend to attract pedants rather than fighting men whereas the new institution desperately needed to establish a favourable reputation among the regiments.

Indeed, to a large extent the new scheme depended on the cooperation of regimental commanding officers, many of whose military horizons were extremely confined. Would they recom-mend their ablest young officers for the Staff College, with the risk of losing them for good, or take the opportunity to push forward the claims of someone the regiment would rather be without? Similarly, the potentially valuable scheme of attaching newly graduated staff officers to units of the other arms would be a waste of time under commanders out of sympathy with such new-fangled ideas.

Above all, the successful development of the Staff College would depend on the attitude of the Commander-in-Chief and the men he appointed as Commandant and instructors. It would be astonishing if personal merit were allowed to prevail in the one sector of staff appointments while 'interest' operated everywhere else and the purchase system continued to give great advantages to wealthy officers in all but the Ordnance Corps.

Finally, in all these discussions little attention had been given to Sidney Herbert's important points that not only had the British Army no General Staff, but also in peacetime there had hitherto been no permanent organization higher than the regiment. How, in short, could it profit to develop the 'brain' of the Army if the limbs and body were to remain weak and stunted?

CHAPTER 2. NOTES

1 S. G. P. Ward, *Wellington's Headquarters* (London, 1957). See also Richard Glover, *Peninsular Preparation: the Reform of the British Army, 1795–1809* (London, 1963).

2 R. H. Thoumine, *Scientific Soldier: a Life of General Le Marchant, 1766–1812.*

3 *Hansard's Parliamentary Debates,* Third Series, Vol. 142, col. 996. See also Ward, *op. cit.,* Appendix I.

4 Select Committee on the Royal Military College, Sandhurst (Sandhurst Report), Parliamentary Paper 317, 1855, Appendix 2, p. 186.

5 Ward, *op. cit.,* p. 44 and Appendix I. Ward significantly lists only one ex-R.M.C. man in the Adjutant-General's department to 27 in the Quartermaster-General's.

6 *Ibid.,* p. 37. Brigade majors were in a limbo between regimental officers and the headquarter's staff. They were often drawn from regimental adjutants and some had been aide-de-camps. Their definite duties included drawing up duty rosters, placing picquets and liaison within the brigade.

7 *Ibid.,* pp. 55, 122, 152.

8 Sandhurst Report, Minutes of Evidence, paras 2286–7 (General Sir Howard Douglas). Documents relating to the setting up of the Royal Military College, General Jarry's qualifications as an instructor and an outline of his course for the Senior Department are to be found in W.O. 1/943. The following provides a clear indication of General Jarry's notion of the training required for the staff of the Quartermaster-General in the field:

> The instruction shall principally consist in explaining the nature of country, and forming the eye to that judicious choice of position and the conduct of offensive and defensive war. It shall comprise the manner of reconnoitering a country, so far as concerns military operations; of laying down a plan of it with expedition, of making choice upon the ground, of the situation for camps, of marking out and constructing of field works and intrenchments which are to defend a given position; together with the methods of encamping, of guarding camps and of marching armies. Those theories shall be enforced and exemplified by different applications of them, made upon the ground by positions taken and by imaginary marches from one camp to another . . . All orders relative to those different duties shall be given and explained in the same manner, as would be required on actual service.

Draft of a Warrant for the purpose of establishing a Royal Military College, 1800, *Ibid.,* ff. 97–101.

9 Ward, *op. cit.*, p. 159.

9b B.M. Add, MSS. 54540 (Napier MSS.), ff. 1–2. For Lt-Col C. J. Napier's further criticisms of the Senior Department in 1817 see his letters to his mother in Bodleian MSS. Eng Lett. C236, ff 192–243. I am indebted to John W. Shy for these references.

10 Ward, *op. cit.*, pp. 109–10.

10b Report of the Commissioners on the Purchase and Sale of Commissions in the Army, 1857, p. xxii.

11 Sandhurst Report, Minutes of Evidence, para. 1277 (Lt-Col W. H. Adams).

12 See Lord Stanmore, *Life of Sidney Herbert* (London, 1906), Vol. II, pp. 375–86. And entry in *D.N.B.* by J. A. Hamilton K.C.

13 Sandhurst Report, Appendix 5.

14 Stanmore, *op. cit.*, p. 378.

15 Brevet-Major A. R. Godwin-Austen, *The Staff and the Staff College* (London, 1927), pp. 88–9.

16 The Prince Consort's Memorandum on the Army (duplicate) dated 17 January 1855, and remarks on it by Sidney Herbert and Lord Panmure. RA E5/5,9,36. For MacDougall's career see Jay Luvaas, *The Education of an Army: British Military Thought, 1815–1940* (London, 1965), pp. 101–29.

17 From February 1855 the offices of Secretary at War and Secretary of State for War were combined; and responsibility for the Colonies was transferred from the latter to a new office. Lord Panmure and his successors were referred to as Secretary of State for War.

18 Sandhurst Report, Minutes of Evidence, para. 1284 (Lt-Col W. H. Adams).

19 *Ibid.*, para. 432 (Col Prosser), 2289–93 (General Douglas). See also Godwin-Austen, *op. cit.*, p. 88.

20 Military Parliamentary Papers (War Office Library), Vol. XL, 1856, Part I, pp. 211–27, 233.

21 Sandhurst Report, Minutes of Evidence, paras 2121–77 (Mr J. Godwin).

22 Sir George Douglas and Sir George Dalhousie Ramsay (eds), *The Panmure Papers* (London, 1908), Vol. II, p. 288.

23 Sandhurst Report, Minutes of Evidence, para. 2374 (General Douglas).

24 Sandhurst Report, Appendix 3, p. 189. Lt-Col. Adams strongly defended the purchase system because 'it favours the poor man at least as much as the rich man'.

25 Committee on the Training of Officers for the Scientific Corps (Report on the Scientific Corps) 1857. Report, pp. XXIV-XXVI, XXXVII-XXXIX.

26 Rough draft of a Memorandum on Military Education by the late Field-Marshal Viscount Hardinge. Dalhousie Muniments (Scottish Record Office), GD 45/8/322. Also in RA E8/94.

27 *Hansard*, Vol. 142, cols 980–1023.

28 See Godwin-Austen, *op. cit.*, pp. 94, 101 and illustration from *Punch* on p. 63 (above).

29 Col Willoughby Verner, *The Military Life of H.R.H. George, Duke of Cambridge* (London, 1905), Vol. I, p. 139.

30 Lefroy was born in 1817, the son of the rector of Ashe in Hampshire. He was commissioned from Woolwich in 1834, and five years later sailed to St Helena to carry out a magnetic survey. Between 1842 and 1853 he made his scientific reputation by remarkably enterprising and accurate work in the same field in Canada, in the process covering thousands of miles with only one companion. In 1854 he compiled a *Handbook of Field Artillery for the use of Officers* which remained valid for thirty years. On Lefroy see *Autobiography of General Sir John Henry Lefroy* (ed.) Lady Lefroy (c. 1895); article by Col. R. H. Vetch R.E. in the *Dictionary of National Biography;* and Major D. D. Vigors R.A., 'General Sir John Lefroy K.C.M.G., C.B., F.R.S., LLD., F.S.A.', *Royal Artillery Historical Society Proceedings,* Vol. XI, no. 1, January 1967. The Lefroy Papers contain nothing on military education but several of his memoranda and letters are to be found in the Dalhousie Muniments.

31 'On the Organization of a Department of Military Organization' signed 'J. H. Lefroy' and dated 8 November 1856. Dalhousie Muniments, GD 45/8/389. Lefroy also proposed that a quarter of the Ordnance Survey team (then composed of 18 Royal Engineer Officers) be taken from graduates of the Staff College.

32 The distinction p.s.c. first appeared in the Army List in February 1864. At the same time officers possessing the old Military College Certificate were distinguished by the letters m.c.c.

33 Dalhousie Muniments GD 45/8/392, Lefroy to Panmure, 29 December 1856. Douglas and Ramsay, *op. cit.*, Vol. II, pp. 377–8, Panmure to Palmerston, 19 January 1857.

34 See *The Panmure Papers*, Vol. II, pp. 337–8, 340–2, 351–6, 369–72.

35 In 1859 Lefroy was a member of the Royal Commission on the Defences of the United Kingdom. He subsequently held various posts in the Ordnance department, becoming Director-General of Ordnance in December 1868. In 1870 he resigned in protest against Cardwell's comptroller scheme, and left the Army. He was Governor of Bermuda (1871–7) and Governor of Tasmania (1880–2) and died in 1890.

36 Lefroy, *Autobiography*, p. 193.

37 Memorandum by H.R.H. Duke of Cambridge, and Lefroy's comments in a separate paper. Dalhousie Muniments, GD 45/8/398.

38 General Order no. 685. See Godwin-Austen *op. cit.*, pp. 97–9.

39 *The Panmure Papers,* Vol. II, p. 373.

40 *Hansard*, Vol., 147, cols 569–608.

41 *Report of the Commissioners on the Purchase and Sale of Commissions in the Army*, 1857.

42 RA E10/13, 14. The predominance of mathematics was a general feature in nineteenth-century military institutions. For the subject's exceedingly long reign at West Point, for example, see Stephen E.

Ambrose, *Duty, Honor, Country: a History of West Point* (Baltimore, 1966).

43 Dalhousie Muniments GD 45/8/152, the Duke of Cambridge to Panmure, 3 November 1857.
44 Copy of Memorandum by the Council of Military Education dated 6 November 1857, RA E10/14.
45 War Office Papers W.O. 33/6/37, 38.
46 The original Staff College regulations are summarized by Godwin-Austen, *op. cit.*, pp. 103–7.
47 In 1861 the Duke of Cambridge stated in a letter to the Prince Consort that it would be 'a positive waste of time for Engineer officers to go to the Staff College since training at Chatham was equal, if not superior, to the Staff College'. In the same year he approved the addition of two Royal Marine officers as supernumeraries to the complement of the Staff College. RA E13/39, 84, 87.
48 Dalhousie Muniments GD 45/8/398. 'Remarks on the Commander-in-Chief's Memorandum' by J. H. Lefroy, 24 January 1857, para. 47.
49 Godwin-Austen, *op. cit.*, p. 108.

CHAPTER THREE

Growing Pains
1858–1870

Although the Staff College acquired its name in 1858, four
years were to elapse before it became established in its permanent habitation at Camberley, about a mile from the Royal
Military College. In the meantime, since the latter housed only
about 180 cadets in buildings originally designed for 412, the
officers temporarily occupied the west wing. James Pennethorne
was invited to design the new College, and in May 1859 his
plans for an imposing building in the modern Italian style were
approved by the Queen. The site selected was on the brow of a
slope, falling gently to an ornamental lake and well screened
by trees from the busy London to Portsmouth road. It was to
measure 265 feet in length, 110 in width and 55 in height,
built of brick faced with stone, and designed to accommodate
40 students – albeit in spartan conditions. The College 'prior
to comparatively recent desecration', Godwin-Austen was to
write in 1927, 'was a noble building with a beautiful vista over
the placid lake, surrounded by beech, rowan, chestnut and
alder'. Most visitors would probably concede that it still provides an admirably peaceful environment for the arduous study
of war. When the Duke of Cambridge came down to lay the
first block of masonry on 14 December 1859, the day's proceedings were recounted enthusiastically and at considerable
length in a leading article in *The Times*.[1] The new College was
virtually completed when the first batch of students moved
there in the autumn of 1862.

By this date, unfortunately, public and parliamentary interest
in military reform, which had reached its flood tide in the years
immediately after the Crimean War, was already fast ebbing.

Consequently, military education, along with such other aspects as administrative re-organization, conditions of service and field training, failed to make such progress as might have been expected in the 1860s.

Nor indeed did Britain's disillusioning experiences in the Crimea stimulate reforms in `every branch of military affairs. In particular it failed to initiate much serious thought within the Army about its strategic role or tactical doctrine. As to the discussion and formulation of strategy, the Army was severely handicapped both by the absence of any political direction as regards its role in a major war and by the lack of 'a brain' in the shape of a General Staff. Tactically, too, the ghost of Wellington had still not been wholly exorcised. Two of the main tactical innovations in the Crimea – field entrenchments and the increased firepower of rifled muskets – were largely ignored. 'A reliance upon field works was considered injurious to discipline and élan; while the continued success of the Brown Bess doctrine during the Indian Mutiny tended to encourage its use.'[2] The tendency to disperse the regiments in companies or even smaller detachments whether serving at home or overseas, and the shortage of money for worthwhile field training, also militated against the serious study of war. 'Thus,' as Dr Adrian Preston has written, 'on the eve of the American Civil War, the development of British military thought had barely begun. The approved pattern seemed to be to look at military history as a great quarry of principles and examples to be judiciously selected to bolster pre-conceived ideas or traditional doctrines.'[3]

It would consequently be altogether anachronistic to look to the infant Staff College to produce a 'school of thought' in these early years. It is significant, however, that of the handful of serving officers who by their pens and their lectures were struggling to develop the professional study of war in Britain, two of the most distinguished and influential, Lt-Col (later Maj.-Gen. Sir Patrick) MacDougall and Col (later Lt-Gen. Sir Edward) Hamley, were both closely connected with the Staff College from its earliest days.

Patrick Leonard MacDougall belonged 'to the first form in

what Lord Wolseley described as a "new army school".[4] He had returned in 1854 from ten years soldiering in Canada to become superintendent of studies at the Royal Military College, whence he returned once more after serving in the Crimea. Conscious of the British officers' shortcomings in professional education and of the lack of a manageable textbook on the broader aspects of war, he published, in 1856, *The Theory of War*. This was an appropriate moment for the distillation of the essential ideas of the classic European military writers. The volume enjoyed an immediate success and, together with a pamphlet he published in the following year entitled *The Senior Department of the Royal Military College*, made him a natural choice as the first Commandant of the Staff College. Though *The Theory of War* temporarily filled an important gap and soon became a standard textbook, it had little claim to originality, nor was it a treatise on modern developments in warfare. For the most part MacDougall was content to expatiate on what he regarded as the unchanging principles of strategy as applied by Frederick and Napoleon, and expounded by such commentators and historians as Jomini or his own favourite – Sir William Napier. In a later book, *Modern Warfare and Modern Artillery*, published in 1863 after he had left Camberley, MacDougall displayed more originality as well as topicality in analysing the probable effects of improved ordnance on the operations of war. In the opinion of a modern military historian the two chapters that deal specifically with the influence of weapons upon war and tactics 'deserve consideration as the most succinct indeed classic forecast of modern warfare'.[5]

At the Staff College, MacDougall lectured on the campaigns of the great captains and also wrote a book on Hannibal. His main task, however, was to implement the recommendations of the Council of Military Education and to set the new institution on its feet. This he seems to have done successfully if unspectacularly before relinquishing his post in September 1861.

Probably of greater importance in the early shaping of the Staff College was the influence of the personality and literary reputation of the first professor of military history, Edward Bruce Hamley.[6] For Hamley was that comparative rarity among mid-Victorian regular officers: a gifted and prolific writer. Originally he had turned to literature with the unprofessional motives of supplementing his pay and amusing himself during periods of dreary regimental soldiering in Canada and Gibraltar. *Blackwoods* magazine provided his main outlet throughout his career. Hamley, who was present at every major battle in the Crimea, defended the Army against its civilian detractors in *The Story of the Campaign of Sebastopol Written in Camp*, which was published in 1855. In his view, responsibility for the Army's shortcomings lay chiefly with the political authorities who had so starved it of money and auxiliary services before the campaign. Rather surprisingly for an officer whose subsequent career was to be so much involved with military education, Hamley rejected the allegations of incompetent leadership in the Crimea and poured scorn on the first hesitant steps to improve officer education by obliging all candidates for a first commission to submit to examination. Thus a combination of distinguished service in the Duke of Cambridge's division and sound conservative views on politics and army reform made Hamley an acceptable choice as the first professor of military history.

At Camberley, Hamley's task was 'to point out to students the objects of the various campaigns . . . as well as the manner in which these operations were conducted, showing when and why they were successful and where and why they failed'. Amongst less attractive or digestible fare, military history was likely to be a popular subject, but in any case Hamley was a great success as a lecturer. He was later to complain that 'for every lecture I write I have to read twenty résumés or parodies of it'; yet this was apparently what he encouraged since he evidently expected his students to accept his conclusions as well as his facts and he did not encourage original research. Sir Evelyn Wood, who was in the class of 1863–4, relates the case of a fellow-student who was preparing superficially for an essay on the battle of Blenheim but rejected Wood's offer to lend him Cox's *Life of Marlborough*, which was not in the College library, with the glib rejoiner, 'No, I shall serve up Hamley, Hamley,

SPOON FEEDING

The last week before the final examination at the Staff College.

nothing but Hamley; that always gets me full marks'.[7] Hamley has been aptly dubbed 'the strategic pedagogue'.[8]

The fruit of six years teaching at Camberley was Hamley's monumental volume, *The Operations of War*, which he completed early in 1866. The author was evidently a disciple of Jomini rather than Clausewitz. Like the former, he believed that warfare could be satisfactorily subjected to rational analysis from which permanently valid principles – such as the strategic offensive, concentration at the decisive point, surprise and pursuit – could be derived. His method of presentation, likewise reminiscent of Jomini (who was still living when the book was first published), was to illustrate the principles of war from representative campaigns. While such an approach had obvious advantages for teaching, it was, as Professor Luvaas points out, 'better calculated to reaffirm established truths than to discover new ones'. Though by no means indifferent to contemporary campaigns, Hamley was to some extent blinkered by his devotion to the classical battles of the eras of Frederick and Napoleon. In particular he displayed little insight, compared with, say, his contemporary MacDougall or Henderson later, into the enormous significance of tactical developments in the American Civil War. In this respect 'one can almost accuse him of backing into the second half of the century of iron and steam with his eyes still focused, however sharply, on the past'.[9]

The Operations of War enjoyed a remarkable success and established Hamley's reputation as Britain's leading authority on military thought. It was adopted as the official text not only at Camberley but also in the United States, where the second edition was introduced as a textbook in the military history department of the Artillery School in 1870.[10] Though the book went through five editions in Hamley's lifetime and continued to be printed until 1923, a reaction against it is observable in Britain as early as the 1890s. In 1894 it was discontinued as the sole text in military history for the Staff College entrance examination. Soon afterwards Lt-Col G. F. R. Henderson, then professor of military history at Camberley, referred to it in a lecture at the Royal United Service Institution as 'a great book' but went on to expose its limitations.

It is an aid to study, not to practice. In the description of campaigns the keynote, that is, the aim of the commander, seems often wanting; and the real objective of the operations is obscured by the number of side issues . . . He [the student] has read a great deal about rectangular bases, re-entering frontiers, parallel and transverse obstacles, but he has heard little of great principles; and if he is set to solve a strategical problem he finds that he has no clear idea of what to do or how to do it . . . Again Hamley deliberately omitted all reference to the spirit of war, to moral influences, to the effect of rapidity, of surprise, and secrecy; and these . . . not mere manoeuvres, are the best weapons of the strategist.[11]

Despite Hamley's limitations as a student of war, he was by general agreement a popular figure and a successful teacher at the Staff College. The same cannot be said of some of his colleagues. The French teacher's one idea of imparting knowledge of his language was to read the Emperor's letters to his brothers and subordinate generals. The professor of topography, though himself an accomplished surveyor, continued to demand the same high standard of technical precision and embellishment as had been insisted upon in the old days at High Wycombe. Hours were devoted to brush and line drawing which produced some splendid soldier artists[12] but might have been better spent on rapid sketching and other tactical exercises. Instruction in fortification was almost entirely theoretical and dealt only with defences applicable to static warfare. Geology, though of questionable professional importance, remained an optional subject until 1882 because the professor, Rupert T. Jones, had been given life tenure. Godwin-Austen paints a particularly unattractive pen portrait of the Reverend Mr Twisden, professor of mathematics and astronomy, 'a pedant of the old school', a sour unbending character whose enthusiasm had probably been quenched by too many years of attempting to teach higher mathematics to unresponsive cadets at the Royal Military College. Mr Twisden was guilty of unintentional irony when he defended his main subject on the grounds that 'it tends to impart to reasoning that habitual precision and exactitude in which (many) papers are reported to be deficient'. In fact, the great majority of officers relied on preparatory cramming at such famous establishments as Capt. Lendy's at Sunbury, a wise precaution since even those who had learnt Euclid and algebra at school were likely to be appallingly rusty after five to ten years' soldiering. Capt. Lendy concentrated frankly on the memorizing of facts; thus the first four books of Euclid were learnt by heart with no attempt at understanding them.[13] Moreover, it is most unlikely that Hamley was the only instructor who favoured learning by rote, or that habits acquired at the entrance examination were easily put aside. Indeed, the grading system put a premium on the amassing of marks as an end in itself, and this constituted perhaps the darkest blemish on the course in its first decade.

Hamley's successor as professor of military history, Lt-Col Charles Chesney (a brother of Sir George Chesney, the author of *The Battle of Dorking*, and well known himself for his *Waterloo Lectures*) was ahead of his time in his teaching methods. After his first lecture Evelyn Wood remarked to the assiduous note-taker and repeater of Hamley that henceforth he would have to think for himself:

> Charles Chesney's ideas of teaching were diametrically opposed to those of his predecessor. He mentioned the salient points in the standard authorities who had written on the campaign or battle, and then said, 'And now, gentlemen, no doubt you will be good enough to read all these authors and give me the advantage of your studies'. The result showed my forecast was correct, for my friend the précis writer, who had hitherto got one or two marks out of a hundred more than anyone else, now came down to our level.[14]

Inevitably, as in any new institution, various adjustments and changes in the regulations and syllabus were made in the early years of the Staff College, but rather than enumerate these it is worth describing how the College generally operated.

At the end of the first year all students sat a probationary examination to ensure that they were worthy to complete the course. This appears to have been a formality since the Council

STAFF COLLEGE – A LECTURE AFTER LUNCH

(Staff College Officer nervously alive to the approaching Examination.)

"Don't you think Mr Twisden you might give the Examiner a hint that we are rather a weak lot in Mathematics"?

(Mr Twisden with great politeness). "There is not the slightest occasion for me to do this as he will very soon find it out."

of Military Education reported in 1865 that 'no case has yet occurred of rejection at this examination'. At the final examination at the end of the second year the student was examined in, at most, seven subjects: military history, military administration and law, fortification, and military surveying and reconnaissance. The two additional subjects could be chosen from mathematics, modern languages (French, German and Hindustani), natural and experimental science. Until 1862 students had been allowed to take up all the subjects taught at the College and some had been examined in as many as ten subjects. Not surprisingly this system had led to superficiality, carelessness and mental indigestion – not to speak of ruined health in a few cases. The Council of Military Education hinted that even five compulsory subjects might be too many.[15] By 1869, mathematics had been divided into higher and lower courses, either or both of which could be taken as additional subjects. The underlying snag was that although a p.s.c. could be obtained by passing in five subjects it was essential to take two more in order to pass high in the list. In effect the tendency to 'mark grubbing' was increased since mathematics carried high marks and a good result in the subject was deemed crucial to qualify for a coveted post in the Topographical Department.[16] In short, the Council 'sardonically hanging up the whip, had slily substituted scorpions'.[17]

The difficulties encountered by the College instructors in preparing their students to grapple with the practical problems that confront an army in war are nowhere better illustrated than in the case of military administration – an uninspiring subject perhaps but arguably the most important in the syllabus. Although the Board of Ordnance had been abolished and the Commissariat separated from the Treasury as a result of the Crimean War, the precise responsibilities of the military branch in a future war remained ill-defined. Consequently, in the 1860s administration still remained largely a mystery to the Army officer. The unfortunate instructor at Camberley had to train his class to study problems to which there was no approved answer. Therefore, in the one hour per week devoted to this vast subject he could do little more than describe in a general

way such matters as the medical and supply services, embarkation, entrainment and the planning of standing camps. Such
vital aspects as the organization of a line of communications
and the military uses of railways received no attention whatso-
ever. Furthermore, the course was plagued by examinations;
the internal examiners set three a year which unfortunately
bore only the vaguest resemblance to the external examiner's
questions at the end of the course. The students attempted to
pass both on the strength of their lecture notes. Lt Evelyn
Baring (later Lord Cromer), who was shortly to pass out first
in the class of 1869, told the Royal Commissioners that 'officers
cram up for an examination just a few hours before it comes on,
and then forget all about it'. He regarded military administration as the most important subject and urged that its teaching
should be made more practical. How could a staff officer be
trained for rapid decision-making under the present system?
He had been asked to prepare a plan for the defence of a village
which was to be attacked in six hours and was given a month
to do it in.[18]

Though early graduates testified to the benefits they had
derived from the course, in its first decade Camberley remained
too academic in a pejorative sense, and in atmosphere was too
much like a school. It was the restrictions of the schoolroom
and the pedestrian attitude to study which prompted Brevet-
Maj. G. P. Colley to drop lectures, teach himself, and successfully complete the course – passing out first – after only one
year.[19] A cursory glance at almost any of the examination papers
from these years reveals the pedantic or unrealistic nature of the
questions put to mature men who were supposedly training to
be staff officers.[20]

It was also symptomatic of the uncertainty of the proper
ingredients of staff training at both the Horse Guards and the
War Office that small financial grants for outdoor training were
only grudgingly made; while certain of the most valuable proposals of Lefroy and others were steadily whittled away. For
example, the second Commandant, Col. W. C. E. Napier, a
believer in the importance of military topography and reconnaissance, had encouraged the senior division of 1865 to make a

AFTER 18 MONTHS AT THE STAFF COLLEGE, VISIT TO CHATHAM TO SEE THE LATEST INVENTIONS.

"this a spade"! gentlemen

The intense curiosity the faces of the officers is impossible to depict.

very accurate sketch of 32 square miles of the country around
Dorking and Guildford. In 1869 the Council of Military Education expressed regret that the financial vote had been so reduced
that this work had practically ceased.[21]

Another aspect in which the original instructions of the
Council of Military Education were soon disregarded was the
period of attachment to other arms after graduating from the
Staff College. In 1860 the period of attachment was reduced
from six months to four, in 1863 to three and in 1864 to six
weeks with the cavalry and artillery and one month with
infantry. Moreover, attachment to the artillery at Woolwich
was arranged in the winter months when there was little opportunity to practise gunnery in the field. As the jurisdiction of the
Council of Military Education ended when the officers left
Camberley they could only deplore this attenuation of what the
Report on the Scientific Corps of 1857 had shown to be one of
the most important aspects of staff training in Continental
armies.[22]

Among the most important questions to be asked about a
competitive and specialist institution in its formative years are,
does it attract a sufficient number of well-qualified candidates,
and do many of its graduates distinguish themselves in their
subsequent careers? To take the latter criterion first: the Staff
College in its first decade did attract to Camberley a few of the
ablest men in the service, and by no means all of these were
'military intellectuals' unsuited to command in the field. Lt
Evelyn Baring of the Royal Artillery, soon to leave the service
to become Private Secretary to his cousin Lord Northbrook as
Viceroy of India, has already been mentioned. So too has Maj.
Colley who, after his brilliant results at the College, returned as
Professor of Administration in 1871, made his name as organizer
of the transport in the Ashanti War, and met a tragic death on
Majuba Hill in 1881 as Governor and Commander-in-Chief in
Natal.[23] Robert Home of the Royal Engineers, like Colley,
passed the final examination in only one year, passing out third
in 1860. In 1864 he assisted in drawing up a plan for the
defence of Canada's frontiers. Then, as a captain in the Topographical and Statistical section of the Intelligence Branch at

1. The Staff College today.

Isaac Dalby, mathematician and surveyor.

John Narrien, F.R.S., F.R.A.S., mathematician and astronomer.

2. Distinguished Professors at the old Senior Department.

the War Office during the Franco-Prussian War, he wrote a
number of detailed and scholarly reports on various features of
both armies. His semi-official manual, *Precis of Modern Tactics*,
which appeared in 1873, 'rapidly became a by-word for
accepted doctrine' and remained a prescribed textbook at the
Staff College until 1914. Home died prematurely as a colonel
in 1879 as a result of contracting typhoid fever in Bulgaria
where he served as British commissioner for the delimitation
of boundaries.[24] Maj. C. O. Creagh, who graduated in 1861,
was later (as Col Creagh-Osborne) to become the first ex-Staff
College student to become Commandant – and also the longest
holder of the appointment (1878–85). Evelyn Wood, already
holder of the V.C. and later a Field-Marshal, passed out in
1864. H. M. Hozier R.A., who passed out first in 1863, accompanied the Prussian Army in 1866 and wrote *The Seven Weeks
War*. He enhanced his reputation as *The Times*' military
correspondent during the Franco-Prussian War. Four years
later his brother, Lt J. W. Hozier, also passed first, receiving
commendation for his examination in French, Italian, Dutch,
Modern Greek and Spanish.[25]

It does not follow, of course, that these few bright swallows
made the Camberley summer. To be sure, the flow of candidates was too small for it to be claimed that the Staff College
was getting anything like the pick of the best brains in the Army.
After an encouraging start with 56 candidates for 15 places in
1858 the number of entries over the next nine years were 34,
33, 32, 23, 28, 27, 34, 28, 23.[26]

The entry regulations allowed the Royal Artillery two officers
in each annual intake, the remainder being supplied from the
cavalry and infantry. Significantly, Royal Engineers were not
admitted to the College from 1861 to 1872 inclusive on the
grounds that their cadet training at Woolwich, followed by a
practical course after being commissioned at Chatham, was
held to be at least the equal of a Staff College certificate and
they were considered eligible for any staff appointment. Next,
although officers serving overseas were allowed to compete for
entrance, they usually did so at a great disadvantage as regards
preparation, and a high proportion of them failed. There was as

E

yet of course no equivalent of Camberley in India or anywhere else in the empire. Furthermore only one officer could secure entry to the College from one battalion in any year. Although this regulation had the sensible aim of preventing battalions losing too many of their best officers, it was hardly the way to get the best men in the Army for the staff. It happened quite frequently that more than one officer from a battalion qualified at the same entrance examination, in which event the one with the fewer marks had to compete again 'from scratch' at a later date. Thus it could (and did) happen that men who qualified high up the list were passed over, though it is hard to say if many were permanently lost to the Staff College through this rule. In 1862, officers of the 64th regiment were placed second and third, so that 'the loser', Brevet-Maj. G. D. Barker with 2,509 marks, failed to qualify, while an officer with 1,429 marks was admitted. (Barker, however, passed in first two years later and in 1874 became professor of military history.) Evelyn Wood was 'pipped' by a single mark by another officer in the 17th Lancers and had to exchange into the 73rd Foot – at considerable financial loss – in order to gain entry.[27] As was to be expected, artillery officers suffered most from this regulation, which at least succeeded in preventing the better-educated members of the Scientific Corps from obtaining a monopoly. Lastly, it was discovered that an excessively high proportion of the candidates (and of p.s.c.s) were still only subalterns. Apart from the desire to train mature officers for the staff, this presented the practical problem that many staff appointments – such as brigade majorships – were not open to these officers for several years after graduation. In 1869, the Council of Military Education expressed regret that 'officers of more standing in the service do not come forward to compete for admission'; while the Duke of Cambridge forthrightly told the Royal Commission on Military Education that in his opinion no subaltern officer should be allowed to go to the Staff College at all.[28] This overlooked the fact that there were experienced and intellectually able officers who remained subalterns simply because they lacked money to purchase promotion.

The details of the officers who attended the Staff College in its early years unfortunately do not provide answers to many of the questions that spring to mind. How many applied for unworthy motives, seeking at Camberley a haven rather than a testing ground? How many ambitious officers were held back by the disapproval of their colonel or brother officers for this hot-bed of personal competition? There is no reason to doubt Ian Hamilton's recollections of his subaltern days in India in the 1870s, when 'it was the proud boast of the Gordons that none of their officers had ever entered the Staff College or ever would. To permit oneself even to breathe the name of such a place was held to be excessively bad "form".'[29] Whether their commanding officers saw them off with a blessing or a curse is seldom possible to say, but at least it can be shown that the majority of line regiments did not deter at least one of their members from going to Camberley. In the quarter-century between July 1856 and February 1881 only 8 infantry regiments had no successful officer at Camberley, though 22 had only 1. (Of course, long service abroad on remote campaigns such as the Maori Wars, rather than apathy or hostility, is another possible explanation for some of these.) Some single-battalion regiments (the first 25 had 2 each) seem to have been proud to get officers into Camberley: the 26th for example sent 6, the 59th and 62nd 5 each, and several 4. The cavalry with 38 was on the low side, as might be expected.[30]

Towards the end of the 1860s, military education again began to receive adverse publicity in the press. This was probably due in part to the spectacular development of the public schools which once again cast doubt on the need for cadet academies since the schools could produce an adequate flow of 'officers and gentlemen'. But the Staff College did not escape criticism. *The Times* published a long leading article on the College on 16 January 1867. After asking rhetorically whether success at the College had been appropriately rewarded with staff appointments, it continued:

> Notwithstanding the efforts made after the Crimean War to raise the standard of military science among our Staff Officers, and notwithstanding the public belief that by the

establishment of the Staff College we have realized that object, the fact is that favour, and not scientific attainments, is still the passport to prizes in the Staff service . . . The very highest distinction that it [the College] can confer meets with the least possible recognition, and constitutes no claim to preferment, at least in time of peace . . . Our Staff system humiliated us before the eyes of all Europe in the Crimea, not because we had no officers qualified by their ability for staff employment, but simply because they had not been previously designated or trained for it, while the smart young aides-de-camp who surrounded our Generals were shamefully ignorant of their scientific duties.

It was high time that public criticism be brought to bear on this neglect of merit 'in a profession in which promotion by merit ought to be the very life and soul, and in which the incompetence of a single individual may involve national disaster . . . The German war [against Austria] which has suggested to us so many other misgivings about the organization of our army, has left no more instructive lesson than the paramount importance of the scientific corps (*sic*).'

This drew a letter printed on 18 January, signed 'Sunbury', which was a transparent pseudonym of Capt. Lendy, the crammer. 'Sunbury' underlined *The Times* indictment by arguing that in fact the Staff College had failed to attract 'the most rising men' or *élite* in the Army. 'A great number,' he alleged, 'join to avoid going to India; others to get married. Some who are already married join in order to have two years' rest. The professional men with love of their profession have been few.' Though he may have hit the mark in a few cases, two years' 'rest' under the weight of instruction offered by Mr Twisden and his colleagues was not the kind of holiday which many officers of that era can have relished. 'Sunbury' attributed the low number of candidates for entrance to the following reasons:

1 The appointments on the Staff are not given exclusively to Staff College men.

2 While at Sandhurst (*sic*) the students, so far from receiving an increase of pay, as in Continental armies, are actually out of pocket.

3 Only one man per regiment can be admitted.

Maj. Godwin-Austen cavalierly dismisses the rejoinder from Maj.-Gen. Sir W. C. E. Napier, lately Commandant and now Vice-President of the Council of Military Education, on 21 January as 'containing little worthy of note'. In fact, Gen. Napier pointed out that only 99 officers had successfully passed through since 1858 and 58 of these had been employed on the Staff. Allowing for some of the remainder being lieutenants, or serving in India, only 22 had not yet been so employed, and some of these had only recently become eligible. Thus the problem seems to have been in part one of a persisting bad reputation rather than a great prevalence of interest over merit. But Napier did not address himself to the question of how many staff appointments had gone to non-p.s.c.s. This suspicion certainly rankled, and the Royal Commission would shortly reveal that a number of senior generals were indeed prejudiced against the Staff College.

On 27 February Col. Charles Chesney (Professor of Military History at the Staff College) penned a belated answer to 'Sunbury' on returning from vacation. What obviously irritated him was the assertion that 'the *élite*' did not as a rule compete for entrance to the College, and he challenged 'Sunbury' to define his terms. He was less persuasive in attempting to rebut the view that the Staff College was only attracting a moderate number of competitors.

> Few men like to go up and be marked afterwards in their regiments as having failed. The candidates are of mature age, have to prepare often under great difficulties, and seldom appear unless hoping for success. It is a matter of pleasing surprise, and shows a movement pervading the whole Service, that with such conditions two are found for every vacancy in the College.[31]

In rallying to the support of the institution where he was employed, Chesney seems to have overlooked the fact that the

Staff College was not without defects and that *The Times* and Capt. Lendy, though sometimes inaccurate in their criticisms, were essentially on the side of reform.

Sir John Pakington, who had succeeded Gen. Peel as Secretary of State for War in Derby's government in March 1867, decided that something must be done to reassure the public that *The Times'* strictures were unfounded. He saw the basic problem as to define the qualities of mind and character needed in a staff officer and then to tighten the reports demanded of the candidates' commanding officers. At the same time the Staff College course must be revised and if any subjects were thought to be superfluous they and their instructors should be removed, thus reducing expenditure. On 2 July 1867, therefore, Pakington wrote to the Governor of the Royal Military College inviting suggestions and requesting a return showing the time devoted by each member of the Staff to his tutorial duties.

Among the proposals submitted to improve the course, Hamley urged that more emphasis should be given to practical training: a brigade of infantry, a battery of artillery, and a regiment or part of a regiment of cavalry should be placed for a time under the Commandant as brigadier, and the duties of the Staff performed entirely by the students. Col. T. E. Lacy, the Commandant, pressed for the abolition of personal competition for place in order to end 'the all-engrossing scramble for marks which has become a reproach to this College'.[32] In forwarding the reports to the Commander-in-Chief, the Council of Military Education remarked pointedly on the Secretary of State for War's ambition to reduce the annual expenditure of £8,600 on the Staff College, that 'the value of a well-educated Staff is not to be estimated by a mere reference to the cost of their instruction'.

In November 1867, a month after Sir John Pakington had received suggestions for reform, only 23 candidates presented themselves for the 15 vacancies. Something clearly had to be done, but the Secretary for War could not make up his mind on the merits of the various alternatives suggested by the Council of Military Education. After several months of inaction he adopted the traditional solution of indecisive ministers and called for a Royal Commission. This was appointed on 23 June 1868 to inquire generally into the present state of Military Education, including the course of instruction at the Staff College.

The Commission comprised twelve members. Lord Ripon, who as Earl de Grey had been Secretary of State for War from 1863 to 1866, was the first choice as chairman, but his place was taken by Lord Dufferin before the inquiry began. Maj.-Gen. J. H. Lefroy also resigned before the completion of the inquiry, but a strong board of commissioners remained, including Lord Eustace Cecil, Lord Northbrook, Sir Charles Russell, Lt-Gen. D. A. Cameron, Maj.-Gens. Haythorne and Eardley-Wilmot and Lt-Col Charles C. Chesney. The Secretary was John W. Hozier, 2nd Dragoons, whose achievement in passing out first from the Staff College in 1867 was thus speedily recognized.

The Commission examined the views of a cross-section of officers and instructors concerned with military education, ranging from the Commander-in-Chief and older generals who had commanded in the Crimea, through past and present members of the Staff at Camberley to junior officers such as Lt Baring, who was still a student at the College. The Commission's First Report, devoted exclusively to the education of officers, was submitted on 9 August 1869.

The Report was particularly severe in its criticisms of Sandhurst. The Governor possessed too little authority; the Queen's and Indian Army cadets provided an idle element; military instruction predominated too much over education proper; staff–student relations compared unfavourably with the public schools; and there was far too much 'cramming'. Woolwich, where the course lasted two and a half years as against Sandhurst's one and a half, was considerably more efficient, though – as at Sandhurst – the hospital returns showed that there was 'considerable immorality'. Once again, however, Sandhurst was reprieved: it should neither be amalgamated with Woolwich nor abolished. 'The moral and proper mental training of a body of 200 young men between the ages of 16 and 19 ought not to be an insoluble problem.'[33]

The Report also noted that, after obtaining their commissions, British officers usually received less professional instruction in their regiments than those of other large armies; a defect which was becoming daily more critical. It was recommended that sixty garrison instructors, all with 'p.s.c.s', should be appointed, and in addition every regiment should have its own instructor, who eventually would also all be Staff College graduates.[34]

Despite these and other strictures, the Report's concluding remarks verged on the euphoric. Taking into consideration 'the peculiar system of purchase which regulates promotion, and the social characteristics of the class from which our army is officered', it was neither possible nor desirable to introduce a rigidly uniform system of instruction such as prevailed in some Continental armies.

> In the officers of the army Your Majesty already possesses a body of gentlemen of the highest spirit and inspired by the most devoted sense of duty. Eminently endowed, as they are, with natural aptitudes which go so far to constitute the excellence of the military character, we have perfect confidence that when once the requisite facilities are afforded them of superadding technical knowledge to their other qualifications, they will carry the perfection of military training to a point which has never yet been exceeded in any army in the world.[35]

This conditional approach – that with certain developments all would be well – also characterized the Commission's verdict on the Staff College:

> Of all the establishments maintained by Government for purposes of military instruction, few probably might be rendered more capable of exercising a beneficial influence than the Staff College. As originally organized it was thought likely to become an institution to which the ablest men in the army would resort for the purpose of acquiring a thorough education in the higher and more complicated subjects

connected with the military profession . . . it would appear that these expectations have not been quite fulfilled. Although it undoubtedly discharges many useful functions, the Staff College is apparently not popular with the army. It sometimes fails to attract those most likely to prove themselves most efficient when serving on the Staff. Of those who obtain admission, only a proportion appear adequately to represent the higher intellectual ability of the army; while some have been found wanting, when called upon to perform Staff duties, in certain qualifications essential to officers in such a position.[36]

Nevertheless, the Commissioners, with one exception, were convinced that the foundation of a Staff College had been a sound idea and that it was well worth improving. Maj.-Gen. W. C. E. Napier, now Vice-President of the Council of Military Education, stressed that the cost of the Staff College was a small premium to pay in order to obtain an efficient organization for war. Maj. Adams (Chesney's successor as Professor of Military History, who had served thirteen years in the Austrian Army and had fought in the campaigns of 1848–9 and 1864) pleaded for patience: 'we have not yet had time to establish a course of sufficient value . . . You require perhaps another generation of instructors to get the full value.' Lt Baring held strongly that the Staff College, 'imperfect though it be, is much better than no College at all. A large proportion of the officers . . . receive their commissions direct; they know nothing of their profession beyond the ordinary routine of military duties.' Except at the Staff College 'scarcely any opportunity is afforded to them [of gaining theoretical knowledge] should they be willing to do so . . .' Col. Lacy was conspicuously ahead of his time in his broad vision of the College's future contribution to the Army and the empire. Not merely should it provide staff for the Adjutant-General's and Quartermaster-General's departments: 'I think you look to the Staff College for educating your future general officers, your military administrators, your service in the colonies, and all the varied duties which fall to an officer in our service.'[37] Capt. A. B. Tulloch, who passed

out of the Staff College in 1869, was later to defend the course
on the eminently sensible grounds that it enabled young officers
to exchange ideas with a great variety of men, and that the
habit formed during those two years of working steadily for
some eight hours a day proved to be an enduring influence.[38]
Among many other witnesses who defended the Staff College,
the most prominent were Lt-Gen. Sir James Yorke Scarlett,
commander of the Aldershot division and famous as the commander of the Heavy Brigade at Balaclava; Lt-Gen. Sir James
Hope Grant, Commander-in-Chief of the China expedition of
1860 and now Quartermaster-General; and Col. E. B. Hamley,
currently a member of the Council of Military Education.[39]

There was, however, one strident dissentient voice among
the Commissioners. Lord de Ros, Deputy-Lieutenant of the
Tower, was a veteran with fifty years of service but no experience of battle. In 1854 he had been appointed Quartermaster-
General to the Expeditionary Force but had been invalided
home from Varna with sunstroke. In his opinion, widely shared
so he claimed in 'military circles', 'no such institution [as the
Staff College] is required for the army'. He cited the view of
Field-Marshal Sir John Burgoyne, 'an officer of European
celebrity for scientific attainments, and who, moreover, has
seen more service in the field than any officer now living', who
denied that 'the Staff had hitherto shown itself inferior to any
other in the world, or that individuals competent for it are not
always available from the regimental officers of the army'.
Other veterans who shared Lord de Ros' views were Sir William
Mansfield (Commander-in-Chief in India), Lord William
Paulet (the Adjutant-General), Lord Strathnairn (Commander-
in-Chief in Ireland) and Lt-Gen. W. F. Forster (Military
Secretary to the Duke of Cambridge).[40] But Lord de Ros'
trump card was undoubtedly the evidence of the Duke of
Cambridge himself. Lord de Ros argued that, apart from Gen.
Scarlett, none of the supporters of the Staff College had held
any important command on foreign service – which was
patently untrue of Gen. Hope Grant for one – and that many
of them could be discounted as objective witnesses because they
would naturally 'plead and advocate the cause of an institution

of which they had been, or still continued to be members'. He applauded the Commissioners' proposal to appoint garrison instructors, and hoped they might achieve what 'the Staff College (wandering into a sort of fool's paradise of abstract learning and science) had failed to accomplish'.[41]

The reactionary views of a minority of elderly generals might be dismissed as the inevitable accompaniment to any far-reaching innovation; indeed it has been shown that the course needed to be improved in many respects. But the thinly-veiled hostility of the Commander-in-Chief (then aged only fifty) was a more serious matter, not least because he had played so prominent a part in establishing the Staff College only a decade previously.

The Duke expressed his opinions with customary forthright-ness in answer to a question from the chairman.

I have the very best feelings towards those gentlemen who have been at the Staff College, and I have always considered that they have done remarkably well; but I prefer for the Staff to have regimental officers. I am quite satisfied that the best staff officer is your regimental officer, and that the whole system of the Staff is entirely based upon the regimental principle, and on matters of detail connected with the regiments, and that any amount of study will never make up for a thorough proficiency and knowledge of his business which a regimental officer has … If you can educate a sufficiency of young men at Sandhurst at the Cadet College, to go through surveying and field fortification to a limited extent and matters of that sort, which are most essential for a staff officer, and can give them the advantage of a thoroughly good regimental system, you may depend upon it that that is far better for a staff officer than any education which you may give at the Staff College. At the same time I wish it to be clearly understood that I do not give any opinion adverse to those gentlemen who have passed the Staff College, and who I believe have worked extremely hard, and have done their very best to do what is right by themselves and by the public; but still I think that the class of officers who go to

the Staff College are not always those whom we should wish
to see on the Staff.

Not surprisingly, the Duke reacted indignantly to Col. Chesney's suggestion that more officers might be sent to Camberley
in order to widen the pool of trained staff officers from which
selection could be made: it would take more officers away from
their regiments and increase the number of grumblers. 'We
shall have more grumblers than we have now, and I am sorry
to say we have quite enough already.' The Duke admitted that
some officers on his own staff were not p.s.c.s, but many qualified officers were not in staff posts simply because they were
still too junior in rank. 'When these officers get to the rank of
field officer we shall have much more difficulty than we have
now in selecting officers who have not passed the Staff College.'
But most significant of all was the emphatic answer to Lord de
Ros' leading question: 'From your Royal Highness' long experience in the army, have you ever known any case of a good
regimental officer breaking down as a staff officer?' – 'Never,'
replied the Duke.[42] Not only had the Commander-in-Chief
evinced a very restricted understanding of the possible roles of
trained staff officers – which he clearly equated with regimental
duties; he also came very close to saying there was no point in
having a Staff College at all.

The first main criticism levelled at the Staff College in the
evidence supplied to the Royal Commission, already quoted,
was the unsatisfactory quality of a proportion of the officers
who applied, entered and even successfully completed the
course. Lt Baring's frank personal impression was corroborated
by more senior witnesses, including Col. Hamley: 'since I have
been at the College, I have been thrown intimately with about
fifty officers destined for future staff employment . . . I should
say that about one-third of these would make excellent staff
officers, about one-third mediocre, and about one-third would
from one cause or another be unlikely to form useful staff
officers.'[43] At the root of the problem of securing officers with
at least some of the necessary qualities for the staff, such as

'tact, presence of mind, a military eye for country, skill and hardihood in riding, promptitude of comprehension and readiness of speech', was the reliability of the certificate required of every candidate's commanding officer. No point emerged more clearly from the evidence than the futility of this precaution. 'The certificates do not appear to possess more than a conventional value, granted as they are with such facility as to afford a most imperfect guarantee of the fitness of the individual.' The Commission suggested ingenious remedies such as making the questions more definite and searching, and requiring them to be signed by the three senior officers of the regiment.[44] Nevertheless, the same complaint continued to recur over the next thirty years and the problem was evidently two-sided; that is, the regiments were likely to shunt the idle, overtly ambitious or otherwise unwanted officer to Camberley – or at least would not stand in his way – until the Staff College attained such a high reputation throughout the Army that it became rather an honour to have an officer accepted.

As in the era of the old Senior Department, the greatest single handicap under which the Staff College still laboured in 1869 was the uncertainty of its graduates obtaining an appointment as a reward for two arduous and expensive years at Camberley during which they forfeited their prospects of promotion through purchase. Even if the chances seemed to be improving in peacetime, there was a widespread feeling that on active service paper qualifications would be disregarded.[45] Maj.-Gen. Napier admitted that 'a fair number' of p.s.c.s had not yet obtained appointments, and urged once again that 'the Staff College should be the only portal to the staff in peacetime', and this was echoed in the Report.[46] Royal Engineer officers, substantive field officers who had attained the rank of lieutenant-colonel before 1 January 1860, and officers of proven ability in the field had been and would remain qualified for all staff appointments without passing the Staff College. Moreover, 'until the Staff College was in a position to supply all vacancies on the Staff' (an equivocal statement), officers without p.s.c.s could be appointed directly not only as brigade majors and to the personal staff of General officers, but also to

the Adjutant-General's and Quartermaster-General's departments. Except for military secretaries, a qualifying examination
was necessary. The significance of this 'back-door' entry to the
staff is shown by the fact that thirty-six officers passed qualifying
examinations between 1865 and 1869.[47] True, the majority
became aides-de-camp for which a p.s.c. was not necessary,
but the War Office's patent reluctance to make the p.s.c.
obligatory even for junior staff posts was naturally resented by
Staff College graduates who failed to obtain any such appointment.

As to the course itself, opinion was virtually unanimous that
there was far too much emphasis on personal competition and
that this had various disagreeable effects.[48] The Commission
consequently recommended that, apart from a probationary
examination at the end of the first year, success would depend
solely on proficiency in the final examination; personal positions were abolished and henceforth success would be denoted
simply by the two classes of 'honours' or 'pass'.

The other major criticism was that the course was far too
theoretical and unpractical. Lt Baring, for example, pointed
out that part of the training in fortification was more appropriate
to the specialist engineer. 'A good deal of time is lost in drawing
plans of permanent fortification. If in practice such plans had
to be executed, they would be drawn by engineers and not by
staff officers.' Maj. Adams considered that at least another six
months should be allowed for the study of the telegraph and
railway systems. Col. Hamley, too, made a strong plea for much
greater attention to modern means of transport. But, as Godwin-
Austen wryly remarks, 'the Commissioners as a body seemed
incapable of comprehending the conditions of modern warfare.
Reading their questions to the witnesses, one sees their minds
"wrapped as it were in cotton wool".'[49]

One of the most important changes that took place as a
result of the Royal Commission was the abolition of the Council
of Military Education and its replacement, on 31 March 1870,
by a Directorate of Military Education. To ease the transition,
Maj.-Gen. W. C. E. Napier, lately Vice-President of the
Council, became the first Director-General. According to

Godwin-Austen, the object of the change was to put the Director-General under, and make him directly responsible to, the Commander-in-Chief and the Secretary of State for War: 'military education ceased to be controlled by a consultative body with little connection with the War Office'. Since, however, the Commander-in-Chief had from the start been President of the Council of Military Education the reform would not appear to have been momentous.

The majority of the recommendations of the Royal Commission were implemented by General Order 41, dated 14 April 1870. As regards admissions, the number of students at the College was increased from 30 to 40. Royal Engineer officers were again to be admitted (a significant recognition of the potential value of the College), and 5 of the 20 annual places would be reserved to officers of the Scientific Corps. The curious anomaly whereby the p.s.c. could be obtained without attending the full course was retained, but very few officers in practice attempted to take advantage of it.

The main objectives in the reform of the syllabus were the related ones of making the course more professional and practical, and reducing the emphasis on mathematics, which would henceforth be taught only as preparation for a qualifying examination at the end of the first year. The subjects were divided into 'obligatory' and 'voluntary', the former comprising:

1 Fortification and field engineering.
2 Artillery.
3 Military drawing, field sketching, and surveying, with the addition of photography as applied to the copying of maps and plans. Road-making, as at present, to be combined with this course.
4 Reconnaissance.
5 Military art, history, and geography.
6 Military administration and legislation.
7 Either French, German or Hindustani.
8 Military telegraphy, with the employment of the field telegraph, and signalling.

The voluntary subjects were:-

1 The two languages not selected as obligatory.
2 Geology, limited to its military applications and exclusive of mineralogy.
3 Experimental sciences, viz. chemistry, heat electricity, and magnetism in their practical applications to military science.

The only credit to be gained by taking voluntary subjects was an honourable mention in the final examination and in the personal report.[50]

In an attempt to inculcate the importance of more practical instruction, the Report descended to detail. The course should provide practical experience in laying out encampments (including the construction of field ovens, etc.); the transport of troops, arms and material by railway; the transport of the sick and wounded, and the embarkation and disembarkation of troops, horses and artillery. More time should be devoted to military history, administration and law, and greater attention should be paid to the style of framing military reports. The value of understanding telegraphy and learning foreign languages was also underlined. Finally, since the elementary point that staff officers must be good horsemen had been far from universally ensured, every officer at the Staff College was strictly required to keep a horse.

The status of the Staff College was enhanced by the Report's recommendation that it should form an entirely distinct establishment from the Cadet College with an independent Commandant whose normal tenure would be seven years with the power of re-appointment. None the less, the College remained, for administrative purposes, under the Governor of the Royal Military College until 1911.

Lastly, the practice of attaching recently graduated staff officers to the other arms was recognized to have been a failure and was discontinued. Instead, all p.s.c.s (including those who had not attended the full course) were to be attached for three months during the following summer drill season to the staff of a General Officer at a camp where all three arms were represented. The General Officer would forward a confidential report to the Director-General on the officers' performance and suitability for staff employment.

Thus, apart from a continuing reluctance to make full residence at the College and a p.s.c. obligatory qualifications for staff employment, the Royal Commission (and the subsequent Army Order) went far towards meeting the criticisms of well-informed witnesses such as Col Hamley. A small increase had been approved in the number of students, while the re-admission of Engineers showed that specialist training at Chatham was no longer thought to produce a fully-qualified staff officer. Should the emphasis on practical outdoor work be carried out with enthusiasm then Camberley would begin to turn out officers whose value would at once be appreciated in war.

The Staff College's equivocal achievements and reputation in its first decade closely reflect the uneven progress of military reform generally between the end of the Crimean War and the beginning of Cardwell's tenure of the War Office in December 1868. After the enthusiasm for army reform generated by the Crimean War and reinforced by the shock of the Indian Mutiny and the fear of French invasion, the 1860s constituted a lull or trough during which Britain's military authorities were slow to grasp the significance of developments in the American Civil War and the Austro-Prussian War. In particular, though graduates, instructors and a few senior officers were prepared to testify to its indispensability, the Staff College was clearly not regarded with enthusiasm by the Army as a whole during this period. Indeed, as has been emphasized, no less a person than the Commander-in-Chief had thrown cold water on the value of such an institution. Though much of the criticism and pessimism were attributable to ignorance and prejudice, in several respects the College was open to indictment. It must also be remembered that down to 1870 Britain's strategic position appeared to be comparatively secure; and also that the Staff College graduates had as yet had no real opportunity to prove their competence in the field since the one considerable campaign of the later 1860s – in Abyssinia – had been mounted from India.[51]

When the Royal Commission issued its first report in 1869, the Army was on the brink of a unique and hectic period of reform associated with the name of Edward Cardwell. Prussia's ascending scale of victories in 1864, 1866 and 1870 were generally acknowledged to be founded on a superior staff system; while in Britain Sir Garnet Wolseley and a progressive 'school' of young officers – including several p.s.c.s such as Colley and Baring – assisted Cardwell in preparing a series of far-reaching reforms. Among these, the abolition of the purchase of commissions in 1871 would at last prepare the way for a really professional officer corps in which promotion and coveted appointments would depend far more on merit and professional distinctions such as the p.s.c.

To what extent would the Staff College succeed in throwing off its early defects, and what contribution would it make to the reformed army of the 1870s? Much would depend on the selection of a Commandant of intellectual distinction, progressive ideas on officer education, and prestige with the senior generals at the Horse Guards.

CHAPTER 3. NOTES

1 *The Times*, 15 December 1859. Godwin-Austen, *op. cit.*, pp. 111, 118–19. The College crest, an Owl surmounted by a crown, and the motto '*Tam Marte quam Minerva*', were adopted in 1868, the joint work of Capt. J. N. Crealock and Maj. A. S. Jones V.C. (then Adjutant of the College). Although the device is not recognized by the College of Heraldry it is a doubly appropriate one, for as well as being the symbol of the goddess of wisdom the owl also appears on the family arms of Le Marchant, the founder of the Royal Military College.

2 A. W. Preston, 'British Military Thought 1856–1890', *The Army Quarterly*, Vol. LXXXIX, no. 1, October 1964, pp. 57–74.

3 *Ibid.*, p. 60.

4 Luvaas, *op. cit.*, p. 101.

5 Preston, *op. cit.*, p. 65.

6 On Hamley's career see Alexander Innes Shand, *The Life of General Sir Edward Bruce Hamley K.C.B., K.C.M.G.* (Edinburgh and London, 1895), 2 vols; E. M. Lloyd's article in the *D.N.B.* (Vol. XXII Supplement) and Luvaas, *op. cit.*, pp. 130–68.

7 Evelyn Wood, *From Midshipman to Field Marshal* (London, 1906), Vol. I, p. 215.

8 Luvaas, *op. cit.*, p. 130.

9 *Ibid.*, pp. 149–50.

10 Shand, *op. cit.*, pp. 191–3. The Council of Military Education refused to allow the book to be adopted at the Royal Military Academy, Woolwich on the grounds that it would be improper to recommend the work of a colleague, and that anyway it was beyond the capacity of the cadets.

11 Lt-Col G. F. R. Henderson, 'Strategy and its Teaching', *Journal of the Royal United Service Institution.*, Vol. XLII, July 1898, p. 775.

12 A few examples of students' sketches from this period are preserved at the Staff College. See also Rawlinson's illustrations to his diaries in the National Army Museum.

13 'A few tags of Lendy's geological patter' gained Ian Hamilton 200 marks in his Sandhurst entrance examination. "Naturally, these tags, pumped into me as you might pump porridge down the throat of a young goose (before Michaelmas), had long since turned into manure, and I could not for the life of me explain what exactly was clay and what was chalk." General Sir Ian Hamilton, *When I was a Boy* (London, 1939), pp. 173–9, 222. For Lendy's priming of Staff College candidates see Wood, *op. cit.*, pp. 203–4.

14 Wood, *op. cit.*, p. 215.

15 *Second General Report by the Council of Military Education* (c3502), 1865, pp. 8–9.

16 *Third General Report of the Council of Military Education*, (c4153), 1869, p. 6. Wood, *op. cit.*, pp. 208–9. Royal Commission on Military Education, First Report, 1869, Minutes of Evidence, 9179–83.
17 Godwin-Austen, *op. cit.*, p. 129.
18 Royal Commission on Military Education, Minutes of Evidence, 9185–91.
19 Lt-Gen. Sir William F. Butler K.C.B., *The Life of Sir George Pomeroy-Colley* (London, 1899), p. 79.
20 See, for example, the examination papers taken by the Senior Division in December 1864. *Second General Report of the Council of Military Education*, pp. 135–51.
21 *Third General Report of the Council of Military Education*, p. 7.
22 *Second General Report of the Council of Military Education*, p. 10. Godwin-Austen, *op. cit.*, p. 142.
23 Brian Bond (ed.), *Victorian Military Campaigns* (London, 1967), pp. 201–40.
24 Preston, *op. cit.*, pp. 72–3. Col. R. H. Vetch R.E., *Dictionary of National Biography*, Vol. IX.
25 *Roll of the Staff College 1858–1887* (1887). War Office Library, pp. 13, 19.
26 Royal Commission on Military Education, Minutes of Evidence, 1385.
27 Wood, *op. cit.*, p. 205.
28 Royal Commission on Military Education, 9540.
29 Gen. Sir Ian Hamilton (edited by Maj. A. Farrar-Hockley), *The Commander* (London, 1957), p. 50.
30 *Roll of the Staff College, passim.*
31 *The Times*, 16, 18, and 21 January and 27 February 1867. Extracts are quoted by Godwin-Austen, *op. cit.*, pp. 145–8.
32 Godwin-Austen, *op. cit.*, pp. 149–52.
33 Royal Commission on Military Education, First Report, pp. 14–15, 21.
34 *Ibid.*, pp. 26–7, 49. By General Order No. 26 of March 1871, 27 p.s.c.s were to be appointed garrison instructors, 16 at home and 11 in India.
35 *Ibid.*, p. 28.
36 *Ibid.*, p. 23.
37 *Ibid.*, Minutes of Evidence, 1497–9; 8831–2; 9196; 8408.
38 Maj.-Gen. A. B. Tulloch, *Recollections of Forty Years Service* (Edinburgh and London, 1903), p. 147.
39 Royal Commission on Military Education, Minutes of Evidence, 5958; 5975–8, 6025–6; 8630.
40 *Ibid.*, 5922–3; 9483–4; 9363–8; 9409. I am indebted to John Sweetman for the explanation of Lord de Ros' return from Varna before the Crimean campaign began. The information is to be found in the Raglan Papers.
41 *Ibid.*, pp. 29–30.
42 *Ibid.*, Minutes of Evidence, 9529; 9531; 6490–2; 9553.
43 *Ibid.*, 9196; 8604–5.
44 *Ibid.*, p. 24.

45 *Ibid.*, 9196. Majors or lieutenant-colonels who received staff appointments had to go on half-pay and lose their regimental position. Thus after five years the ex-staff officer would be likely to have lost both his full pay and regimental advantages. See letter signed 'Ex-staff officer on half-pay' in *The Times*, 17 December 1859.
46 Royal Commission on Military Education, pp. 11, 23. Minutes of Evidence, 8386; 1566; 1571–2; 9196. According to Col. T. E. Lacy, of the 144 officers who had passed since 1858, 81 had held staff appointments; a few of the remainder had resigned or died or were still subalterns.
47 *Report of the Council of Military Education*, 1869, p. 39. On leaving Camberley, Evelyn Wood was quite satisfied with the appointment or aide-de-camp. See Wood, *op. cit.*, pp. 216–17.
48 *Report of the Royal Commission on Military Education*, Minutes of Evidence, 8381; 8610; 8804; 8979; 9030; 9109; 9174–7.
49 *Ibid.*, 9208; 8815; 8608. Godwin-Austen, p. 154.
50 *Ibid.*, Report, p. 51.
51 See the editor's introduction and chapter by D. G. Chandler in Brian Bond (ed.), *Victorian Military Campaigns*.

CHAPTER FOUR

The Staff College in the Wolseley Era
1870–1890

By 1870 the Staff College was beginning to surmount some of its protracted 'growing pains' when the Franco-German War underlined the need for such an institution to many more senior officers who had remained unconvinced by Britain's own experience in the Crimea.

Taking first a *tour d'horizon*, the next two decades were to witness several improvements: the number of students at the College was increased and there was generally a keener competition for entry; the syllabus was gradually made more practical; and the methods of recruiting and evaluating potential staff officers became more sensible. Most important, Staff College graduates were given incentives and encouragement to demonstrate their value both in peacetime and on campaigns, with the result that by 1890 the Army was coming to appreciate the distinction represented by the letters 'p.s.c.'.

Nevertheless, imperfections remained in the course at Camberley and, more seriously, the precise role of the Staff College remained uncertain. In the absence of a genuine General Staff and of an army at home permanently organized for war, the openings for trained staff officers were too few and a logical system for advancement, such as that developed by von Moltke in Prussia, was lacking. Also, on a wider view, Britain's military policy remained remarkably ill-defined until a furious debate erupted in the late 1880s, and in these circumstances it was exceedingly difficult for the Staff College to provide what Sir Henry Wilson was later to call 'a School of Thought' – as distinct from more limited education for staff duties.

In this combination of undeniable improvements and continuing anomalies and defects, the Staff College in these decades faithfully mirrors the uneven progress of army reform in general after the spate of controversial measures enacted by Edward Cardwell as Secretary of State for War, 1868–74. While these reforms collectively constituted a decisive break from the old Wellingtonian army, in the short run they failed to yield the full benefits either expected by their authors or subsequently claimed for them by some later historians. As a Canadian scholar has recently remarked: 'A detailed study of army organization between the Crimean and Boer Wars leads to the conclusion that much of the old continued while many of the changes made under Cardwell failed to take hold. It is time that more emphasis was placed on this conservative aspect of British military history rather than on the liberal and novel features of army reform in the late Victorian period.'[1]

The significance of developments at the Staff College would thus be difficult to appreciate without first briefly describing some of the more important aspects of army organization in the aftermath of the Cardwell reforms. Above all it is essential to clarify the division of responsibility among the high officials at the War Office, and to trace the emergence of an embryo General Staff.

Cardwell faced the difficult task of improving the efficiency of the Army while simultaneously reducing expenditure. Three broad problems confronted him. First, he had to continue the process of departmental reconstruction begun during the Crimean War. Second, though initially he had not determined on abolition, he had to check the growing scandals connected with the purchase system. And, third, recurrent recruiting crises suggested that radical changes were necessary in military organization and the soldier's terms of service. These three facets of the Cardwell reforms will be discussed in turn.[2]

(i) *Reorganization of the War Office*

By the War Office Act of 1870 and an Order in Council dated 4 June in the same year, the long dispute over the

TABLE I

Central Army Administration after the War Office Act of 1870

Secretary of State for War (normally a member of the House of Commons)
Parliamentary Under-Secretary (normally a member of the House of Lords)
Permanent Under-Secretary (a civil servant)

Supply Dept | **Military Dept** | **Finance Dept**

Supply Dept

Surveyor-General of Ordnance (normally an M.P.)

Maintenance of all supplies, transport, clothing, munitions. Purchase, construction and charge of *matériel*

Military Dept

Commander-in-Chief (A serving officer, no fixed term of office)

Branches of Military Department

- Military Secretary
- Adjutant-General's Dept.
  - Intelligence Dept. (from 1882)
- Quartermaster-General's Dept.
  - Intelligence Dept. (1873–82)
- Inspector-General of Fortifications and Engineers
- Director of Artillery
- Military Education
- Inspector-General of Cavalry
- Medical and Veterinary Depts.

Finance Dept

Financial Secretary (normally an M.P.)

Appropriation, accounting and audit of Army estimates Control of Army Pay Department constitutional position of the Duke of Cambridge as Commander-in-Chief was formally settled. The subordination of the Commander-in-Chief to the Minister for War was tangibly demonstrated by the enforced removal of the former's office from the Horse Guards to the War Office, even though the Duke insisted on a separate entrance and obstinately headed his letters 'The Horse Guards, Pall Mall'.

The main effect of the War Office Act was to concentrate military administration under the Secretary of State in three great offices; those of the Officer Commanding-in-Chief, the Surveyor-General of Ordnance and the Financial Secretary. The Commander-in-Chief was the principal military adviser. He was responsible for the raising, training and discipline of all regular and auxiliary forces, and his empire was enlarged by the addition of the department for Military Education, and the recently created Topographical branch, soon to become the Intelligence Department. To the Surveyor-General was entrusted the control of all civil administrative duties, including transport, supply, clothing and munitions, with complete responsibility for the purchase, construction and charge of *matériel*. The Financial Secretary was responsible for the estimates presented to Parliament; the appropriation, accounting and auditing of funds; and the control of the Army Pay Department. Thus, in short, all purely military work was concentrated under the Commander-in-Chief, but he in turn was made directly responsible to the Secretary of State. With only minor modifications this system continued until 1888.[3]

The two highest staff officers under the Commander-in-Chief were the Military Secretary and the Adjutant General. Lt-Gen. W. F. Forster, as Military Secretary between 1860 and 1871, controlled the vast majority of appointments and promotions. In 1871, tenure of this office, along with other staff appointments, was limited to five years, and the Military Secretary became more directly responsible to the Secretary of State. Nevertheless, until the Duke of Cambridge became too old and infirm in the 1890s, it was his influence – and through him the Crown's – which continued to predominate in the distribution and control of army patronage. Politically there was much to be said for this continuation of royal authority; militarily it became increasingly open to criticism.

In Continental armies it was natural for the Quartermaster-General to take responsibility for the general staff when it developed in the course of the nineteenth century.[4] In Britain, however, the status of this officer declined: after 1870 he was nominally subordinate to the Adjutant-General and, since his chief duties were regarded as being performed only in wartime, his peacetime responsibilities were very restricted. They consisted mainly in keeping the register of regiments for service abroad, and the moving, quartering or embarking of troops. Writing in 1880, Maj. Arthur Griffiths noted that one Assistant and one Deputy-Assistant comprised the Quartermaster-General's entire staff within the War Office.[5] However, the Quartermaster-General was also for a few years responsible for the Intelligence Department, created in 1873, and at first housed in St James's Square, an important forerunner of the General Staff.

The Adjutant-General, then, was the unofficial deputy of the Commander-in-Chief, and his functions most closely approximated those of a chief of staff. In the 1870s the Adjutant-General provided close support for the Duke of Cambridge, particularly during the tenure of the able Crimean veteran Sir Richard Airey. Between 1881 and 1897, however, the post was held successively by Viscount Wolseley and Sir Redvers Buller, neither of whom was in close sympathy with the Duke. Though Wolseley and Buller have the merited reputation of being army reformers in many areas, their unrivalled experience in colonial warfare may have made them averse to radical alterations in the central administrative organization. Whatever the reason, it was certainly the case that the Adjutant-General's office 'tended to develop along lines of administration and routine rather than along those of strategic planning'.[6]

The first tentative step towards a future British general staff was made in 1855 when, as a result of the acute shortage of maps and information about the Crimean theatre, a Topographical branch was created at the War Office. Two years later Lord Panmure united the Topographical branch, the

Ordnance Survey and the Quartermaster-General's Military Depot as 'The Topographical and Statistical Department of the War Office'. For the next decade, as Sir George Aston remarked, the Department concerned itself rather narrowly with the topography of foreign countries: 'the nature and strength of their armies were treated as minor matters [and] relegated to the background', until the Prussian victories roused the department from its slumbers.[7] In 1870, Capt. (later Maj.-Gen. Sir Charles) Wilson reported to Cardwell that the collections of foreign maps were very incomplete and that there was no means of keeping the office supplied with information from abroad. Even after the Franco-German War, in 1871, Wilson noted, 'There is not at present in the possession of Government a trustworthy account of any foreign army'. Had hostilities with France occurred in 1870, information about the enemy would have had to be sought in translations of German works. Cardwell agreed that the office must be expanded and on 24 February 1873 he announced the creation of an Intelligence Department under Maj.-Gen. Sir P. L. MacDougall, the first Commandant of the Staff College. The following year, the Department was placed under the Quartermaster-General, only to return to the Adjutant-General's charge in 1882.

The two-fold duties of the Department were: first, 'the collection of all topographical and statistical information which it would be useful to possess in event of invasion or foreign war' and, second, 'the application of such information, in respect to the measures considered and determined on during peace, which should be adopted in war, so that no delay might arise from uncertainty and hesitation'. In 1875 the staff comprised MacDougall, Wilson his deputy, five assistants and ten attached officers.[8] In the late 1870s Col. Robert Home, a brilliant Engineer officer and Staff College graduate, began, for the first time in peace, to grapple with the enormous problems of mobilization; but his premature death in 1879 seems to have halted this important work, because the Department showed no further marked developments until the mid-1880s.[9]

When, in 1886, Wolseley resumed his duties as Adjutant-General, he discovered that the Intelligence Department still consisted of a handful of officers working in cramped quarters (now in Queen Anne's Gate) and was regarded as 'a harmless but rather useless appendage to the War Office'. He promptly succeeded in getting a larger financial grant for the Department and appointed as its Chief (later styled Director of Intelligence) Maj.-Gen. Sir Henry Brackenbury, whom he had described as 'not one of the cleverest, but *the* cleverest man in the British Army'. Brackenbury was instructed to draft a full and precise programme showing the exact number of men, horses and guns, and the amount of transport and material of all kinds, required to mobilize at home a force of two army corps and a cavalry division.[10] Brackenbury's work in narrowing the enormous gap between paper plans and the troops and material available, and his considerable refinement and expansion of intelligence work will be referred to later, and here we need only note that the rapid rise in prestige and scope of the Intelligence Department under Wolseley's encouragement, provided openings for many of the most able Staff College graduates of the 1880s, including A'Court (Repington), Aston, Callwell and Grierson.

(ii) *The Abolition of the Purchase of Commissions*

The abolition of the purchase of commissions in 1871 was chiefly memorable for the bitter and prolonged dissatisfaction with the War Minister and his supporters which it provoked in conservative circles of the Army, the clubs and Parliament. For numerous reasons – financial, military and constitutional – purchase had to be abolished sooner or later – and for Cardwell it clearly stood in the way of other military reforms. In the long run too, abolition of purchase was an essential preliminary to the emergence of a professional officer corps. Whether abolition, by itself, effected significant changes in the short run in either the social composition or the spirit of the officer corps may seriously be doubted. The social classes from which officers were drawn probably did not alter conspicuously down to 1914; while very low financial rewards, an artificially high cost of living, and powerful regimental traditions went far to ensure that the vast majority of officers would continue to be ex-public schoolboys from well-to-do families.

Abolition of purchase could not, by itself, secure higher standards of appointment or promotion. Sandhurst in those days has been perhaps over-harshly described as 'among the least effective and the least inhabitable of the public schools',[11] but it is nevertheless true that the College underwent no radical reforms between 1880 and the South African War. After that conflict a War Office Committee commented on the promotion of the commanders of battalions, brigades and divisions: 'It is deplorable that an officer who goes through his career in a dilatory, slovenly, unenterprising manner should be permitted, as he is now, . . . to rise to positions of trust and responsibility so long as he does not commit any grave error or show marked incompetence.'[12]

The majority of subalterns were recruited from the public schools, a few of which now allowed military or modern sides in their classes. Their function was generally seen as the development of character and inculcation of the qualities of the gentleman. It is probably true that few of the intellectually ablest boys opted for the Army, where the general level of officer education would have appeared very low but for a leavening of engineer and artillery officers who had received a sound scientific education at Woolwich.

Nor were service conditions at home conducive to serious professional training after commissioning. Garrison instructors had been set up after 1870 wherever large bodies of troops were assembled. Attendance at these classes remained voluntary, however, because the Duke of Cambridge insisted that the British officer must never be coerced into school like the Prussian. The small size of most depots, the lack of large-scale permanent organizations (except at Aldershot), the persistence of parade-ground drill and the shortage of training grounds, all militated against young officers taking their profession seriously. Even the annual autumn manœuvres, started by Cardwell, ceased between 1873 and the mid-1890s because of Parliamentary economy. Viewed in this way, the role of the Staff College takes on even greater significance as a flickering light amid the surrounding gloom, but it is also easy to understand why it continued to experience difficulty in recruiting suitable students.

(iii) *Military Organization and Recruiting*

The linking of battalions, begun in 1872 and carried to its logical conclusion in 1881, at least brought an element of order and rationality where none had existed before; while short service, introduced in 1870, did eventually produce a reserve of some 80,000 troops by the outbreak of the South African War. But these reforms failed to overcome some of the inherent problems raised by Britain's military policy and national attitude to the Army. The need to provide and constantly replenish with drafts a large garrison in India ruled out the possibility of really short service, except through conscription which was politically unacceptable. Parliamentary economy frequently reduced the establishment of battalions at home below the level at which military efficiency could be maintained and, moreover, the same battalions were periodically raided for relief drafts or overseas expeditions. The balance of battalions at home was never in fact brought up to equal those abroad, while after 1882 the need to find extra garrisons for Egypt and the Sudan tilted it hopelessly against the home force. Parliament ignored the pleas of its chief military advisers (the Duke of Cambridge and Wolseley were united on this issue) to raise additional battalions and keep up the establishments of those at home; recruiting failed periodically to provide sufficient men to meet the high turn-over of the Cardwell system; and the Reserve could not be called upon for anything but major national crises. The result was that by the 1890s the home battalions had become, in Col. Henderson's striking metaphor, 'squeezed lemons', virtually reduced to the role of training cadres for the Army in India and the colonies; while the reserve, so far from providing additional strength to an efficient army, was mostly used up on the outbreak of war to replace young or unfit soldiers in the home units. As Albert Tucker rightly concludes: 'One of the tragedies of Buller's leadership in 1899 was that he had to command an army two-thirds of which was not adequately prepared. The Boer War proved, in fact, that while Britain was capable in 1899 of calling more men to arms than had been possible in 1854, yet the old dilemma had not been removed of an army initially too small, too poorly trained, and too lacking in inventiveness to achieve the success which might have been expected from a great power.'[13]

In the field of military thought, the 1870s and 1880s witnessed a great outpouring of literature in Britain. The intense interest of at least a significant minority of officers in virtually every conceivable aspect of recent military history and contemporary or professional developments can be appreciated by looking through the contents of the *Journal of the Royal United Service Institution*. But in the absence of a General Staff, or of clear directives from government, both tactical and strategic doctrine remained extremely confused.

Through the 1870s and 1880s the British Army was deeply influenced by Prussian writings, particularly in the tactical sphere, and it is significant that an English translation of Clausewitz's *On War* was first published in 1873.[14] In general, Prussian authors laid great stress on the offensive as the superior form of war and, more remarkably, they mistakenly believed that the confusion which had fallen on the skirmishing line when under fire in the war with France had been a necessary feature in their victories. Their basic doctrine, therefore, was to take advantage of the confusion caused by breechloading weapons by giving both the preparatory and the assaulting roles to the skirmishing line, which would be continually fed with reserves. This differed little, as Dr Adrian Preston observes, from 'the combat of savages, who, fighting without any regular order, rush in masses upon the enemy, wishing to come as quickly as possible to single combat'.[15] There were, of course, individual writers, such as Wolseley and MacDougall, who deplored blind pursuit of foreign fashions, but not until the 1890s was the baneful Prussian influence largely discredited.

Strategically, the first serious attempts to work out a coherent policy of colonial defence dates from the late 1870s. For the Army generally, however, small wars in Africa and India seemed to provide its most frequent duty, while home defence against invasion loomed largest in theory. Thus, somewhat unrealistically, the Intelligence Department before Brackenbury took over in 1886, 'was mainly devoted to how to deal with a foreign invading army, after it had landed, leaving the British Navy out of account'.[16] The famous Stanhope Memorandum, issued by the Secretary of State for War on 1 June 1891, expressly discouraged the notion that the Army ought to be prepared to fight on the Continent of Europe. After providing effective support to the civil power at home, providing a garrison for India and all the fortresses and coaling stations, the aim was to be able to mobilize rapidly for home defence two Army Corps of Regular troops and one partly composed of Regulars and partly of Militia. Subject to these considerations and to financial restrictions, the Army should aim at being able to send abroad two complete Army Corps, with a Cavalry Division and Line of Communication. 'But,' the Memorandum concluded, 'it will be distinctly understood that the probability of the employment of an Army Corps in the field in any European War is sufficiently improbable to make it the primary duty of the military authorities to organize our forces efficiently for the defence of this country.'[17]

Whether or not the Staff College should or could have played a more positive role in clarifying national strategy must remain a matter of opinion. Col. F. N. Maude, an Engineer and himself a p.s.c., was later to write astringently that 'Instead of making the Staff College into a true University, for experimental and original research, we made it a kind of repetition school for the backward'.[18] Such an attitude overlooks the painful struggle which the Staff College had still, in 1890, not fully overcome to banish conservative military prejudices; and even given more progressively-minded commandants than Hamley's three successors it is not clear how such research could have been undertaken without an open clash with the Duke of Cambridge. Such original thinking about defence policy was, by 1890, being encouraged, albeit on a small scale, in the Intelligence Department. What was lacking was any properly constituted body, such as the later General Staff or Committee of Imperial

Capt. John Henry Lefroy in 1853. After the Crimean War he drafted a comprehensive scheme for military education but as a lieutenant-colonel was considered too junior to implement his ideas.

H.R.H. George, Duke of Cambridge, Commander-in-Chief 1856–1895. He played an important part in founding the Staff College but his enthusiasm was short-lived.

3. Scientific Soldier and Bow-and-Arrow General.

Lt.-Col. P. L. MacDougall (1858–61)   Col. W. C. E. Napier (1861–4)

Col. T. E. Lacy (1864–70)   Col. E. B. Hamley (1870–7)

4. The first four Commandants.

Defence, entrusted by the Government to carry on a continuous examination of national and imperial security matters so as to be always ready to provide the Cabinet with up-to-date and carefully considered advice on broad questions of policy.

Few military historians, except perhaps partisan supporters of Lord Roberts,[19] would object to calling the period 1870–90 'the Wolseley era'. In 1870, Col. Wolseley, as he then was, received his first independent command – the Red River expedition in Canada to relieve the British settlers imprisoned by Louis Riel. In 1873, now Sir Garnet, he added to his laurels with the militarily very successful Ashanti campaign; and the remainder of the decade was filled with military and pro-consular appointments in Cyprus and South Africa in which his record was somewhat less than brilliant. By 1880 his name had become a household word: 'All Sir Garnet' and 'Our only general' were phrases that betokened his popular renown through the publicity of the Press and the comic opera. In 1882 he was created a baron and awarded £30,000 by Parliament (less than he had hoped for) after the most brilliant of his campaigns, against the nationalist Col Arabi in Egypt. Three years later his active campaigning career ended in anti-climax with the failure of the Gordon relief expedition, for which Wolseley was remarkably successful in getting the blame transferred to other shoulders. Thus, although he continued to play a prominent part in the Army hierarchy until 1900 as successively Adjutant-General, Commander of the Forces in Ireland (1891–5) and Commander-in-Chief (1895–1900), the period after 1885 was rather a sad denouement.

Wolseley combined to a remarkable degree the roles (unusual in that era) of fighting soldier and intellectual army reformer. As the son of an impoverished Irish officer he had obtained a free commission, and by reckless bravery and professional ability in the Crimean, Burmese and China Wars he achieved his majority without purchase. In 1868, at the remarkably early age of thirty-four, he was appointed to the senior staff position in Canada and there, under Col. MacDougall, he commanded a camp of young Canadian officers and first dis-

F

played his zeal for military instruction and reform. One product of this tour was *The Soldier's Pocket Book*, a *vade mecum* packed with commonsense information and advice and the forerunner of the official *Field Service Pocket Book*.

Although the extent of his contribution to the Cardwell Reforms has been challenged,[20] there can be no denying that he was sympathetic to Cardwell's basic objectives and remained a tireless (and provocative) propagandist for many aspects of military reform for the rest of his active life.[21] Wolseley was very much a man of his age, and antipathy to his personality and attitudes makes it difficult for the modern historian to do justice to his very substantial professional achievements. He was blatantly ambitious, intolerant of men of lesser ability and a snob. He saw most issues (especially political ones) in black and white, and had no doubts about Britain's right and duty to conquer and govern 'lesser breeds without the law'. If, in turn, historians have tended to portray his own relations with the Duke of Cambridge in over-simple terms of reformer versus reactionary,[22] the fact remains that on the specific issue of military education he was clearly a fervent advocate for a more professional officer corps.

Wolseley himself was never at the Staff College either as student or instructor, but from the Ashanti campaign onwards he openly favoured p.s.c.s on his staff. Indeed, several of the most brilliant members of the original 'Ashanti Ring' – including Colley, Wood, Buller and Maurice – had recently been at Camberley.[23] In his autobiography, Wolseley remarked that he had been given a free selection of his staff, and the majority he picked were Staff College officers, 'which in itself was a new departure in such matters. I do not believe that any general ever left England with an abler or more daring body of assistants . . .' 'Wolseley is of course wise to get the best aid he can,' Hamley wrote from the Staff College to his publisher in November 1873, 'but it is cutting blocks with a razor to send highly instructed officers into the bush to fight savages.'[24] An examination of the semi-official history of the campaign[25] reveals that 4 out of the original headquarters staff of eight were Camberley men (Colley, Buller, T. D. Baker and G. L.

Huyshe), and also 6 of the 22 officers specially employed. Ten out of 30 was a very good proportion considering the size of the expedition and the youth of the College.

It was in the Egyptian campaign of 1882, however, that the Staff College really came into its own. At least 34 Camberley men held staff appointments, excluding active field commanders such as Sir Edward Hamley (Second Division) and his 2nd brigade commander, Sir Evelyn Wood. Wolseley employed no less than 14 Staff College men on his headquarters staff, including 5 out of 7 in his Intelligence department under Buller. The remainder came from the Cavalry Division (1), the First Division (9), the Second (8) and the Indian Contingent (2).

Although only 20 p.s.c.s held staff appointments in the Gordon Relief Expedition (including 2 who remained with the troops in Egypt), this should not be taken as evidence of waning enthusiasm for Staff College products. Some of Wolseley's protégés had died or were holding field commands, but more important the lack of organized divisions largely accounts for the lower number in comparison with 1882. Wolseley employed 6 p.s.c.s (counting Buller) on his headquarters staff and 7 (including Wood, the G.O.C.) on the Line of Communications Staff.[26]

Wolseley's attitude towards the selection of staff officers is plain from a rather sharp exchange of letters with the Duke of Cambridge. The latter made a sensible point in criticizing Wolseley for clinging to a small group of proven officers: 'if you never go beyond this particular batch of men, you work these and bring *nothing on*; and this I think another serious misfortune to the interests of an Army called upon . . . to serve in every part of the globe'. After apparently heeding the Duke's advice, Wolseley replied that he had selected 'a host of new men' compared with 1882. 'My idea is to give every Staff College officer and every one strongly recommended by a good commanding officer a chance . . . of showing what he can do and what he is worth.'[27] Further evidence of Wolseley's keenness to make use of Staff College men lies in the fact that eight were summoned from the College during 1884–5 for active service, in the Sudan, though not all held staff posts.

From one point of view, however, Wolseley's influence on staff training and organization was probably harmful. He was, *par excellence*, an individualist commander in small wars relying greatly on his own initiative and judgement, and on a few chosen subordinates such as Wood, Buller, Butler and Herbert Stewart. Although these staff officers performed admirable tasks in such matters as communications and supply, Wolseley – rather like Wellington – was not one to encourage genuine initiative in a 'chief of staff'. As Godwin-Austen writes,

> So far as the Staff were concerned, it [the Army] required a high standard of efficiency in certain directions, reconnaissance and local intelligence in particular. But as regards the general plan, and even the preparation of operations orders, there was still little expected of the Staff, particularly in the lower grades. These, the more important matters, were retained almost exclusively in the Commander's own hands ... And if we peep behind the scenes we find administration so defective as to fill us with horror, like the foul slums lurking behind a prosperous square. It is rare to find adequate medical arrangements, for example ... However brilliantly our little campaigns might be conducted, there was room for a good deal of improvement in our Staff organization and training.[28]

Moreover, the 'Ring' system, though in part forced upon Wolseley by the absence of a General Staff – or even of a special force prepared for overseas expeditions at short notice – had a bad effect on the Army as a whole, savouring as it did of favouritism; it could result in harsh injustice to individuals who offended its chief, such as Sir John Glover in Ashanti and Sir Charles Wilson in the Sudan; and eventually in the latter campaign it led to the command becoming top heavy with eminent soldiers who could not work in harmony together. Wolseley's diary for the Nile expedition reveals that major errors and incompetence in staff work played a significant part in the failure to reach Khartoum in time.[29]

Although there is little evidence that Wolseley did much directly for the improvement of the Staff College, indirectly he demonstrated his support for it in two ways. First, so far from believing that experience in colonial wars was sufficient for the staff officer, he urged able young officers to compete for Camberley. Thus he advised Lt John Adye, who had served on his Staff in the Sudan as an aide-de-camp, 'to pass through the Staff College as the surest avenue to professional advancement'.[30] More important, perhaps, he exerted himself to secure first-class appointments to the Camberley Staff. Col. J. F. Maurice, who as a subaltern had won the Wellington Prize Essay competition in 1872 (Wolseley being placed fifth), was appointed Professor of Military Art and History at Camberley in December 1885, and seven years later chose as his successor Col. G. F. R. Henderson, whom Wolseley had placed at Sandhurst after reading his book on the *Campaign of Fredericksburg*.[31] Both C. F. Clery, the author of *Minor Tactics* (Commandant, 1888–93), and H. J. T. Hildyard (Commandant, 1893–8) had served on Wolseley's staff on active service.

Sir Edward Hamley, the renowned author of *The Operations of War*, became Commandant of the Staff College in 1870 and during his seven years there did much to raise the College's status in the Army, quite apart from making it known to his wide circle of friends in literature (who included 'Tony' Trollope and George Eliot), publishing and society. He was in many ways ideally suited for the post and Godwin-Austen has appropriately entitled his chapter on this period 'A Breath of Fresh Air', though he somewhat spoils the effect by spending the first seven pages on a eulogy of the College Drag, concluding that Hamley 'would as soon find a student reading *Jorrocks* as the *Operations of War*, and would alter the programme of study to suit the convenience of those who would go a-hunting'![32]

Hamley was probably never happier than in his seven years as Commandant. Although essentially a London man, and a man of society 'who loved the sharp contact of flint and steel in the flashes of sparkling conversation', he also delighted in the role of country gentleman. He was a somewhat reserved man who found it easier to censure than to praise. He possessed little sense of humour and did not suffer fools gladly. 'Any suggestion of unmanliness drove him to exasperation, while boldness and strength of character always won approval unless that strength was pitted against his own opinion. Opposition he could not endure, and he expected all subordinates and students to accept his views without question ...'[33] On the other hand he went to enormous trouble to get to know his students personally and took great care over the correction of written work. These personality traits were, in 1882, to bring him into conflict with the equally domineering Wolseley and to end his army career, but they did not prevent him from having a tonic effect at Camberley.

Within a year, Hamley infused a completely new spirit into the College. Supported by Cardwell, who had secured an increased training grant, he greatly extended the scope of out-door exercises, particularly in reconnaissance and sketching. He also gave his students a practical taste of staff duties by having them take part in the Army manœuvres of 1871. Three divisions were concentrated at Hartford Bridge Flats, Woolmer Forest and Chobham and the students prepared sketches, reconnoitred, studied the scheme of operations and made notes. The healthy change of emphasis towards practical outdoor work is further evidenced in Hamley's book, *Staff College Exercises* (1875), which provides a detailed account of two exercises held by Hamley in 1874. When, in 1879, Hamley was appointed Chief of the Turco-Bulgarian Delimitation Committee, he chose six of his former students as his assistants.[34]

Following the recommendations of the Royal Commission of 1870, certain changes were made in the course. Practical mathematics was made obligatory for all students in their first year but after an examination at the end of that year the subject was dropped.[35] Personal competition at the final examination was abolished and successful students were returned in the order of the seniority of their corps. Officers who excelled in particular subjects would receive the distinction 'Honours', otherwise there was only the one class of 'Pass'. Surprisingly, however, officers were still allowed to take the final examination without attending the course. Marks for course work were discontinued so as not to handicap these non-residents.

When Hamley became Commandant it is little exaggeration to say that the College was 'in danger of perishing from infantile debility'. By 1877 the academic emphasis on mathematics was at last dying out and slowly being replaced by outdoor reconnaissance and staff schemes. Also, in the year Hamley left, the parochial atmosphere was lessened with the admission of six officers from the Indian Army. Above all, Hamley had given Camberley a touch of military distinction which had long been needed to reassure an army traditionally suspicious of educated officers. When, for example, Lord Gleichen confided to a fellow-Guardsman that he intended to compete for Camberley, 'He looked at me severely and said, "Well, I will give you one piece of advice, and that is to say nothing about it to your brother officers, or you will get yourself jolly well disliked".'[36]

Nevertheless, it would be an exaggeration to imply that Hamley by himself could effect a complete transformation of the College. It was still possible to obtain a 'p.s.c.' without attending the course. Also, although Hamley secured the abolition of a published list showing successful candidates in order of merit, his successors were required to place every officer exactly in the order in which he thought they should be employed. This was an absurd idea since, it was generally agreed, most batches contained two or three excellent staff officers, and half a dozen indifferent ones while the rest were suitable for general staff appointments.[37]

Although Hamley's successors[38] were Staff College graduates, they made far less impression in the 1880s, and this highlights the problem of finding the right man for such an important post, since the Army generally remained averse to study, particularly if there was a chance of active service. Evelyn Wood, then only a major, was offered the succession to Hamley in 1877. Apart from thinking Col. Colley better qualified, Wood was tempted by the appointment. As against 16s a day as a major he would receive £1,000 a year, a good house and the proximity of Wellington College where he intended to send his sons. He consulted Gen. Sir Alfred Horsford who advised him: 'accept it; and if your regiment goes on service you will be a miserable man for the rest of your days'. Wood rejected the offer.[39] A few years later Col. J. F. Maurice was apprehensive – rightly in his own case – that to accept a professorship at Camberley would bar him from future field service. Giving evidence before a Committee on the Military Educational Establishments in 1888, Maurice contrasted the British attitude unfavourably with Germany's. In the latter, military instructors were not thought of as a separate breed to serving officers, whereas in Britain there was a tendency to assume that an officer who took up educational duties was thereby ceasing to be a soldier connected with the active work of his profession.[40]

Col. Creagh-Osborne (Commandant, 1878–85) had seen active service in Scinde in 1845, in the North West Provinces in 1858 and in the Hazara War of 1868 when he had commanded the 1st battalion of the 64th Foot. At Camberley he acted the martinet and became unpopular for treating the officers as if they were cadets or schoolboys, especially in the matter of occasional leave.[41] His successor, Maj.-Gen. E. H. Clive (Commandant, 1885–8) was a Grenadier Guardsman, who had been commissioned as long ago as 1854 but had unfortunately seen no active service. He was a genial, pleasant man with no pretensions of being a very scientific soldier. Gen. Clive was at least determined to know every student personally by constantly visiting the mess and regularly 'dining in'. Clive's successor, Col. Clery, well known in the Army at that time as the author of *Minor Tactics*, was seldom seen by the students and knew few of them by sight.

Possibly the prospects of active service in India or South Africa in the late 1870s caused the numbers competing for entry to the Staff College to decline. From an average of over 40 it sunk to 33 in 1878 and to 27 in 1879. This, and continuing criticism of a few 'black sheep' among Staff College graduates, caused a Committee to be set up under the Director-General of Military Education, Lt-Gen. Sir Beauchamp Walker, to examine the method of admission, the nature of the course and the conditions on which a p.s.c. was awarded.

The Committee reported in March 1880 that the College not only failed to attract all it was desirable to attract, but also still managed to accept officers who were quite unsuitable. A few candidates appeared to be 'more desirous of escaping regimental duty and disagreeable foreign stations than of qualifying for Staff service'. The chief defect was still the laxity with which regimental certificates were granted. The other criticisms were:

1 The deterring effect of the competition.
2 The allotment of too much of the course to theoretical work.
3 The failure to realize the importance of the course as a necessary training for the Staff on the one hand, and a period of strict probation on the other.
4 The tendency to make the final examination the sole test of fitness, rather than to regard it as a necessary evil required to ensure application to the regulated studies and practical exercises.

As regards entry, the Committee attempted once again to ensure that only good potential staff officers were recommended. For the first time the Commander-in-Chief was given the power to nominate two officers provided they had passed a qualifying examination. A second officer from a regiment might also be allowed to enter provided he qualified in the top half of the list. The standard of qualification was to be considerably raised, and it was hoped that mathematics could soon be dropped as an obligatory subject after a satisfactory entrance level was attained (this was adopted in 1885). The level of the probationary and final examinations was also to be raised.

Apart from minor changes directed towards making the course more practical, the chief recommendation was that the award of a p.s.c. be made dependent on a satisfactory report from the Commandant as well as success in the final examination. Lastly, the Committee reported emphatically against awarding the certificate to anyone who had not undergone the course. The final examination they considered 'the least valuable portion of the Staff College test'.[42] The Report was sensible but hardly inspired. It laboured once again the old problem of ensuring by written affidavits that the Staff College was getting suitable candidates, and it spent rather little time on the more

urgent problem of making the course provide better practical
training for staff duties. Indeed, the Committee's underlying
assumption appeared to be that the course should remain
largely theoretical and that practical staff work would be learnt
during the brief period of attachment to other arms.

The outstanding influence at the Staff College in the later
1880s was the Professor of Military Art and History, Col. J. F.
Maurice. Maurice had accepted the post with some reluctance,
for he not only disliked the title of Professor but also the prevailing view on the method and purpose of study which he found at
Camberley. In his view, only pedants could believe in an 'art of
war' which could be reduced to systematic 'rules'. What mattered for Maurice was the careful study of past campaigns and
the comments of great generals. For the studious soldier the
object was not merely to acquire information about battles 'but
to improve his judgement as to what ought to be done under
the varied conditions of actual war'. In the study of military
history it was necessary first to ascertain accurately what the
facts really were; second, to ascertain the causes that led to the
facts; and third, to endeavour to draw sound conclusions for
the future.

    This summary may not sound particularly original to the
modern student, but it conflicted sharply with the idea of
military history which Maurice discovered at Camberley. He
heard of a zealous student who had gained a high place in the
examination by devising a *memoria technica* which enabled him
to place the troops in full detail just as they were on every day
of importance in the prescribed campaign. Maurice agreed with
Arnold that 'a man is likely to acquire a much better knowledge
of general history by the close and intimate study of one particular section of it, as a preliminary to all his reading, than he
is likely to acquire by merely covering a very large amount of
ground'. The superficial study of numerous campaigns could
produce the type of officer, said to have passed through the old
Senior Department, who found himself unable to perform a
specific duty because he had not learnt to move bodies of less
than 100,000 men. Whereas Hamley had digested military

history for his students, Maurice believed that all that could be accomplished at the Staff College was to teach the student how to digest it for himself.[43]

Maurice was a most conscientious teacher, sometimes using as many as sixty books in the preparation of a single lecture. In 1888 he told a Committee that his two years on the staff of the Royal Military College, Sandhurst after 1870 had been among the most interesting in his life, though he had worked so hard that he had almost got brain fever. His point was that soldiers of the very highest calibre were needed as Commandant and instructors otherwise they would do more harm than good: 'even now, in the Staff College, the greatest thing against which I have always to fight is the natural tendency to cram for their examination, and I look upon that as the greatest enemy to education that there is'.[44]

Maurice probably inherited his ability as a teacher, for he was the son of Frederick Denison Maurice, divine, lecturer and Cambridge don. Yet he also displayed a tendency to absent-mindedness and unpracticality which, while no more than amusing foibles in an academic, hardly set a good example for a future staff officer, and much less for a commander. It was these defects, and a violently argumentative nature, which, in Wolseley's view, made him increasingly unfitted for an active command. Sir John Adye, who studied under Maurice, thought his lectures, though interesting, belied his great ability and learning since he would confuse the Archduke Charles with Prince Frederick Charles, and 'told his class twice a week that Lord Wolseley had won the battle of Waterloo'.[45]

Maurice continued and extended Hamley's innovation of conducted tours round the battlefields of Western Europe with the opportunities this brought of contact with foreign officers. Imperfect French added to absent-mindedness provided a source of great amusement as well as inconvenience. '"Bouleversez la voiture!" he would cheerily cry to the driver when he wished him to turn back', while his misreading of Continental time-tables frequently landed the party at a remote station in time to catch a southbound train when their destination lay towards the north.[46]

Although Maurice's approach to the teaching of military history and the instructive battlefield tours – by now financed out of public funds – represented a more progressive spirit at Camberley, comparatively little attention was being given as yet to the writing of orders or the performance of Staff tours. It is revealing that in the 1880s, apart from the foreign tours, the students spent only one night away from College while under instruction.

In 1882 the retirement of the Professor of Geology, Rupert Jones, at last enabled the study of that subject to be confined to its practical use for military purposes. A similar curtailment was made of the study of Experimental Sciences and the two were combined under the head of Applied Sciences, which was also to embrace a study of forage and veterinary work. No marks would henceforth be awarded for this course. Four years later the Reverend Mr Twisden, the formidable Professor of Mathematics, also left, a year after the subject was finally abolished as part of the course and made compulsory in the entrance examination. With the departure of these two veterans and Maurice's replacement of Col. T. E. Hall, the orthodox and unimaginative Professor of Military Art and History, the old pre-Cardwell spirit was dying out and a more practical and progressive philosophy began to seep in, though this was to become more apparent in the 1890s. From 1885 onwards the maximum age at the date of the examinations for entry was fixed at thirty-seven. In fact, a large number of the students entered in their mid-twenties. When Lt C. E. Callwell entered the College in 1885 he was twenty-six years old and 12 more of his 24 colleagues were subalterns. Seventeen out of 25 were bachelors.[47]

The period 1870–90 witnessed a significant increase in the number of students at the College and also some changes in the regulations governing entrance. In 1870 the establishment had been 40: 20 were admitted each year, purely by results in the examination, and no regiment could provide 2 students in any one year. By 1884 the establishment had risen to 48 and in 1886 it was raised to 64. The annual entry was made up as follows:

Cavalry and Infantry	18
Royal Artillery and Royal Engineers	6
Indian Army	3
Royal Marines	1
Nominated by the Commander-in-Chief	4
	32

In every alternate year the Commander-in-Chief was also empowered to nominate one of the officers of the Indian Army from a short list of three. The number of competitors showed considerable fluctuation, and there was a marked decline of interest in the mid-1880s as a result of the strong temptation of active service in the Sudan.[48]

The admission of the Indian Army officers, the relaxation of the rule barring more than one entrant from a regiment, and the introduction of nomination, may be taken as evidence of a more sophisticated search for the best staff material in the Army. Nevertheless, the selection system was (and for that matter still is) open to criticism, particularly in the deliberate handicapping of officers from the Ordnance Corps. A ludicrous situation occurred in 1886 when Royal Artillery officers filled 7 out of the top 8 positions and an Engineer the eighth. At the other end only 13 infantry and cavalry officers qualified for 18 places, so that 5 who had failed to qualify were admitted. Maj. John Adye R.A., who was placed fifth, was at first excluded as there was no further vacancy for a gunner, but he was later admitted as the first officer to receive a nomination. Still the gunner officer who came seventh with 2,407 marks was excluded while a Rifleman who came thirty-second and 'failed' with 1,585 marks was admitted. In the previous year, Ordnance Corps officers occupied 10 of the first 12 places and 4 of them were excluded by the same rule.[49] Clearly, without some such restriction there would have been the serious disadvantage of the Ordnance Corps virtually monopolizing first the Staff College, and later the senior staff posts throughout the Army, but on the other hand it could hardly be claimed that Camberley was getting the best brains when such anomalies occurred nearly every year.

Certain other changes were made in the College regulations after consideration by a Committee in 1886 presided over by the Commandant, Maj.-Gen. E. H. Clive. Among the more important of the results the weight of the final examination was reduced by distributing the award of marks over the two years. The term 'Honours' was abolished and replaced by the term 'distinguished' for candidates who attained ninety per cent in any subject. The languages that could be taken at the final examination were limited to those actually taught at the College, *viz.*, French, German, Russian (a significant recent innovation) and Hindustani. It is interesting to see the subjects studied at the end of the 1880s and the comparative importance attached to them in terms of marks:

Military History and Geography	750
Fortification and Artillery	750
Staff Duties and Administration and Military Law	800
Military Topography	750
Reconnaissances during final term	300
One Foreign Language	400
	3,750

(Qualifying mark 2,250)

The Director-General of Military Education commented inelegantly on the new scale of marks in 1889: 'The effect of these changes has not rendered the course more difficult ... and failures to pass the examinations are of rare occurrence. It may be doubted whether this does not indicate that the standard is not sufficiently high.'[50]

Before about 1880, ex-students' impressions of the Staff College course are fairly sparse, which is not surprising since the College had yet to establish its reputation and not all that many distinguished officers passed through. After that date, however, most of the well-known names of the 1890s and 1900s were there and a considerable number of them devote a chapter or at least a few pages of their memoirs to 'the Staff College'. What kind of memories of the two years at Camberley had they retained into their mature years as soldiers?

Inevitably there are minor differences of attitude and opinion, but on the whole there is a remarkable degree of conformity; so much so indeed that after reading about a dozen memoirs it is hard to remember which was which or to resist the feeling that there is no point in searching for further evidence. The general impression of those who were students in the 1880s is that these were two very happy years, that they were of some professional value, but that the work did not make very rigorous demands.

Capt. C. A'Court Repington, whom many regarded as the most brilliant young staff officer of the 1890s, and who was at the Staff College in 1887–8, has left these typical recollections: 'We had a particularly nice set of young fellows there, and I do not remember any two years of my life which were more profitable or more pleasant. We had all served in different parts of the world, and we learnt a great deal from each other . . . The Staff College was a valuable institution. The healthy open-air life, the drag and the games, the interesting companionship, the good teaching, and the never-to-be-forgotten Library, combined with the two years of freedom from regimental duty in which we wasted so much of our time without much profit, were all a great attraction, and we finished up our course by being attached to other arms of the service and learning something of their ways.' The dominating personality of that year was Horace Smith-Dorrien, who recorded laconically: 'I enjoyed every minute of my two years there. I do not think we were taught as much as we might have been, but there was plenty of sport and not too much work.' Smith-Dorrien was a popular Master of the Drag and got on so well with the Commandant that it was made theoretically possible for officers to hunt six days a week. According to his biographer, Smith-Dorrien 'seems to have spent most of his time between the kennels and the stables, except when at Epsom, Ascot, or Hawthorne Hill. Legend says that after he had been there three months he was found wandering about the corridors asking the way to the library.'

Lt Charles Callwell R.A., who passed in comfortably first in 1884 and was later to become a prolific historian and military

biographer, thought (like so many others) that the most valuable aspect of the course was mixing with intelligent and
variously experienced officers from other arms. In being more
critical of the course than A'Court he was typical of Ordnance
Corps officers who often found at least part of the work elementary compared with what they had done at Woolwich or Chatham, or during their service. Callwell felt that the instructors'
posts were not eagerly sought after by the ambitious; some were
inexperienced in staff work and were therefore like the blind
leading the blind. 'That the course as a whole stood sorely in
need of fundamental reform, most of us probably instinctively
recognized . . .' for even in the second year 'one learnt next to
nothing about the duties which a Staff officer actually has to
perform either in war or in peace . . . we became paper strategists . . . even the elementary task of drafting orders was never
practised and staff tours were unknown.' Adye agreed with
Callwell that the first year was largely wasted. 'For instance,
we spent a great deal of time over the theodolite, an instrument
I had never seen before and have never had occasion to use
since.' But he took a more favourable view of the second year
in which 'more advanced practical work was done, schemes
were worked out on the ground, and I especially enjoyed the
horseback sketching . . .' Lt John Cowans, who joined the Staff
College in 1890 and at twenty-eight was one of the youngest
officers of the batch, felt that the College had now passed the
stage when it was widely regarded as a dangerous experiment;
and noted that entrance was now keenly contested since it was
seen to open the door to speedy advancement. Not only was the
p.s.c. of professional value: 'From the wider point of view it was
then also beginning to be realized that we had no Army in the
correct sense of the term. That is, no body of men representative
of every necessary branch of the Service with its own transport
and equipment, its own brigades, divisions and so on, and,
above all, with its own Staff; in fact no complete independent
unit, every officer of which knew how to work in with the Army
as a whole.'[51]

In these circumstances it was hardly surprising that the abler
or more experienced officers at Camberley criticized the elemen-

tary and over-theoretical aspect of the course. This view was expressed by Capt. George Aston, Royal Marine Artillery, who was at the College in 1890–1 with many officers who were later to gain distinction, including Charles Monro, Bruce Hamilton, Spencer Ewart, John Cowans, F. J. Davies and Lord Edward Gleichen. Aston concludes: 'The few names I have mentioned are a sufficient guarantee of the value of the course, but somehow there was undoubtedly a feeling in the Army that the tests should be more practical. It was assumed of Army officers in general that they were good practical men; but a p.s.c. officer was assumed not to be so, unless he proved it.'[52]

Towards the end of the 1880s a major public controversy arose over the unpreparedness for war of the armed services. Criticism was initially focused on the Navy by the resignation of Lord Charles Beresford from the Board of Admiralty in January 1888; but a Select Committee on the Service Estimates, chaired by Lord Randolph Churchill, soon brought military administration into the limelight as well. Lord Wolseley, while retaining the post of Adjutant-General, boldly supported Beresford in public speeches. He attributed the weakness of the services to the party system, 'that curse of modern England', and stated before the House of Lords that 'as long as the Navy is as weak as it is at the moment, Her Majesty's Army cannot hold its own over the world, dispersed as it is; that our defences at home and abroad are at this moment in an unsatisfactory condition, and that our military forces are not organized or equipped as they should be to guarantee even the safety of the Capital in which we are at the present moment'.[53]

One important result of this agitation was the appointment of a Royal Commission under the chairmanship of the Marquess of Hartington to examine the civil and professional administration of the naval and military departments. The Commission's report was published in March 1890 but the evidence was never made public.

The Report emphasized that lack of cooperation between the War Office and the Admiralty was a potential source of disaster: 'While in action they must be to a large extent dependent on each other, and while in some of the arrangements necessary as a preparation for war, they are absolutely dependent on the assistance of each other, little or no attempt has ever been made to establish settled and regular inter-communication or relations between them, or to secure that the establishments of one service should be determined with any reference to the requirements for the other.' The evidence had revealed that 'no combined plan of operations for the defence of the Empire in any given contingency has ever been worked out or decided upon by the two Departments . . .' The Commission's solution (with Lt-Gen. Sir Henry Brackenbury and Lord Randolph Churchill dissenting), was a Naval and Military Council composed of the Prime Minister, the Parliamentary heads of the Services and their principal professional advisers, and other specialist advisers who might be summoned to attend on particular occasions.[54] Although not immediately adopted, this proposal in many respects foreshadowed the Committee of Imperial Defence which was not established until after the salutary shock administered by the South African War.

When they turned to the internal administration of the War Office, the Commissioners discovered that recent enactments had effected by far the greatest changes since Cardwell's War Office Act of 1870. In 1887, as part of the Jubilee celebrations, the Duke of Cambridge had been made Commander-in-Chief in both name and in fact.[55] By an Order in Council of 21 February 1888 the Duke's responsibilities were enormously increased. The office of Surveyor-General of the Ordnance was abolished and the Commander-in-Chief was charged with all the duties previously entrusted to him; namely, 'with obtaining, holding and issuing to the Army all supplies and munitions of war'. In short the command and the supply of the Army, hitherto kept carefully distinct, were now concentrated under a single official and he a Royal Duke who had already held the highest office for thirty-two years. At the same time the Quartermaster-General suffered a further loss of status and all but two of his subordinates were absorbed into the Adjutant-General's branch.

In theory there was much to be said in favour of thus combining responsibility for command and supply, but in practice the Commission found overwhelming reasons against it. First, this was simply too much responsibility for any one man to deal with efficiently. Second, it weakened the responsibility of the heads of departments. Third, and most important, it deprived the Secretary of State for War of a board of advice, for in effect the Commander-in-Chief became his sole responsible adviser in military matters.[56]

After making diplomatically polite remarks about the long and honourable services of the Duke of Cambridge, the Report eventually recommended that the office of Commander-in-Chief should *not* form part of the permanent constitution of the War Department. Britain needed to follow the example of the military systems of all the great Powers of Europe and create a special Department of the Chief of the Staff 'freed from all executive functions, and charged with the responsible duty of preparing plans for military operations, collecting and co-ordinating information of all kinds, and generally tendering advice upon all matters of organization and the preparation of the army for war'.[57]

At last the British Army was poised on the threshold of a new era, thanks to the Hartington Commission's wise and far-reaching recommendation in favour of a General Staff. The prospects of success seemed enhanced when this important proposal was given additional publicity by the appearance of Spenser Wilkinson's brilliant popular account of the German General Staff, *The Brain of an Army*, on the very day that the Report was published.[58]

Unfortunately, the Duke of Cambridge's obstinate clinging to office made it impossible immediately to create a Chief of the Staff with a genuine General Staff under him.[59] When the Duke was eventually prised out of office in 1895, the title of Commander-in-Chief was retained and inherited by Wolseley, but with greatly reduced powers which, in effect, made him just one of a board of professional advisers, and produced intense friction that goes far to explain the heedless way in which Britain blundered into the South African War.[60]

The creation of a Chief-of-Staff appeared to be as far off as ever. The Duke of Cambridge and Queen Victoria had made plain their bitter opposition. Sir Charles Callwell and Sir William Nicholson later asserted, plausibly, that Wolseley joined forces with the Duke in opposing implementation of the Hartington Report because they knew that Sir Henry Bracken-bury, a former protégé of Wolseley's and then Director of Military Intelligence, had played a major role in drafting that section of the Report and feared that he would be chosen as the first Chief of Staff.[61]

What also needs to be emphasized, however, is the existence among politicians, particularly Liberals and Radicals, of a strong antipathy to the creation of a Chief of Staff on political, indeed almost ideological grounds. This apprehension was forcibly expressed in a dissenting memorandum to the Harting-ton Report by Henry Campbell-Bannerman, who had already briefly occupied the War Office and was to do so again from 1892 to 1895. Campbell-Bannerman gave two reasons for his opposition to a Chief of Staff, the second of which was entirely logical and sensible: he favoured the replacement of a Com-mander-in-Chief by a Council of General Officers and feared that a Chief of Staff, as the adviser on general policy, would overshadow his co-equals and resurrect the present problem. His first reason, however, aptly reveals the prejudice and obscurantism against which the Staff College and a staff system could make but slow headway. In Campbell-Bannerman's view a Chief of Staff was simply unnecessary in the British Army. Continental armies were constantly engaged in suspiciously watching their neighbours and preparing contingency war plans against them, 'but in this country there is in truth no room for "general military policy" in the larger and more ambitious sense of the phrase ... I am at a loss to know where, for this larger branch of its duties, the new Department could find an adequate field in the circumstances of this country.' He hinted darkly that an idle General Staff might be tempted to indulge in unauthorized war planning on its own initiative.[62]

Spenser Wilkinson, rather surprisingly, did not press for the creation of a Chief of Staff in 1889 and 1890 because he hoped that if Wolseley or Roberts could replace the Duke of Cam-

bridge the reforms he advocated might still be implemented by
a Commander-in-Chief. Maj.-Gen. C. B. Brackenbury, elder
brother of Henry and a key figure in the development of the
Intelligence Department in the 1870s, urged upon Wilkinson
the vital importance of a Chief of the Staff:

> The fact is that we have no General Staff in the German
> sense, and we want one. All our staff officers, so called, are
> only what the Germans would call *Adjutantur* and are swal-
> lowed up in a sea of documents and red tape. . . .
>
> If we sent an army on a campaign the chief of its Staff
> and the highest staff officers might be absolutely un-
> acquainted with the design of the whole business, and be
> selected by a bevy of Dukes. All this would be put to rights
> if once we had a General Staff Department, for it would be
> too strong to be sat upon, and the very appointment of a
> Chief of Staff would cause the Duke's resignation. We don't
> want a peace Commander-in-Chief but we want one all
> ready for war. It is too absurd to have a Commander-in-
> Chief permanently on our necks and never intended to take
> the field at all . . . We want a working Inspector-General,
> real commanders of Corps in Districts administering their
> own commands, and a Chief of the Staff to take the field
> with the staff he has trained to carry out the strategy he has
> devised.[63]

In reaction to sweeping (and sometimes uninformed) con-
demnations of the Duke of Cambridge as a complete reactionary
and a disastrous head of the Army, some recent writers have
rightly attempted to restore the balance by pointing to the
Duke's good personal characteristics and the importance of his
disinterested role as the barrier between rival political parties
and direct civil control of the Army with the enormous patronage that conferred.[64] Certainly, Lord Wolseley, who made the
most rude and bitter remarks about the Duke in letters to his
wife, paid tribute on his retirement to that 'honesty of purpose,
loyalty to the Army, devotion to duty, sincere patriotism and
deep and real attachment to his Queen and country [which]
pervaded all he did'. 'Within his limits,' writes the historian of

the War Office, 'he was a keen and discriminating soldier, a good judge of men, and his minutes and correspondence are full of admirable good sense conveyed in clear, and sometimes quite forcible language.' Col Willoughby Verner's biography presents ample evidence of the (mostly vain) struggle which the Duke put up throughout his career against ill-considered reductions of the military establishment.

Nevertheless, severe historical judgements do not always deserve to be mitigated, and from the viewpoint of his relationship with the Staff College and higher military administration there seems to be no call for drastic revision. Memoirs of the Staff College are full of references to the Duke's conservatism and eccentricities, but there is little to show that he did anything positive to develop the institution which he had helped to establish. He had, it has aptly been said, the temperament of a first-class autocrat without a full measure of corresponding ability. But for the firm control exerted over him by several strong War Ministers he would probably have become a military autocrat of the most unprogressive description, and would have filled the Army with 'bow and arrow' generals like himself.[65] The new progressive spirit apparent at the Staff College in the 1890s owed much to the Royal Duke's belated departure from the War Office.

1 Albert V. Tucker, 'Army and Society in England 1870–1900: a Reassessment of the Cardwell Reforms', *Journal of British Studies*, Vol. 2, May 1963, pp. 110–41. See also Brian Bond, 'The Introduction and Operation of Short Service and Localization in the British Army, 1868–1892' (Unpublished M.A. Thesis, University of London, 1962). 'The Effect of Cardwell Reforms', *Journal of the Royal United Service Institution*, November 1960, pp. 515–24, and 'The Late Victorian Army', *History Today*, Vol. XI, September 1961, pp. 616–24.

2 Captain Owen Wheeler, *The War Office Past and Present* (London, 1914), p. 187. Cardwell's pragmatic approach to the purchase problem is exhaustively examined by N. H. Moses in 'Edward Cardwell's abolition of the purchase system in the British Army, 1868–1874: a study of administrative and legislative processes' (Unpublished doctoral dissertation, University of London, 1969).

3 Wheeler, *op. cit.*, pp. 189–95. Hampden Gordon, *The War Office* (London, 1935), pp. 58–9. The latest and most penetrating study of military administration in this period in W. S. Hamer, *The British Army: Civil Military Relations 1885–1905* (Oxford, 1970).

4 See Chapter I, p. 31, *et seq.*

5 Major Arthur Griffiths, *The English Army: its past history, present condition and future prospects* (London, *c.* 1880), pp. 67–8.

6 Tucker, *op. cit.*, pp. 116–18.

7 Sir George Aston, *Secret Service* (London, 1930), p. 17.

8 Sir C. M. Watson, *Life of Major-General Sir Charles Wilson* (London, 1909), pp. 74–84.

9 Col. R. H. Vetch, R.E., 'Colonel Robert Home (1837–79)', *op. cit.* See also A. W. Preston, 'British Military Thought, 1856–90', pp. 72–3.

10 Sir Frederick Maurice and Sir George Arthur, *The Life of Lord Wolseley* (London, 1924), pp. 223–4. Alfred Cochrane, 'General Sir Henry Brackenbury 1837–1914', *Dictionary of National Biography*.

11 Tucker, *op. cit.*, p. 127.

12 W. O. 32/1014/107 Gen/1609 quoted by Tucker, *op. cit.*, p. 126.

13 Tucker, *op. cit.*, p. 127.

14 Preston, *op. cit.*, Colonel F. N. Maude, *War and the World's Life* (London, 1907), Ch. IX, *passim*. The first English translation of Clausewitz's *On War* was Col J. J. Graham's in 1873.

15 Preston, *op. cit.*, p. 70.

16 Aston, *op. cit.*, p. 20.

17 The Stanhope Memorandum is printed in full as Appendix A in

J. K. Dunlop, *The Development of the British Army, 1899–1914* (London, 1938).

18 Maude, *op. cit.*, p. 171.

19 Field-Marshal Lord Roberts (1832–1914) served 41 years in India and made his name with the march from Kabul to Kandahar in the Second Afghan War (1878–81); subsequently Commander-in-Chief in India, South Africa (1899–1900) and Britain (1900–4).

20 Adrian Preston (ed.), *In Relief of Gordon: Lord Wolseley's Campaign Journal of the Khartoum Relief Expedition, 1884–1885* (London, 1967), p. XVIII.

21 See Maurice and Arthur, *op. cit.*, *passim.* Jay Luvaas, *op. cit.*, particularly the essays on Maurice and Henderson; and Joseph Lehmann, *All Sir Garnet: a life of Field-Marshal Lord Wolseley 1833–1913* (London, 1964).

22 A failing which Professor Lehmann does not always avoid in a volume which is much better on Wolseley's early and middle years as an active soldier than on his later career at the War Office.

23 For a concise recent account of the Ashanti War see Brian Bond (ed.), *Victorian Military Campaigns* (London, 1967), Chapter IV.

24 Field-Marshal Viscount Wolseley, *The Story of a Soldier's Life* (London, 1903), Vol. II, p. 276. Hamley to Blackwood 23 November 1873, 4304, ff. 125–7, Blackwood Papers.

25 H. Brackenbury, *The Ashanti War* (Edinburgh, 1874), Vol. I, p. 113.

26 Col. J. F. Maurice, *Military History of the Campaign of 1882 in Egypt* (London, 1887), pp. 112–19. Col. H. E. Colvile, *History of the Sudan Campaign* (London, 1889), Part I, pp. 270–6.

27 Col. W. Verner, *op. cit.*, Vol. II, p. 272, quoted in part by Godwin-Austen, *op. cit.*, pp. 207–8.

28 Godwin-Austen, *op. cit.*, p. 203.

29 See Adrian Preston's trenchant comments in his introduction to *In Relief of Gordon*. To mention just one of the numerous internecine feuds among the Wolseleyites, Sir Evelyn Wood and Sir Baker Russell had been bitterly at odds ever since an incident in the Ashanti Campaign, see Lord Edward Gleichen, *A Guardsman's Memories* (Edinburgh, 1932), p. 118.

30 Sir John Adye, *Soldiers and Others I have known* (London, 1925), p. 136.

31 Maurice and Arthur, *op. cit.*, pp. 235–6.

32 Godwin-Austen, *op. cit.*, pp. 170–7. However, Hamley did write to his friend Blackwood – during a vacation – that he preferred writing poetry to celebrating the operations of war, adding, 'I am enjoying solitude most misanthropically – seeing my species only on hunting days'. 11 January 1873, 4304, f. 73, Blackwood Papers.

33 *Ibid.*, p. 181 and A. Innes Shand, *op. cit.*, Vol. I, pp. 120–8, 198–204.

34 Godwin-Austen, *op. cit.*, p. 186. When Cardwell left the War Office, Hamley wrote: 'He was a friend to enlightened change and progress in the Army and I could look to him confidently for support in whatever was for the benefit of the College.' 20 February 1874, 4318, ff. 88–9, Blackwood Papers.

35 *Ibid.*, p. 181. *First Report of the Education of Officers* by the Director-General of Military Education (London, 1873), p. 23 ff.
36 Gleichen, *op. cit.*, p. 110.
37 Adye, *op. cit.*, p. 140.
38 Maj.-Gen. A. Alison succeeded Hamley in January 1878 but was posted in May. He was followed by Col. C. O. Creagh-Osborne (May 1878–Dec. 1885) and Maj.-Gen. E. H. Clive (Dec. 1885–Aug. 1888).
39 Wood, *op. cit.*, Vol. I, p. 294.
40 *Report of the Committee on Military Educational Establishments*, A 117, 1888, Minutes of Evidence, paras 3618–19. Lt-Col F. Maurice (ed.), *Sir Frederick Maurice: a record of his work and opinions* (London, 1913), p. 58.
41 Adye, *op. cit.*, pp. 139–40.
42 *Report of Committee on the Working of the Staff College, 1880* (Confidential Paper 0774). The report is summarized by Godwin-Austen, *op. cit.*, pp. 190–3.
43 Maurice, *op. cit.*, pp. 58–61; Luvaas, *op. cit.*, pp. 191–3.
44 *Report of the Committee on Military Educational Establishments*, A 117, 1888, Minutes of Evidence, paras 3608, 3611, 3682.
45 Adye, *op. cit.*, pp. 141–2, cf. Repington 'Maurice I loved. He lectured well and was most helpful to us all . . .', *Vestigia* (London, 1919), p. 76.
46 Godwin-Austen, *op. cit.*, pp. 209–10. Maj.-Gen. Sir C. E. Callwell, *Stray Recollections* (London, 1923), Vol, I, p. 278.
47 *Ibid.*, p. 273. *Third Report on the Education of Officers* (c3818), 1883, pp. 24–5; Godwin-Austen, *op. cit.*, p. 206.
48 *Fourth Report on the Education of Officers* (c5793), 1889, pp. 29–32. In 1883 there were 67 competitors, in 1884 – 68, in 1885 – 43, in 1886 – 50, in 1887 – 73, in 1888 – 68. In 1891 two officers from the 2nd Battalion East Surrey Regiment were admitted.
49 *Ibid.*, pp. 51–4. Col. F. N. Maude is particularly scathing about the Staff College's entrance regulations, possibly because he had been excluded in 1884, though placed 15th out of 47, as there were no further vacancies for officers of the Royal Engineers. See *War and the World's Life*, pp. 171–5.
50 *Fourth Report on the Education of Officers*, p. 34.
51 C. A'Court Repington, *op. cit.*, p. 77. Gen. Sir H. Smith-Dorrien, *Memoirs of Forty-Eight Years' Service* (London, 1925), p. 68. Brig. Gen. C. Ballard, *Smith-Dorrien* (London, 1931), pp. 46–7. Callwell, *op. cit.*, Vol. I, pp. 273–92. Adye, *op. cit.*, p. 148. D. Chapman-Huston and O. Rutter, *General Sir John Cowans: The Quartermaster-General of the Great War* (London, 1924), Vol. I, pp. 74–80. See also, for example, Maj.-Gen. Sir George Younghusband, *A Soldier's Memories* (London, 1917), and Lord Edward Gleichen, *op. cit.*
52 Sir George Aston, *Memories of a Marine* (London, 1919), pp. 97–118. 'In those days,' Aston recalls, 'soldiering was not taken quite so seriously as it was after the South African War. There was an un-

written rule that all field days at Aldershot should end before the sacred dinner-hour, and I have seen an attack pushed at a rate which verged on absurdity when there was a doubt whether the battle would be over in time for a certain train to London.'

53 Maurice and Arthur, *op. cit.*, pp. 238–40.

54 *Reports of the Royal Commission on the Civil and Professional Administration of the Naval and Military Departments (The Hartington Report)*, (c5979), 1890, paras 7, 10, 20.

55 Strictly speaking, the Duke of Cambridge was 'Commanding-in-Chief' until 1887, since in theory the Sovereign retained command of the armed forces. The title 'Commander-in-Chief' had last been briefly held by the Duke of Wellington in 1827.

56 *Hartington Report*, paras 51–62.

57 *Ibid.*, 67–94.

58 Henry Spenser Wilkinson, *Thirty-Five Years, 1874–1909* (London, 1933), p. 120; Luvaas, *op. cit.*, pp. 256–60.

59 Brian Bond, 'The Retirement of the Duke of Cambridge', *R.U.S.I. Journal*, November 1961. By Army Order 228 of 1888 the term 'General Staff' was revived. See also Godwin-Austen, *op. cit.*, pp. 218–20.

60 Hamer, *op. cit*, Chapter 4, and F. A. Johnson, *Defence by Committee* (London, 1960), Chapter I.

61 Callwell, *op. cit.*, Vol. I, p. 392. Nicholson's view is quoted by Luvaas, *op. cit.*, p. 260n. Sir Henry Brackenbury may have had ambitions to become the first Chief of Staff, but Luvaas does him an injustice here (pp. 259–60), since he is in fact quoting from the correspondence of his brother, Maj.-Gen. C. B. Brackenbury, with Spenser Wilkinson.

62 *Hartington Report*, Campbell-Bannerman's Dissent, pp. XXIX–XXXI. See also Hamer, *op. cit.*, pp. 141–2.

63 C. B. Brackenbury to Wilkinson, 2 June 1889, *Spenser Wilkinson Papers*. For the opinion that in his last few years in office the Duke of Cambridge was 'scarcely being consulted . . . in respect of many things which really mattered, and that he in reality was occupying a position that verged on the undignified . . .', see Callwell, *op. cit.*, Vol. I, p. 290.

64 Tucker, *op. cit.*; Giles St Aubyn, *The Royal George* (London, 1963); Hamer, *op. cit.*

65 Wheeler, *op. cit.*, pp. 248–9.

CHAPTER FIVE

The Staff College
1890–1899

Although the 1890s witnessed no military reforms as far-reaching or controversial as those of Cardwell or Haldane, it was none the less a decade in which a new progressive spirit began to make itself felt. However disappointing his brief tenure turned out to be in practice, Viscount Wolseley's succession to the Duke of Cambridge as Commander-in-Chief on 1 November 1895 clearly signalled the end of an era. Large-scale summer and autumn manœuvres were revived after a break of twenty years. Stanhope's Memorandum on military policy, questionable as were its assumptions, at least gave the War Office the reasonable task of preparing to raise two Army Corps and a Cavalry Division for home defence.

The Staff College made a notable contribution to the Army's enhanced reputation for it had, by 1890, put behind it much of its reputation for pedantry; it was attracting some outstanding students; and, above all, the magic letters p.s.c. were seen to be worth having since they opened up opportunities not only of coveted appointments, but also of accelerated promotion. The true significance of these improvements is apparent in comparison with the recent past; their limitations were soon to be revealed in the South African War.

As Sir Frederick Maurice had emphasized, if the Staff College were to make a significant impact on the intellectual level of the Army, it was essential for it to secure outstanding men for its Commandant and instructing staff. In the 1890s it was fortunate to secure the services of two officers who between them can be said to have left a lasting impression on the educational history of the Army: Henry J. T. Hildyard and George F. R. Henderson.

Hildyard was born in 1846, the son of T. B. T. Hildyard (the Member of Parliament for Nottinghamshire South, 1846–52 and 1866–85), and he spent five years in the Royal Navy before joining the Army in 1867. He served on the Staff in the Egyptian campaign of 1882 and held further staff appointments before becoming Commandant of the Staff College from 1893 to 1898. He had graduated from Camberley himself in 1877 with special credit in German and Spanish and he frequently contributed translations of German articles to the *Journal* of the Royal United Service Institution. Although he went on to command the 5th Division in the South African War and subsequently became Director-General of Military Education (1903–4) and General Officer Commanding in Chief South Africa (1905–8), it was probably in his five years at Camberley that Hildyard made his most valuable contribution to the Army.

Col. Hildyard set out to make the course thoroughly practical and to combat the old evil of cramming: 'We do not want any cramming here,' was his motto, 'we want officers to absorb, not to cram.' He vainly strove to secure the abolition of all written examinations by outside examiners, but did succeed in the radical change of abolishing the final examination.[1] Instead, students were classified according to their work during the course and the impression they had made on the instructors. Up to 1893, as Henderson wrote later, the chief object of the course had been the accumulation of knowledge and preparation for paper examinations. Under the new regime students spent much of their time solving problems of strategy, tactics and organization both in their quarters and in the field. 'This method of training, accompanied as it was by a salutary friction with other brains . . . was undoubtedly a great advance . . . It was more exclusively practical than the method pursued at any Staff College in Europe; and it was the best substitute for the complete experience on which Wellington laid stress, and also the best supplement to the partial experience . . . of one or more minor campaigns.'[2]

The Staff College aspired to little more than laying the

foundations for a useful career, and of course it could not ensure that the habits of study and thought cultivated during two fairly arduous years would be permanent. Nevertheless, it is to Hildyard's credit that he transformed the College into a 'mental gymnasium' for the Army just at a time when the future leaders of the First World War era were passing through.

The British Army has produced few more gifted military historians and teachers than Col Henderson, who is remembered with warm affection as well as admiration in almost every account of the Staff College in the 1890s.

Henderson was born in 1854, the son of a clergyman who was then headmaster of Leeds Grammar School and subsequently became dean of Carlisle. Destined to follow his father into the church, Henderson won a history scholarship at St John's College, Oxford, but he appears to have preferred sport to study for he left the College for Sandhurst without a degree in 1876. He was commissioned into the York and Lancaster regiment (65th and 84th) and commanded a company with distinction in the actions at Kassassin and Tel el Kebir in 1882. This first brought him to Wolseley's attention. The need for more money, and also a burning desire to devote more time to study and writing caused him to join the Ordnance Store Department in 1885. The following year he published a small volume, *The Campaign of Fredericksburg*, which was brought to Wolseley's attention by Col Maurice and resulted in the author's appointment to the instructional staff at Sandhurst in January 1890. In 1891 he published an elaborate tactical study of the battle of Spicheren which revealed Henderson's unique ability to employ military history to train the judgement of the students by placing them in the shoes of various principal actors in the drama. Maurice, who was shortly due to retire as Professor of Military Art and History, urged Wolseley to appoint Henderson his successor and this he accomplished despite objections that he was too junior. 'Rarely,' as Jay Luvaas remarks, 'has publication resulted in more rapid promotion even in an academic atmosphere.'[3]

In a letter written to Henderson shortly after his transfer

from Sandhurst to Camberley, Maurice suggested that the latter was still in much need of improvement: 'I am deeply conscious that at present the Staff College produces a monstrous deal of bread for very little sack. The able men who would make good Staff Officers benefit greatly; so do those who have strong character or practical experience of war to guide them; but from the ruck we have turned out, I fear me, some cranks and not a few pedants. I am sure that under the new regime you will succeed where I have often failed.'[4]

Henderson justified Maurice's expectations but his career was tragically cut short.

Like Maurice, Henderson was apprehensive lest his success as a teacher and writer should militate against his prospects of active service. Indeed, like his hero Stonewall Jackson who had served as Professor of Artillery Tactics at the Virginia Military Institute, Henderson viewed his appointments to Sandhurst and Camberley as an opportunity to fit himself for command. As it happened it was once again a publication – in 1899 – this time of his monumental study of Stonewall Jackson by which he is most widely remembered, which gave him his opportunity. Lord Roberts was filled with admiration by Henderson's sympathetic treatment of his hero's strategic ideas, and on being appointed Commander-in-Chief in South Africa at the end of 1899, took out Henderson as his Director of Military Intelligence. Although well-qualified for these duties Henderson's health was failing even when he accepted the appointment; he broke down from malaria and fatigue when the Army reached the Modder river and had to be invalided home. Appointed to a staff post at the War Office he revised the *Infantry Drill Book* and was then chosen to write the official history of the war. On this unenviable task he struggled bravely through the remaining months of his life, returning to South Africa to examine the battlefields in 1901. Towards the end of 1902 he collapsed again from overwork and went to Egypt for the winter, only to die at Assuan on 5 March 1903. Scarcely a month before his death he completed one of his most brilliant essays on 'The British Army'.[5]

The future Gen. Lord Rawlinson was typical of the p.s.c.s

of the 1890s in being deeply and permanently impressed by Henderson as a man and a teacher. According to 'Rawly's' biographer Henderson was, 'by the charm of his personality and the inspiration of his teaching, an influence which is almost unique in the history of the Staff College'.[6]

The key to Henderson's success as a teacher was his realization that knowledge 'gained by hard labour and independent effort is of higher worth, and much more likely to be permanently absorbed, than that which comes in by the ear';[7] in short, he insisted that the student himself became involved. As Luvaas writes, those who attended Henderson's lectures or read his books 'found themselves expected to replace the actors, to work out the operations step by step with map and compass, to investigate the reasons behind each decision, to ascertain the relative importance of moral and physical factors, and to deduce the principles on which the generals had acted'.[8]

Ironically, Henderson's passionate concern to encourage an inquisitive and objective approach to military history among British officers was undermined by the very success of his *Stonewall Jackson*. Not only at the Staff College but in promotion examinations the campaigns in the Shenandoah Valley were repeatedly prescribed for study and, over the years, stimulated a flood of précis and primers which encouraged the very cramming that 'Hender' had fought against. As Liddell Hart was to write sardonically in 1927: 'to be able to enumerate the blades of grass in the Shenandoah Valley and the yards marched by Stonewall Jackson's men is not an adequate foundation for leadership in a future war where conditions and armament have radically changed'.[9] Serving officers have informed the present author in 1969 that the Army still tends to take a circumscribed, 'Jacksonian' view of the American Civil War.

Sir Henry Hildyard paid a generous tribute to Henderson's zeal and thoroughness as a teacher, and as an officer acutely conscious that he was forming the minds of the future leaders of the Army. 'He considered that his mission was not restricted to the mere teaching of the subjects that entered into the curriculum, but extended to the extraction from those subjects of every lesson that should go to the making of an efficient commander in the field, and to its complete assimilation by the officers under his instruction . . . He showed great clearness of perception, simplicity and correctness of demonstration, a practical mind that discarded at once methods impracticable in war, and untiring industry and patience.'[10]

Surviving essays and papers from Staff College students of this period, including those of Haig, Edmonds (official historian of the First World War), Ellison, Robertson and Hunter-Weston, amply demonstrate the meticulous pains which Henderson took over marking. 'There was no paper, however crude,' wrote Hildyard, 'wherein he did not notice points for encouragement towards renewed effort; so there was no paper, however complete, to which his practical and well-thought-out remarks did not add value. To him it was a labour of love, and each memoir, good or indifferent, received the same measure of attention from him . . .' Some of the other instructors were as zealous in their marking as Henderson – and the Commandant also added comments to many of the papers – but the old pedantic spirit died hard. Sir George Aston, who was at Camberley just before the Hildyard era, criticized the excessive amount of time spent on military surveying in which two days a week and many leisure hours were spent in converting sketches of little bits of country into highly artistic drawings. He relates how one Royal Engineer, famous for his surveys of large areas of the North West Frontier of India, had one of his best productions returned to him with the advice written across it, 'You should practise gravel-pits'.[11]

Henderson always delighted, both at Sandhurst and Camberley, to play an active part in student sports and recreations. He was, for example, a keen cricketer and follower of the Staff College Drag. Hildyard, as well as some of his students, has pointed to the value of these informal contacts – perhaps inspired by memories of the Oxford tutorial system – which he fostered at the College, using his rare leisure hours to discuss disputed points raised by the latest lecture or the most recent work on military literature. 'And it would be difficult to say now where most was really learned by the officers anxious to

5a. The Professors, 1864.
Col. Lacy is standing in the centre, Rev. Twisden (Mathematics) is seated centre, and Col. Chesney (Military History and Strategy) is on his right.

5b. The Senior Division, 1875.

1. Lieut A. de la Voye, 56th Foot
2. Lieut. A. G. Walker, RA
3. Lieut. T. B. Hitchcock, 53rd Foot
4. Lieut. G. W. Hawkins, RA
5. Capt. G. L. Le M. Taylor, 16th Foot
6. Capt. J. C. Ardagh, RE
7. Lieut. N. Y. Lloyd, 82nd Foot
8. Lieut. E. J. Courtney, 35th Foot
9. Capt. W. F. Gatacre, 77th Foot
10. Capt. E. S. Creek, 23rd Foot
11. Maj. The Hon. H. J. L. Wood, 12th Lancers
12. Lieut. W. A. H. Hare, RE
13. Maj. C. J. Burnett, 15th Foot
14. Capt. S. Boulderson, 17th Lancers
15. Lieut. S. C. Pratt, RA
16. Lieut. E. J. Lugard, 4th Foot

Major-General Sir A. Alison (1878)

Col. C. O. Creagh-Osborne (1878–85)

Col. E. H. Clive (1885–8)

Brig.-Gen. C. F. Clery (1888–93)

6. Commandants in the Wolseley Era.
Creagh-Osborne was an unpopular martinet, Clive was handicapped by lack of campaign experience while Clery, though the author of a text book on *Minor Tactics*, was seldom seen by the students.

acquire knowledge in the military art – in the lecture-hall or in the ante-room of the Staff College Mess.'[12]

As for Henderson's influence on the future leaders in the South African and First World Wars, *The Times* in its obituary notice made a flattering comparison with von Moltke's influence on the Prussian Army and predicted that Henderson's influence would be felt in the next great war. Field-Marshal Sir William Robertson, who was at the Staff College in 1897–8, believed that all his contemporaries, including Haig and Allenby, who achieved fame in the First World War, would 'readily admit that such successes as attended their leadership were largely due to the sound instruction and inspiring counsel which they received from their old tutor some twenty years or so before. Of the different causes which are alleged to have given us the victory over Germany, not one should be assigned a more prominent place than the influence and teaching of Henderson at the Staff College.'[13] Whether or not the Professor would have been entirely enthusiastic about the qualities of generalship displayed by his former students between 1914 and 1918, Robertson's statement is important testimony to the formative influence of the Staff College and its most distinguished teacher in the 1890s. When Viscount Esher read Henderson's posthumously published essays, *The Science of War*, he lamented to his son that the author did not live to be Chief of the Staff. 'Now, that type is exactly what is required, and yet apparently it does not exist in the Army.'[14]

For a vivid and, for the most part unflattering, description of the Staff College in the 1890s, we turn to the reminiscences of Brig.-Gen. Sir James Edmonds, a very learned Royal Engineer who is best known as the Official Historian of the First World War.[15] At Camberley he acquired the enduring nickname of 'Archimedes'. He and a fellow sapper captain, G. M. W. Macdonogh, passed in so far ahead of the rest that there was a delay in publishing the results and a change was made to alphabetical order to try to conceal the gap between these two and the rest. Not surprisingly both found a large part of the course unexacting and some allowance must be made for this in Edmonds's rather mordant criticism. Edmonds, in fact, used

G

some of his ample leisure to compile a weighty history of the American Civil War, while Macdonogh spent his in London qualifying as a barrister.[16]

As a married officer Edmonds lived in his own house in Camberley and described the College, unromantically, as 'a single large hotel-like looking, rectangular, two-storeyed, dirty yellow building, with long corridor passages most difficult to warm ... It contained a mess, halls of study, a library and quarters for 16 bachelor officers ...' It was entirely inadequate for the needs of 64 officers and staff not to speak of India and the Dominions who by this time were interested in sending officers to it. On the other hand it should be remembered that the Kriegsakademie possessed no residential accommodation whatever.

Edmonds's pay as an engineer captain was £750 p.a. but his pay was stopped during the course on the curious grounds that he was not employed on Corps works. He paid £50 p.a. for a partly furnished house, £18 to the cook, £16 to the parlour-maid, 30s a week to the groom, and he gave his wife £5 a week for housekeeping. He estimated that a bachelor at the College required about £200 a year in addition to his pay as a captain.

The class of 1896–7 was exceptional not only in containing a high proportion of men of ability, but also because its members were at the peak of their careers when the great opportunity came in 1914. Of the batch of 32, 4 were killed in action or died of wounds; 1 was wounded and died of enteric in Lady-smith; 1 died in France of exposure; 2 were wounded and invalided home. Of the remainder, 2 became field-marshals and peers (Haig and Allenby), 15 became generals (of whom 8 were knighted); 1 got no further than colonel; 3 retired for reasons of health before 1914; 1 resigned because he had inherited a fortune; and 1 shot himself, his mother-in-law and her lawyer in *une drame passionelle*.[17] Although Edmonds agreed with the popular view that the cream of the intellect of the country did not go into the Army, he challenged a critic who asserted that the majority of Staff College students were of mediocre talent. The fact that candidates had to go through several weary months of preparation for the entrance examination, survive two years' hard work with no certainty of even a trial on the staff, and spend about £300 of their own money was strong *prima facie* evidence of zeal, ability and perseverance. In his year there were about six 'rank duffers' thanks to the efforts of crammers and the power of the Commander-in-Chief to nominate, but the rest 'were all men of exceptional ability and by contact with them even the duffers improved'.[18]

Edmonds was not alone in thinking that a Staff consisting of one Commandant, six military instructors and two civilians (one of whom was bone idle) was inadequate for the thorough criticism of the work of 64 students. 'The staff in my time slaved to get through the mass of paper handed in to them. They made the lectures not only instructive but stimulating, but I shall never consider the Government returned me value for the two years of my life, the engineer pay I gave up, and the additional £400 I had to spend.' He pointed out that the Kriegsakademie then had a staff of 44 professors and instructors. Moreover, only one of the Camberley lecturers, Maj. C. R. Simpson, had served on the Staff, in the Intelligence Division, and he was 'conspicuously silent about the working of that institution'.[19]

Again Edmonds was voicing a common criticism when he complained that the first year was largely wasted on elementary lectures; the object being apparently to complete a neglected military education rather than to prepare for staff work.

What actually happened in the first year was that we sat at a few lectures – the good boys in the front row, the idle asleep in the back row – and heard what amounted to no more than the reading of some paragraphs of the regulation books (mostly out of date) and some pages of military history; but we did a great deal out of doors mostly making ordinary sketch maps, with compass and plane table and by eye, on foot, on horseback and on bicycle. With our own fair hands, under an artillery instructor, we dug trenches, put up wires, made temporary bridges . . . and amid a scene of indescribable confusion we laid a few railway rails. There was a written marked examination at the end of the first year, but nobody regarded it seriously.[20]

In the second year, however, there was a great improvement as Col. Hildyard made his influence felt.

> We worked on a number of 'schemes' out of doors, comprising most of the small tactical operations of war, writing little appreciations and operation orders for a small mixed force, not for a brigade or division. Students of the year which left as mine entered told me that they did not write a single operation order while at the College. Hildyard sent us long distances on the recently discovered 'pneumatic' bike, to the disgust of some of my stout friends.[21]

In theory it had always been an aim of the Staff College to prepare officers for higher command as well as for staff duties, though the former objective had never been systematically or thoroughly pursued. By the 1890s, however, it is clear that the College was recruiting some of the ablest – and also some of the most ambitious – young officers in the Army, many of whom went on to obtain field commands in South Africa and to become the commanders of armies, corps and divisions in the First World War. Future First World War generals at the College between 1890 and 1893 included Spencer Ewart, Bruce Hamilton, F. J. Davies, Charles Monro, Samuel Lomax, Henry Wilson, Henry Rawlinson and John Cowans. It was in the years 1895–8, however, that a galaxy of future stars passed through. The Senior Division in 1897, for example, included Allenby, Haking, Edmonds, Haig, Macdonogh, Dyer, Capper and Forrestier-Walker; and the Junior Division, A. J. Murray and W. R. Robertson. Among others to gain distinction from the later 1890s were Hunter-Weston, Godley, Hubert Gough, Braithwaite, Maude, Herbert Lawrence and de Lisle.

In some cases officers who later rose to the top were already picked out as outstanding at Camberley but, as at school, the future leader sometimes lay well back in the ruck. As an example of the former, the outstanding personality of 1887–8 was Horace Smith-Dorrien, who fully justified his high rating in South Africa and in 1914. On the other hand, in 1890–1, Sir George Aston described one man as 'head and shoulders above the rest, and an inspiration to every one . . . In brains and in sound judgment he was in a class by himself, far ahead of everyone . . .' This was the Hon. Milo Talbot R.E. who retired as a colonel before the First World War to assist Lord Roberts with his national service campaign.[22]

According to Brig.-Gen. Sir James Edmonds the ablest soldier of his year (1896–7) was H. N. C. Heath K.O.Y.L.I. who died early in 1915, 'worn out by trying to knock into shape during the severe winter of 1914–15 a Territorial division which he brought to France'. Also outstanding in that batch were (Sir) Richard Haking who rose to command the XI Corps on the Western Front and was perhaps unlucky not to get the Third Army in place of Byng; (Sir) George Macdonogh, later Director of Military Intelligence at the War Office and Adjutant-General; and (Sir) Thompson Capper who was killed in command of a division in the battle of Loos in 1915. 'Wully' Robertson, probably the first ex-ranker to go to Camberley, was the dominant personality in the succeeding year.

Edmonds's list omits the two cavalry officers destined to become peers and field-marshals, Edmund Allenby and Douglas Haig. The former was Master of the Drag and very popular at the College but according to Edmonds 'he looked a typical young English fox-hunting squire'; he had not much to say for himself and 'was obviously out of his depth'. C. R. Simpson, then Professor of Staff Duties, later told Edmonds that the staff had considered Allenby dull and stupid and were surprised at the good speech he had made at the Farmers' Dinner at the end of the hunting season. Macdonogh and Edmonds had written the speech for him. These severe judgements of Allenby were wide of the mark. Sir George Barrow, who entered the College a year after Haig and Allenby, was more perceptive in noticing that the former carried the habit of concentration on professional studies to excess, thereby stunting the growth of his imagination. Allenby, by contrast, was an imaginative man of wide interests: he was a passionate student of ornithology, and later became a Fellow of the Zoological Society; he was also widely read and fond of music.

Capt. Douglas Haig, 7th Hussars, had not yet put aside the

taciturn and surly behaviour that had characterized him as a
Sandhurst cadet. At the Staff College he worked harder than
anyone else, kept himself to himself, and was seldom seen in the
mess except for meals. He had not enhanced his popularity
when, on first arriving at the College, he had requested three
days' leave in the Leave Book 'to shoot, to meet the Prince of
Wales' – with whom he was already friendly through his elder
sister Mrs Henrietta Jamieson.[23]

Haig had been fortunate to gain admission to the Staff
College by nomination. He took the entrance examination in
1893 but failed to qualify as he obtained only 182, instead of
the qualifying minimum of 200 out of 400 marks in mathematics
which was an obligatory subject. However, having obtained the
necessary 3/8ths minimum in mathematics in order to become
eligible for a nomination the following year, he received the
Commander-in-Chief's nomination for the course beginning in
1896. This was unusual as, according to the regulations, he
ought to have been nominated in 1894 or 1895. It seems that
the Commander-in-Chief made an exception in his favour.[24]

Edmonds was frequently detailed to work with Haig by
Col. Henderson and, quite apart from Haig's handicap of
colour-blindness, found him 'terribly slow on the uptake'.
On a three-day Staff Exercise on horseback near the end of
the course, Haig and another officer asked if they might ride
with Edmonds. On the third day the latter went off on his
own and, when reproached by Haig, blurted out 'I could not
afford to be handicapped by you and Blair any longer'. Not
surprisingly their relations remained somewhat strained for
many years after this but Haig forgave Edmonds and created a
niche for him at headquarters in France when he became
Commander-in-Chief in 1915.

Edmonds is also the source of another story concerning Haig.
Col. Henderson allegedly one day said to a group of students
sitting round the ante-room fire, 'there is a fellow in your batch
who is going to be commander-in-chief one of these days. No,
not any of you, Capt. Haig.' Henderson would obviously be
aware of Haig's intense application to his studies and of his
blatant professional ambition, but it may not be too cynical to

suggest that he also took into account Haig's friendship with the Prince of Wales which would be likely to ease his ascent of the promotion ladder.

For a final, penetrating comparison of Haig and Allenby, a later Camberley graduate and future Field-Marshal – Earl Wavell – wrote:

In spirit and in body they were fellows – strong, enduring, and upright; but in mind there was a wide difference between them. Allenby had the finer perception and the greater knowledge; his intelligence had, as already shown, a wide range and many interests outside soldiering; he took every opportunity to visit new places and to acquire fresh learning. He was earnest and thorough in his profession, but it was by no means his only, probably not even his first, interest. Haig, on the other hand, had a single-track mind, intensely and narrowly concentrated, like a telescope, on the one object, except his profession of soldiering, and later his family, he had no real interests of any kind, and little knowledge; nor had he any desire for knowledge, unless it bore on his own special subject. Very quick of temper in his youth, he had so disciplined his mind and body to serve his fixed purpose that he seldom showed anger or impatience. Allenby, by nature of a more tolerant humour, indulged as the years went on in frequent outbursts of violent temper. Haig, secure in his own self-confidence, seldom listened to the opinion of others; Allenby, equally strong-willed, would always pay heed to those who had knowledge. Haig recorded all events in a carefully kept diary; Allenby made no note whatever of his acts or thoughts, and destroyed practically every letter or paper he received. Haig had a deeply religious strain, and was a regular churchgoer; Allenby, though a constant student of the Bible, made little observance of the outward forms of religion.

To sum up, Allenby was the more broad-minded and the more human; Haig by virtue of concentration, the more technically efficient. Their differences in character can be attributed partly to their respective nationalities. Haig was

Scottish to the bone, Allenby was English to the core. The two men never understood each other well, nor were easy in each other's company.[25]

Before discussing the advantages and limitations of the Staff College course in the 1890s, some attempt must be made to provide evidence of what sort of problems the students were asked to deal with and what comments they received from the professors.

In Military History, the problem, set by Henderson for Capt. Edmonds in his first year, was 'The Waterloo Campaign: Discuss Wellington's dispositions up to the time he left Brussels on 16 June 1815'. Precise instructions were laid down regarding the lay-out of the answer. Edmonds listed 43 authorities, and his answer ran to 26 pages of an exercise book and two neatly-executed sketch maps. Both Henderson and Hildyard criticized the memoir for being too long and too packed with quotations; the latter concluded, 'I hope on future occasions to see more of your own opinions, and fewer quotations from the writings of others'. In the second year Edmonds compiled an immensely detailed answer to the problem: 'Put forward suggestions for the active defence of India from India itself'.[26]

Field-Marshal Haig appears to have preserved the bulk of his Staff College papers and they provide a monument to his industry.[27] His Military History projects give a very clear impression of the kind of detailed and practical questions which Henderson set. A few examples will suffice:

1 'Report on the Valley of Virginia indicating the strategic points.' Assume that the report is written by one of Jackson's Staff Officers on 10 March 1862.
2 Write General Jackson's orders for the battle of Kernstown on 23 March 1862.
3 An appreciation of the problem to be given by Banks' Chief of the Staff on 25 April 1862.
4 Write the Army of the Valley's orders for the day of the battle of Cross Keys, 8 June 1862.

5 Assuming Blücher was right to occupy the position along Ligny brook, write his Army order for the occupation of that position, placing troops as you please and giving your reason.

6 Write Napoleon's order for attack of the original position at Waterloo with reasons, assuming that the flanks cannot be turned. Dispositions to be in accordance with modern weapons.

Henderson's comments, generally complimentary, reveal his overriding concern to derive and inculcate practical lessons from military history. Thus, on a problem relating to Jackson's orders for 24 May 1862, he wrote, 'What are you to do about the Staffs of units in case you create a new commander? One often finds, in history, that failure resulted from a force suddenly being divided into two commands, and an officer detailed as commander to one of them with an insufficient staff. A case of this nature occurred on 27 June 1862 in Jackson's force. It is worth remembering.' As an example of Henderson's concern for detail, in the same Civil War problem Haig had written, 'Troops reached Front Royal at nightfall, say 8.o. pm', and the instructor noted 'The altitude [sic] is much lower than in England and the sun sets at 7.o. pm in May, and with a very short twilight'. A pedantic point perhaps, but lack of precision can be far more expensive for the general than the scholar.

In Staff Duties, Haig's main project was to draw up a scheme for the mobilization and equipment of an expeditionary force. In 1897 Haig took part in a disembarkation scheme, the general idea of which was that the coast of Sussex represented an enemy's shores, and that the naval conditions were such as to warrant Britain attempting an invasion. He also – as did Edmonds – drew up detailed proposals for an expedition to the Sudan[28] – where of course Kitchener had begun his campaign of reconquest – and this won praise from both markers, Cols Henderson and Fleming.

Finally, a bare summary of the remainder of the contents of the Edmonds' Staff College papers will give a fair idea of the nature of the paperwork in the 1890s. For the Senior Division Staff Duties Scheme the students, working in pairs, were to assume that two armies were to clash in the vicinity of Worplesdon. They were ordered to ride to Chobham Common and reconnoitre three roads practicable for all arms, using a standard map of four miles to the inch. Edmonds's sketch, as Col Fleming noted, was clear, but unnecessarily elaborate. Paring down such reports and sketches to give the essential minimum of information useful to a harassed commander was clearly an art that needed considerable practice. For his Senior Division Railway Scheme Edmonds had to report on Wellington Station with a view to its suitability for entraining troops and for extension by means of extemporized sidings or platforms. A plan on the scale of 60 yards to an inch had to be submitted. Lastly, the Edmonds' Papers contain several very elaborate topographical sketches of sections of country in the Camberley area. None of these papers reveal anything particulary original – though Haig displayed an impressive knowledge of nineteenth-century campaigns – and there would be no point in mentioning them did they not reveal significant progress towards the practical study of staff problems even by comparison with the Hamley era in the 1870s.

Since the Staff College was, before 1900, 'the only school of strategy, of organization, of Imperial Defence, in the Queen's dominions', it seems reasonable to point to its omissions and weaknesses while acknowledging that it was now producing a steady flow of able graduates. In the first place no naval officers participated in the course, and hence what few 'combined operations' schemes there were – such as the disembarkation project studied by Haig – must have been very inadequate single-service affairs. Nor as yet were officers from the dominions represented at Camberley, with the result that problems of imperial defence were viewed entirely through British eyes. Indeed, as a more serious criticism, there is little evidence that the broader issues of 'imperial defence' were studied at the College. The fact that this subject was not treated seriously at Government level, that there was no general staff, and that military education had to steer well clear of political issues, all militated against 'higher defence studies' or what Spenser Wilkinson termed, in *The Brain of an Army*, 'A Military University'. Thirdly, apart from the instructive Continental tours to the battlefields of the Napoleonic and Franco-German Wars, the students spent too much of their time in the all-too-familiar Camberley neighbourhood. Staff tours and war games were coming into vogue in the Army in the 1890s but the Staff College could hardly be called a pioneer: Edmonds, for example, mentions that in his time there was only one annual war game between Seniors and Juniors. Lack of money rather than conservatism was the most likely explanation for this. Fourthly, though Staff duties and military administration were now more seriously taught than in the 1880s, when Callwell had complained that 'one learnt next to nothing about the duties which a staff officer actually has to perform either in war or in peace', still it was difficult to find instructors with experience. Edmonds later wrote that all he learnt of value was 'how to make a march "graphic" and to use the Playfair Cypher'. Much in fact depended on how conscientiously the potential staff officer was instructed during the approximate six weeks' attachment to other arms in each year of the course. Many officers regarded this as the most valuable part of the course but they were sometimes treated most unhelpfully by their hosts.[29] Lastly, though officers possessing a p.s.c. were too few to fill all available staff appointments, there was still no guarantee that the successful graduate from Camberley would receive a staff posting.

Henderson aptly summed up the value and the limitations of the Staff College when he pointed out that it possessed

no cauldron in which folly might be transmuted into wisdom, or ambition purged of the vanity which is as dangerous to soldiers as to angels. But it could make good men better, broaden their views, strengthen their powers of reasoning and improve their judgement.

Field-Marshal Sir William Robertson testified that having a body of staff officers and commanders who had been taught the same basic principles of strategy and tactics, and were accustomed to employing the same methods of administration, had been of inestimable value to him as Chief of the Imperial General Staff in the First World War. In his dealings – purely telegraphic – with Maude in Mesopotamia, Milne in Macedonia, Allenby in Palestine and Monro in India there had never been any misunderstanding such as would almost inevitably have occurred between commanders without a common staff training.[30]

To what extent did the Army, before the shock of the South African War, provide an outlet for the talents of confident and well-informed young officers produced by the Staff College? In the absence of a general staff we must look to the work of the Intelligence Department, and in the absence of war to the staff tours and army manœuvres of the 1890s.

In the early days of the Intelligence Department, when it was ludicrously under-staffed and its officers were still groping after a system, much of its work had been of a humdrum nature, consisting largely of 'cutting passages out of British and foreign newspapers and having them pasted by clerks into vast tomes of the scrap-book order'. By the late 1880s, however, the Department's duties had grown to cover all factual questions of colonial defence and also mobilization. The routine work may be described under four headings as:

1 Collection of information by means of special reports, newspapers, periodicals, books and individual inquiries;
2 Methodical registration of this information so that it could speedily be produced when required;
3 Distillation of some of the information into printed reports;
4 Distribution of such information as might be useful to other departments of the War Office, to military educational establishments, and to the Army at large.[31]

From 1886 to 1891 the Department was in the charge of 'the cleverest man in the British Army', Maj.-Gen. (later Gen. Sir Henry) Brackenbury, who was ideally suited to the post.

As a 'Wolseley man' Brackenbury had the support of the Adjutant-General and used it virtually to double the permanent staff and also to transform attached officers into regular staff officers with the rank of Staff Captain. 'Brack' was not a man to suffer fools gladly and his relations with senior officers, including Wolseley, were apt to be spiced with acrimony, but he was idolized by his staff. As Sir Charles Callwell testified: 'It was a privilege and an education to be his subordinate and to enjoy his friendship, for he made a point of getting to know those under him, out of office hours.'[32]

By 1887, when Callwell joined the Department from Camberley, it was largely, though not exclusively, staffed by officers who had shown promise at the Staff College. Thus there were three other officers from Callwell's year, H. P. Northcote, E. Agar and C. R. Simpson; and other p.s.c.s included James Wolfe Murray (C.I.G.S. during the First World War), Leonard Darwin (subsequently President of the Royal Geographical Society), J. C. Dalton, J. K. Trotter, Charles Barter and 'Jimmy' Grierson. Charles A'Court Repington, Henry Wilson and 'Wully' Robertson were just three more of the many brilliant officers who were to graduate from Camberley to Queen Anne's Gate.

The Intelligence Department was sub-divided into five sections on a regional basis, and a mapping section. Callwell's section, for example, embraced Austria–Hungary, the Balkans, Egypt and most parts of Africa; while the 'French' section covered not only metropolitan France, but the French overseas Empire and other parts of Africa. Although a brilliant chief such as Brackenbury would be well placed to form an overall view of relative military strengths and likely areas of conflict, these were not the Department's official duties. In brief, it was an information gathering rather than an advisory bureau. Indeed, the sub-divisions tended to work in watertight compartments. The Department's information about the worsening military situation in South Africa in the 1890s was largely ignored by the War Office, while during the war it was treated 'as a separate, and not very important, part of the War Office organization'.[33]

The development of the Intelligence Department into a genuine 'thinking department' of the Army was inhibited by the failure to implement the Hartington Commission's recommendation in favour of creating a general staff. Two other bodies, that did enjoy a brief existence before the South African War, might have crowned the edifice for which the Staff College now provided an excellent foundation: namely, the Colonial Defence Committee and the Defence Committee of the Cabinet. Neither, unfortunately, did so.

The Colonial Defence Committee was an inter-service departmental body which was set up on a permanent basis in 1885 and lasted until 1904.[34] It neither undertook strategic planning nor offered advice of its own, but merely gathered and circulated the work of various departments on matters such as the defence of particular ports and the size and training of colonial forces. In 1895, largely on the initiative of A. J. Balfour, a standing Defence Committee of the Cabinet was set up under the chairmanship of the Duke of Devonshire. In the view of Lord Salisbury, the Prime Minister, the Committee's task was to determine 'the work for which the Army and Navy have to be fitted, and how they are to be fitted for it'. Unfortunately, both the First Lord of the Admiralty and the Secretary of State for War took the narrow view that the Committee should only concern itself with those matters in imperial defence which were not the sole responsibility of the War Office or the Admiralty. With this restricted sphere of activity and under a far from dynamic chairman, the Committee met infrequently and accomplished little. When the subject was re-opened in the Cabinet in November 1900, Goschen argued that the Committee had done excellent work: it had dealt with docks at Bermuda, Jamaica and Singapore and similar issues, such as whether the Army or the Navy should control Wei-hai-Wei.[35] A majority of the Cabinet remained opposed or lukewarm to regular meetings, a permanent secretariat and a wider field of activity. Thus, with virtually no encouragement towards systematic thought about strategic problems at Government level, with a minimum of inter-service collaboration – and indeed in the absence of a naval equivalent of Camberley – it is easy to appreciate that the Staff College could exert only an exiguous and extremely indirect influence on the higher levels of military thought before 1900.

One area of military activity in which there was a conspicuous revival and new developments in the 1890s was in the practical preparation of the home army and its auxiliaries for war by means of manœuvres, cavalry rides and staff tours. The Staff College can claim little direct credit for this more professional approach, except that some of the leading advocates of field training, such as Generals Wood and Buller, were ex-Camberley men; that Staff College students sometimes reconnoitred the ground; and that officers with a p.s.c. and also Camberley instructors played a prominent role on the Umpires' staffs and on those of the contending forces.

Apart from the difficulty of obtaining Parliamentary grants for large-scale manœuvres, the greatest obstacle was to secure the use of suitable ground of sufficient extent. Sir Evelyn Wood in particular, as commander of the Eastern District (1886–8) and the Aldershot Division (1888–93), made heroic efforts to gain access to country over which realistic training could take place, but even when the local landlords were agreeable he was frequently baulked by the objections of shooting tenants. Thus, for example, the autumn manœuvres of 1895 were scheduled for Salisbury Plain but had to be switched to the New Forest.[36] Even then the map for these, and other manœuvres, contain outlined 'islands' of country which remained sacred to the pheasant.

In 1893 a young artillery officer was invited to join Sir Evelyn Wood's staff – at his own expense – for the Aldershot divisional manœuvres on the Berkshire Downs, and his vivid account of those enjoyable ten days shows just how much the Army had to learn about soldiering in the field. The troops wore, not khaki, but red and blue uniforms, and to distinguish the opponents one side wore full dress headdresses. 'Guardsmen and fusiliers were to be seen skirmishing and endeavouring to hide themselves in red coats and huge busbies, while I think one of the most imposing sights I have ever seen was the Greys in their red tunics and immense busbies bestriding great grey horses and charging a line of guns.'[37] It might just as well have been Waterloo or the Crimea; yet six years later many of these officers and men would be engaged in battles where it was often impossible to see the enemy at all and where shock action was out of the question.

Although by comparison with the great continental armies British military manœuvres in the 1890s were small-scale and unsophisticated, it is difficult to look through the dusty volumes of reports in the Old War Office Library without being impressed by the progress which was being made by Britain's own standards, both as regards numbers mobilized and lessons learnt – or at least noted. Plenty of mistakes were reported in the Hampshire autumn manœuvres of 1891 in which two divisions took part under Sir Evelyn Wood's direction – the largest manœuvres since 1873. The failing most apparent was that of officers 'considering only the branch of service to which they belong. Many officers have not sufficient confidence to give decided orders to the other arms of the service; thus officers of the same force were observed working in the immediate vicinity but independent of each other. Commanders of units neither asked for nor gave information to other units operating near them. Infantry when joining artillery in action seldom or never inquired as to the range.' Wood also reported that reconnaissance work was poor, and inexperienced officers tended to act in a manner which would not have been attempted in war; remaining mounted, for example, under intense rifle fire. This latter fault was less evident in the manœuvres of 1895.[38]

Quite apart from tactical lessons, however, which can hardly have been well digested in view of the disasters in 1899, these reports show that the Army had an enormous amount to learn about practically every aspect of its profession. Hygiene, commissariat arrangements, march discipline, pitching camp, signalling; all had to be painfully improved by experience since so little attention had been given to them in previous decades. In 1897, for example, the 1st Brigade of the 1st Division was mobilized at short notice under Lord Methuen. Mobilization orders were issued late on 31 July, the Brigade assembled at

Hounslow on 5 August, marched to Chobham and back and disbanded on the 9th. The troop movements were quite successful but they were severely handicapped by reliance on the Woolwich depot for stores and equipment. In response to the mobilization telegram the depot replied that it was closed for the next four days and nothing could be issued![39]

In the autumn of 1896 no less than 5 divisions took the field including 16 Militia battalions: the largest force ever assembled at home for manœuvres. Indeed, there was no training ground large enough for such a force so the exercises consisted of a succession of field days. One fault noted on this occasion was that insufficient attention was paid to the effect of machine-gun fire: units retained unaltered formations when Maxim guns opened fire on them.

In 1895 the first 'Staff Tour' took place in imitation of a system of training that had been in vogue for years in Germany and has been called 'the best means ever invented of teaching officers their duties in the field'.[40]

The Ride was conducted by the Adjutant-General, Sir Redvers Buller, and the idea was that an Army Corps based on Croydon had been detailed to secure the approaches to London through Reigate and Redhill against an enemy who had landed between Brighton and Littlehampton. The two sides did not meet, and even the Directing Staff made unrealistic demands because it was learning its job, but at the end of six days all the exhausted participants agreed that they had learnt a great deal.

In August and September 1898 two Army Corps manœuvred against each other on Salisbury Plain and in Dorset. Although Lord Wolseley concluded his report with praise for the immense improvements made over recent years, he also found much to criticize. 'Full advantage was seldom taken of the conformation of the ground to conceal the advance of attacking columns; nor were the staff officers always successful in ascertaining by previous reconnaissance the best and easiest routes for the march of troops.' Civilian transport and supplies had both fallen far below the Army's needs. Sir William Robertson recalled that some of the umpiring staff were still inclined to look upon the manœuvres as a kind of glorified picnic.[41]

Manœuvres on the scale of those on Salisbury Plain were essential to the well-being of an army in peacetime. The War Office had belatedly come to this conclusion in the 1890s but all too little had been achieved before the outbreak of the South African War. Not only, of course, did manœuvres enable soldiers and officers to gain experience of innumerable practical problems in large units (divisions and corps) containing representatives of all the arms, but they also provided practice for generals and their staffs. Commanders could work out strategical and tactical problems in conditions analogous to those of actual war, discuss solutions and try out modifications in orthodox methods made necessary by improved armaments or other changes. Not least important, even manœuvres, without much of the strain and friction of actual warfare, could expose the incompetence of generals mentally or physically unfit for field command.

> If the senior officers are never tested in time of peace, it is always possible that a man may be appointed to an important command in the field who has lost his nerve, whose brain is rusty, whose knowledge is out of date, who is unacquainted with the tactics of the latest textbooks, or whose claims to high preferment rest upon a brilliant reputation, won perhaps, in a less responsible rank, and on an easier field.[42]

It seems reasonable to suggest that under a better developed system of field training Sir Redvers Buller would have been eliminated from the list of potential commanders-in-chief while, on the other hand, the Duke of Connaught would not have commanded in manœuvres unless he was to be allowed to command in war.

Finally, while it was recognized that education and training on a higher level than the regiment was essential for generals and staff officers who would comprise the 'brain of the Army' in war, the reality fell far short of what was practicable. The Staff College produced only thirty-two graduates a year, insufficient to fill all staff appointments in peacetime let alone in war. Many regimental officers without a p.s.c. doubtless proved competent in staff appointments, but they lacked the common education and mental attitudes which von Moltke had regarded as a crucial cementing element in training officers for the German General Staff. Perhaps even more seriously, the absence in peacetime of divisional organizations with permanent staffs – except at Aldershot – and the infrequency of large-scale manœuvres meant that generals could not become familiar with their staffs. Such a system, relying on improvisation and individuals' past experience of war, had been regarded as adequate for the succession of small colonial campaigns since the Crimean War. Its weaknesses were to be made painfully clear in the long conflict with the Boers which began in October 1899.

CHAPTER 5. NOTES

1 Godwin-Austen, *op. cit.*, p. 231. Aston, *op. cit.*, p. 101. Aston has amusingly described how, becoming confused from overwork just before the final examination, he attempted to light his watch with a match, threw his socks into the bath instead of the sponge and threw an unread letter into the fire instead of the envelope.

2 Col. G. F. R. Henderson (ed. Capt. N. Malcolm), *The Science of War* (London, 1910), pp. 402–3; Godwin-Austen, *op. cit.*, pp. 231–2; Field-Marshal Sir William Robertson, *op. cit.*, pp. 81–2; Sir Edward May, *Changes and Chances of a Soldier's Life* (London, 1925), p. 80.

3 Luvaas, *op. cit.*, pp. 223–4. Luvaas provides an excellent short account of Henderson's publications and the evolution of his military thought. The other principal sources of information on Henderson used here are E. M. Lloyd's article in the *D.N.B.* (1901–11); Lord Roberts's Memoir in *The Science of War*; and Lt-Col R. M. Holden's obituary article in the *R.U.S.I. Journal*, Vol. XLVII (1903), pp. 375–82.

4 Maurice, *op. cit.*, pp. 64–5.

5 See *The Science of War*, pp. 382–434.

6 Maj.-Gen. Sir Frederick Maurice, *The Life of Lord Rawlinson of Trent* (London, 1928), p. 26. For another warm tribute to Henderson as a teacher see Gen. Sir George de S. Barrow, *The Fire of Life* (London, *c*1941), p. 42.

7 *The Science of War*, pp. 48–9.

8 Luvaas, *op. cit.*, p. 242.

9 Capt. B. H. Liddell Hart in *The Remaking of Modern Armies*, pp. 170–1, cited by Luvaas, *op. cit.*, p. 243.

10 *The Science of War*, p. XXIX.

11 *The Science of War*, pp. XXIX–XXX. Aston, *op. cit.*, pp. 100–1.

12 *The Science of War*, p. XXX. A dissentient note is struck by Brig.-Gen. Sir James Edmonds who wrote in old age that Henderson 'was rather lazy and did not make many criticisms of instructional value'. But Edmonds had an uncomfortably long memory and in 1952 he still recalled Henderson's criticism of his eccentric use of commas ('The pepperpot appears to have been used') in his Waterloo memoir of 1897. See Edmonds' 'Four Generations of Staff College Students – 1896 to 1952. I, 1896', *The Army Quarterly*, Vol. LXV, no. 1 (October, 1952), pp. 42–5.

13 *The Times*, 7 March 1903. Robertson, *op. cit.*, p. 83.

14 M. V. Brett (ed.) *Journals and Letters of Reginald Viscount Esher*, Vol. II, 1903–10 (London, 1934), p. 112.

15 Sir James Edmonds, unpublished *Reminiscences*, Chapter XIV, 'The Staff College 1896–7, and his draft reply to an article on the Staff

College in the *World* of 21 November 1900 (Edmonds Papers).

16 Edmonds, *Reminiscences,* Chapter XIV, p. 279. *A History of the Civil War in the United States* by W. Birkbeck Wood and Maj. J. E. Edmonds was published in 1905. Lt.-Gen. Sir George Macdonogh achieved distinction as Director of Military Intelligence 1916–18 and Adjutant-General to the Forces 1918–22.

17 Edmonds published his analysis of the fates of his contemporaries at Camberley in *Owl Pie* (The Staff College Journal) in 1956 and it is reprinted by F. W. Young in *The Story of the Staff College, 1858–1958* (Aldershot, 1958), p. 18.

18 Edmonds' draft reply to article on the Staff College, *supra*, p. 3.

19 *Ibid.* and 'Four Generations of Staff College Students', *Army Quarterly,* October, 1952, *supra.*

20 *Ibid.* Callwell, for example, was equally critical of the first year of the course; see *Stray Recollections,* I, pp. 276–7.

21 'Four Generations of Staff College Students.'

22 Adye, *op. cit.,* pp. 140–1; Aston, *op. cit.,* p. 113.

23 Edmonds, *Reminiscences,* Chapter XIV. The Edmonds Papers contain lists of Staff College students and instructors for 1896–7. The published Staff College Roll ends in 1887, but Godwin-Austen gives a selection of the more important names of the 1890s, *op. cit.,* pp. 227, 233. A full list of past students is preserved at the Staff College. See Barrow, *op. cit.,* pp. 43–5, for a vivid comparison of the personalities of Haig and Allenby.

24 Letter from Sir Herbert Creedy, Permanent Under Secretary of State for War, to Duff Cooper, 21 May 1935, copy in Edmonds Papers with a note 'You will not quote the W.O. as the authority for the above?'

25 *Reminiscences,* Chapter XIV, pp. 266–8. Edmonds could be a waspish critic but it should be remembered that he was writing in old age when, generally speaking, he could be relied upon to support Haig against the attacks of younger writers. See also Gen. Sir A. Wavell, *Allenby: a Study in Greatness* (London, 1940), pp. 62–3.

26 Edmonds Papers.

27 Haig Papers. See especially vols 7–10, 13, 19, 20, 24, 29, 30.

28 The Staff Duties written exercise set by Lt.-Col. E. Fleming concerned the employment of a British force to support or cooperate with the Egyptian Army in the further prosecution of the operations then in hand in the Sudan. The students were invited to discuss 'what should be the organization, composition and strength of such a force' and to give their views 'as to its mobilization and equipment and as to when and how it would be best employed'. Edmonds Papers.

29 See Callwell, *op. cit.,* I p. 277. Edmonds relates that when he reported at the 2nd Infantry Brigade Headquarters the Brigade-Major (John Cowans, Quartermaster-General at the War Office during the First World War) said, 'Well now you've come I'm off on leave'. Edmonds learnt a great deal with the aid of the brigade clerk. See 'Four Generations of Staff College Officers', p. 45.

30 *The Science of War,* p. 402. Robertson, *op. cit.,* p. 88–90.

31 Callwell, *op. cit.*, I, pp. 305, 311–21.
32 *Ibid.*, p. 306
33 Maj.-Gen. Sir Charles Callwell, *Field Marshal Sir Henry Wilson: his Life and Diaries* (London, 1927) I, p. 18. Robertson, *op. cit.*, p. 100. Repington, *op. cit.*, pp. 82–3.
34 John P. Mackintosh, 'The Role of the Committee of Imperial Defence before 1914', *English Historical Review*, Vol. LXXVII, July 1962, pp. 490–503.
35 *Ibid.*, pp. 491–2.
36 Sir Evelyn Wood, *op. cit.*, II, pp. 211–12, 219–20. One objector, the head of a firm of prosperous drapers in Knightsbridge, told Wood frankly that 'he worked hard for ten months in the year, and that no compensation for disturbance of game would make up to him for less sport'. See also 'The Autumn Manoeuvres 1895', Report by the Duke of Connaught (War Office Library).
37 May, *op. cit.*, pp. 171–2.
38 'Autumn Manouevres in Hampshire, 1891', Comments by Lt.-Gen. Sir E. Wood, pp. 8–9, 20, and 'Autumn Manoeuvres, 1895', Report by the Duke of Connaught, p. 6 (War Office Library).
39 *Manoeuvres 1894–97. Report on the Mobilisation of the 1st Brigade, 1st Division, 1st Army Corps* by Maj.-Gen. Lord Methuen, p. 30 (War Office Library).
40 May, *op. cit.*, pp. 186–7.
41 *Report on the Manoeuvres of August–September 1898* by Viscount Wolseley, especially pp. VII, XVII. Robertson, *op. cit.*, pp. 86–7. See also Lt-Col Holmes Wilson R.A., 'The Salisbury Manoeuvres – with the Artillery of an Army Corps', *United Service Magazine*, Vol. XVIII, October 1898-March 1899, pp. 188–95.
42 *The Science of War*, p. 397.

CHAPTER SIX

The impact of the South African War on the Staff College and staff training 1899–1906

'The supremacy of brains and the planning out of all operations of war in time of peace are essential to military success all the world over. They were perhaps more important for the British Army than for any other.'[1] Although the late Victorian Army was engaged almost incessantly in a series of colonial campaigns in the most varied terrain, from the defiles of the Himalayas to the swamps and jungles of Ashanti and the burning sands of the Sudan, the Boers in 1899 provided by far the most redoubtable opposition since the distant Crimean War. They exposed the weaknesses of an Army which had been regarded, in L. S. Amery's words,

> less as an instrument for war . . . than as a state-established institution to be maintained and perpetuated for its own sake. Regarded as an institution or society the British Army of 1899 was undoubtedly a success . . . As a fighting machine it was largely a sham. The number of full-grown efficient soldiers was small, the military training of all ranks inadequate, and the whole organized on no definitely thought out principle of Imperial defence, and prepared for no eventualities.[2]

When every allowance has been made for the difficulties of the terrain, the unorthodox tactics of a skilful and elusive foe and the bewildering impact of magazine rifles and smokeless powder, and when it has been admitted that European armies would probably have fared even worse, the fact remains that generalship and staff work were sadly inadequate. Inevitably, after a long period without a major war, many generals had risen purely by seniority and were nothing more than elderly regimental officers, with brains and will-power atrophied by years of unexacting routine. Such men were alike incapable of devising a plan or of carrying it into execution.

The deficiencies of the generals were too seldom mitigated or remedied by their staffs. As previous chapters have shown, the Army did not lack a nucleus of mentally alert officers trained, at least theoretically, in staff work. What was lacking was an efficient selection system and the experience of working together with their generals in peacetime. 'Englishmen,' as L. S. Amery wrote in *The Times' History of the War in South Africa*, 'who would not dream of sending a crew to Henley Regatta whose members had never rowed together before, were quite content that a general's staff should be hastily improvised at the last moment from officers scraped together from every corner.' The Staff College produced no more than thirty-two graduates annually, which barely sufficed in peacetime. As a result, in 1899 nearly half the staff appointments were filled by untrained regimental officers.[3] Even after the staffs had learnt from bitter experience, older generals frequently had no conception of how to make use of them. Lord Kitchener, who, ironically, was not free from the fault himself, later emphasized the unfortunate tendency of many commanders to do their own staff work.[4] Despite the lessons of the American Civil War and the dazzling successes of Prussia which owed so much to superior staff work, Britain continued to regard a military staff as largely ornamental and exceedingly expensive. If it did nothing else the South African War revealed the foolishness of such an attitude.

Contemporary criticisms of the lack of professional zeal among the junior officers reveal what is obvious, that the 'brain' of an army requires a steady supply of invigorating new blood in the form of well-educated regimental officers. The Staff College reforms of the 1890s had in fact put that institution far ahead of the professional expertise of the Army in general.

Viscount Esher, an acute observer of military shortcomings, noted in 1906 that it was still the exception and not the rule to find a clever and highly educated soldier:

> Compare (not Haig or French or that sort of man) the ordinary young soldier, aged 23–25, with the young professional man of the same age (and you know so many); and put aside their charm, and think only of their attainments. What then? Do not think for a moment that I think less of their natural ability. It is quite on a level with that of any other class. I am thinking of their trained knowledge, and of their grounding in the elements of their business. A soldier requires to be quite as carefully trained in military history (for example) as a lawyer in historical jurisprudence, if he is to be of real use in his profession.[5]

Four years earlier he had estimated that only two out of every forty regimental officers were any good at all. The rest were '*loafers*'. All the competent and ambitious officers tended to gravitate to the Staff. Esher drew a distinction between the Staff and the Staff College asserting that 'Staff *College* men failed in S.A. But all the men who succeeded had been, at some time or other, staff officers.' Nevertheless, he was not against the Staff College in principle. On the contrary, he took the Utopian view that 'Until every regimental officer is forced to go through the Staff College and until the Army is looked upon as a profession, and not as a pastime, the regimental officer will be looked on by commanders of armies as a superior kind of pawn – but not as one of the active and capable pieces in the game of war.' Elsewhere Esher remarked:

> Politicians and others who are brought into contact with soldiers, notice the comparatively low standard of knowledge between the heads of the military profession and others: not in technique, but in general education. Men of fine natural abilities appear stunted. Exceptions there are, of course; but John Morley and Knollys [the King's Private Secretary], for example, are both struck by the comparative inferiority of our best Generals to men of equal standing in other

professions, including the Navy. What is the reason for this? In most walks of life, the strenuous years are from 20 to 30. It is during these years that at the Bar, in Medicine, in the Church – whether at Universities or under special professional conditions – young men acquire the habit of application. In the Navy an officer's education is not completed at 20, but he works hard during the subsequent years.

In the Army, a subaltern, during the first years of his life, and generally until he reaches middle-age, limits his efforts to acquiring such technical knowledge of his profession as can be absorbed between 9 and 1 daily. There is no inducement for him to educate himself, or to do any more than he is obliged. Hence, during the ten most crucial years of his life, he acquires no habits of application, but devotes himself to sport, or sinks into indifference and idleness. Later on, when the responsibilities of the higher command begin to inspire prospective terror, an officer tries to make up for lost time, and regrets lost opportunities.

No doubt some young officers read books, and improve their minds, but spasmodically, and without real incentive. A lad will think, for a week, that in order to be a general he must 'work at' strategy; so he will take real pains to master a campaign of Napoleon. The following week it strikes him that he cannot command armies until he is 40, and he falls asleep in the anteroom . . .[6]

That Esher's strictures on military amateurism were justified is evident from the exceptionally frank report of an Inter-departmental Committee of Enquiry, under the chairmanship of the Rt Hon A. Akers-Douglas M.P., which was appointed in April 1902 and completed its investigation in March 1903. It revealed that the Cadet Colleges were still suffering from some of the defects which had characterized the Staff College in its early decades.

The decisive factor in expenditure on military education, the Report showed, had been economy. Indeed the vote for education comprised only 0·65 per cent of the Army Estimates. Moreover, although the country was spending ever more on elementary education, the money devoted by the Army to technical and professional education was decreasing. Minor criticisms were made of R.M.A. Woolwich, but it was Sandhurst that came under a really heavy fire. The Committee found that there was 'absolutely no inducement to work'. There was too much reason to fear that even cadets who failed to attain the low qualifying standard had been commissioned none the less. Such essential accomplishments as musketry and revolver shooting were neglected, while far too much time was spent in being drilled – not even in learning to *take* drill. Spit and polish were – and long continued to be – the watchwords: 'as examination has been said to govern education, so inspection may be said to govern military training'. Cadets pipe-clayed their belts but did not clean their rifles. 'This is remarkable, for while a cadet might acquire a familiarity with the mechanism of a rifle from being required to clean it, the educational value of pipe-claying a belt is extremely slight.'[7]

If the Committee could find few complimentary remarks to make about Sandhurst, their comments on the military training of young officers was even more scathing. There was remarkable unanimity among the witnesses that junior officers were lamentably lacking in military knowledge and in any zeal to learn. Keenness was out of fashion and to show it was 'not correct form'. The main cause of this apathy was that promotion prospects seemed to bear no relation to zeal and ability.

The examination system at Sandhurst and the two subsequent promotion examinations were admitted to 'encourage the custom of idleness with a brief period of cram'. As for the College examinations,

> Principles have been lost sight of in a mass of detail, and the minds of cadets have been wearied with accumulations of useless formulae and dreary unpractical exercises, with the result that the young officer, while still in the cadet stage, acquires a dislike of all military study which often remains with him throughout his career. At present an attempt is made to cram the mind of the cadet with masses of figures,

and he is taught to regard with horror any deviation from a sealed pattern. Little encouragement is given to originality of mind, and few attempts appear to be made to exercise him practically in the mode of application of the theoretical knowledge with which he is surfeited. The result is that he is inclined to lose interest in his studies, and to regard them as a nuisance which need trouble him no more once he has obtained his commission.[8]

The Committee's caustic criticisms and enlightened recommendations could, however, make little impression on the fundamental factor which determined the social composition of the officer class. Talk of greater attention to study and increased professional zeal soon came up against the snag that an army career was still widely regarded as an amateur occupation for gentlemen. So far from expecting to live comfortably on their pay – except in India – the majority of officers themselves willingly paid for the privilege of belonging to those splendid and leisurely clubs – the regiments. In the cavalry especially expenses were so high (£400 to £700 per annum private income) that the War Office was obliged to accept almost any candidate. As the Akers-Douglas Report succinctly stated: 'Our Cavalry must be officered. We may require from the candidates either money or brains; the supply is most unlikely to meet the demand if we endeavour to exact both.' If the War Department would supply chargers and prohibit frequent changes of uniform and the sporting of unauthorized patterns, there was no reason why young cavalry officers should not be able to live in perfect comfort with a private income of about £200 per annum![9]

The Committee hastened to reassure their readers that they had no intention of turning Army officers into scholars and pedants. 'For the fact must be faced that the military profession has not been hitherto associated with protracted periods of hard work, nor are the habits of industry to be acquired in a day.' The essence of the problem was to secure an honest system of promotion by merit. 'So long as mediocrity is permitted to pass muster, and signal ability to meet with no substantial recognition, it is useless to hope for any valuable results from verbal amendments in the regulations.'[10]

Criticism of staff work in the South African War must be seen in a proper perspective. On the one hand the British Army revealed its unpreparedness for war in almost every conceivable respect from the troopers' fieldcraft to the generals' strategy, and as L. S. Amery – no champion of the Staff – allowed, staff work could have been a great deal worse. On the other hand there was an understandable tendency to blame the staff for what were really the mistakes of the commanders. Thus Esher noted in March 1900 that Buller had been complaining that he was supplied with a rotten staff. Unfortunately for Buller the War Office had unearthed a recent letter from him written from Aldershot saying that he approved of the staff suggested by Wolseley, and adding 'If I can't beat the Boers with such a lot of officers as you propose, I ought to be kicked!'[11]

Nevertheless, there is abundant evidence that the lack of a properly organized staff system was a serious handicap, and that incompetent staff work played a conspicuous part in many of the muddles and disasters. As regards anomalies in organization, one may instance Roberts's headquarters staff. Kitchener was nominally Chief of Staff but neither by training nor temperament was he suited for the appointment. Indeed, he was employed rather as a deputy commander to whom Roberts could delegate difficult missions or send round to hustle up departments and subordinates. This arrangement had its advantages, but its disadvantages were seen in the initial attack at Paardeberg on 18 February 1900 ordered by Kitchener against the wishes of the divisional commander, Lt.-Gen. Thomas Kelly-Kenny. 'The truth is,' as L. S. Amery wrote, 'that at the battle of Paardeberg there was neither a commander nor a directing staff in any real sense of the words. What happened was simply that Kitchener, with the help of a small personal staff and of his own fiery energy and overmastering personality, to some extent succeeded in impressing his will upon a number of scattered and uncoordinated units.' The want of common training and a common theory of war were starkly apparent in this costly action, which Kitchener's latest biographer calls the most controversial episode in his career.[12] Roberts's real Chief of Staff was his Director of Intelligence Maj. (later Col.) G. F. R. Henderson whom he selected straight from the Staff College. Unfortunately, Henderson's health soon broke down and Roberts then relied heavily upon the advice of Col. W. G. Nicholson, a very experienced staff officer who was nominally director of the transport service.

Sir Charles Callwell later graphically sketched the difference between divisions that could be effected by an efficient chief of staff. Callwell's battery was sometimes attached to the 2nd Division and sometimes to the 5th. The latter became far preferable to serve with when Thompson Capper, who had been at Camberley under Hildyard, became its chief staff officer.

> The consequence was that when you were with the 5th Division you got orders that were at once clear, concise, and comprehensive, and that everything ran smoothly. It was almost a revelation after some other experiences one had encountered since landing at Durban. This however by all accounts was not the case only in the Natal Army. The senior staff officers throughout the forces in the field were not properly trained, and although they were competent in peace they did not properly understand their duties in time of war. During the operations for the relief of Ladysmith, deliberate as they were, I never remember seeing a map or plan of any kind except at the time of Vaal-Krantz. Sketches may have been made and reproduced by hectograph or some similar means; but if they were, they were not distributed properly although they were very badly wanted, and there was no proper organization for distributing them and for making sure that every unit had at least one copy.

'What a lot we have to learn from this war in every way!' wrote Col. Grierson from Pretoria on 7 July 1900. 'I think our first lesson is that we must have big annual manœuvres and have our staffs properly trained. We don't seem to grasp anything higher than a division. And we must have "staff journeys" to teach the control of armies in the field. If we take the field with a force the size of this one against an European enemy and continue in our present happy-go-lucky style of staffing and staff work we shall come to most awful grief. There is no system about it, and without a system a large army cannot be properly handled.'[13]

The main defects of staff work, such as lack of maps, faulty intelligence, failure to reconnoitre, vague and muddled orders, can be illustrated from a few incidents in the opening months of the war; though they could easily be multiplied *ad nauseam*.

Lord Methuen, advancing to the relief of Kimberley, launched a suicidal frontal attack at the Modder River on 28 November 1899. He and his staff were completely mistaken as to the course of the rivers Riet and Modder and were utterly ignorant of the Boers' positions and strength. Only the doggedness of the troops and junior commanders mitigated the elementary mistakes of the higher direction. Lord Methuen failed to profit from this experience and committed the same blunder – on a grander scale – of a frontal attack against unreconnoitred positions at Magersfontein.

At Stormberg in north-eastern Cape Colony on 9 December Maj.-Gen. Sir W. F. Gatacre provided a textbook example of how not to carry out an (admittedly difficult) night march.

The first fundamental mistake was to change the route to a longer indirect approach at the last moment. A night march across unreconnoitred and inadequately-mapped ground put the General at the mercy of his native guides; the only officer of the Intelligence Staff who knew the ground intimately was inexplicably left behind. Apart from losing the way it became clear that the guides had completely failed to grasp the General's intentions. Since the change of route had not been explained to the troops – or the commanding officer at the base – the tail of the column, including the field hospital and sundry ammunition wagons took the discarded direct route and would have marched straight into the Boer positions but for the intervention of a party of war correspondents. When the weary troops, who had been made to march for hours with bayonets fixed, eventually stumbled up against Boer outposts all semblance of control was speedily lost. The most astonishing blunder of the whole episode then occurred: neither Gatacre nor his staff seems to have realized that about 600 unwounded officers and men (a third of the infantry) had been abandoned at the foot of the rock on which the Boer camp lay. As *The Times* historian commented, nothing but an extraordinary combination of bad management and bad fortune could account for the failure of an audacious plan against an enemy of such poor fighting quality.

An egregious blunder of a different kind resulted in the loss of an enormous supply column at Waterval Drift on the Riet River on 15 February 1900. Lord Roberts was pressing north to trap Cronje's force on the Modder River and relieve Kimberley, and the loss of his main supply column imposed a serious handicap for many weeks. Despite the knowledge that Christiaan De Wet with a considerable commando was shadowing the column, and despite the requests of three officers accompanying the wagons, Roberts's acting Chief-of-Staff, Maj.-Gen. W. F. Kelly, refused to increase the detachment of 500 men to protect a convoy which, on the move, extended over six or seven miles of road. De Wet timed his attack perfectly when the oxen were scattered along the northern bank just after a long and tedious crossing. Headquarters belatedly sent back reinforcements in driblets but Roberts eventually decided to abandon the whole convoy. De Wet captured 176 wagons containing approximately 70,200 rations of preserved meat, 180,000 rations of bread stuff and groceries, 38,800 grain rations and eight wagon-loads of medical comforts. Most of the ox teams were lost and also 500 slaughter cattle. The obvious criticisms concern the removal of the covering division just when it was most needed and the fatuous assumption that De Wet had left the district because he could not be seen. But perhaps more culpable was the failure of anyone on Roberts's staff to suggest that a small escort should entrench itself round the beleaguered convoy. De Wet could certainly not have got the wagons away (he eventually moved them at a snail's pace) and, more important, he could have been detained at the Drift and so prevented from interfering in the Paardeberg battle on 18 February.

The disaster at Colenso derived from Buller's personal

7. 'Our only General'. Field Marshal Viscount Wolseley (1833–1913). Wolseley, though not himself a graduate, supported the Staff College by employing many of its officers on his staff and by selecting outstandingly able officers, such as Maurice and Henderson, to be professors there.

8. Two officers who inspired a new outlook at Camberley in the 1890s. *Left*: Col. H. J. Hildyard (Commandant 1893–8). His motto was: 'We want officers to absorb, not to cram.' *Right*: Col. G. F. R. Henderson (Professor of Military Art and History 1892–9). Many of the leading commanders of the First World War paid tribute to his teaching and personal influence.

incompetence and pusillanimity and renders criticism of mistakes in staff work largely beside the point, but at Spion Kop, as L. S. Amery noted, there was a most conspicuous failure to realize the importance of acquiring and communicating information.

> No effort was made beforehand to ascertain the shape of the position to be occupied, or to furnish the officers entrusted with its capture with such information. No sufficient effort was made by those officers themselves to discover the shape of the summit before intrenching. No attempt was subsequently made to enlighten Warren as to the tactical position on the hill either by those above or by Buller below. No message was sent to Coke to inform him of Thorneycroft's appointment, or of Warren's change of headquarters. No message was sent to Thorneycroft to inform him that Coke was coming up, or that the 60th were attacking the Twin Peaks. Throughout the day Warren never once communicated to anyone on the summit what arrangements he was making for the next day. Nobody, in fact, made any real, determined effort to transmit information or to discover what was happening'.

And if the overriding importance of information was not realized, still less was the difficulty of securing its transmission. 'The systematic repetition of every message by several orderlies was not attempted, and, indeed, short as were the distances involved, messages by hand seem in many cases to have taken quite inordinate times to reach their destination.'

Behind the failures in the field, however, lay the more important factor of Buller's disorganization of the Army. 'By practically withdrawing himself and his staff from the operations, Buller pulled out the keystone of the whole military framework, and dislocated it from top to bottom.' Buller would not command himself but neither would he delegate full powers to a subordinate. Warren, Coke and Hill were each doing work for which they were not prepared and with an inadequate and makeshift staff. None of them rose to the test but the test was hardly a fair one.[14]

H

The Elgin Commission examined practically everyone concerned with the higher military and civil direction of the war
and issued its monumental Report and Minutes of Evidence
in July 1903.[15]

As Lord Roberts made clear in his evidence, the key factors as
regards the shortcomings of the combatant staff were pre-war
unpreparedness and the unprecedented expansion of the Army.

> For an Army of 90,000 men, we had, probably, as many
> trained staff officers as were required. But when the Army
> grew to 250,000 and 300,000 men, the appointments had to
> be filled by men with whom want of experience was the rule
> rather than the exception. Those officers who had received
> previous training, either in active service or at the Staff
> College, generally did well; but the absence of a definite
> system of staff duties . . . was undoubtedly prejudicial to the
> smooth running of the military machine . . . Many instances
> of indifferent staff work might be quoted, and it seems clear
> that the entire staff should be thoroughly trained; that a
> definite system of staff duties should be laid down; and that
> we should have enough trained staff officers to supply . . . a
> large army . . .

Trustworthy soldiers, the Commander-in-Chief pointed out,
could soon be trained 'But staff officers cannot be improvised
in a few weeks or months . . .' Brains, he declared, were even
more important than numbers, especially in an army like
Britain's which was always likely to contain a large proportion
of men who were not soldiers by profession.[16]

Although a stream of senior officers echoed and elaborated
on Lord Roberts's criticisms of staff officers and staff work, none
of them criticized the role of the Staff College, though Kitchener
made it clear that he preferred officers who had acquired their
experience in the field. Several, indeed, were at pains to
emphasize recent improvements at Camberley. Gen. Sir Evelyn
Wood, for example, praised the transformation wrought by
Hildyard and added: 'I think it is now eminently practical. I
think it is a very good institution. It will be difficult to improve
on it.' It was hardly surprising that former Camberley men

such as Hildyard and Haig should sing the praises of a Staff College training, but the testimony of non-p.s.c.s such as Maj.-Gens. Sir H. E. Colvile and R. G. Kekewich could not be so easily discounted. The former stated in giving evidence: 'I have had no experience of Staff College training, except by its results, and of these I cannot speak too highly. Whether the system is the best possible, I do not know, but I have no hesitation in saying that for staff work a Staff College officer is simply invaluable, and I would never willingly take an officer on my staff who had not been through the College. Every care should be taken that only the best officers are allowed to go to the Staff College . . .'[17]

Compared with earlier inquiries concerning the Staff College a remarkable change of emphasis is apparent in the Elgin Report. Although the members of the Commission occasionally put sceptical questions about the value of education at the College and of the performance of p.s.c.s as against non p.s.c.s, the overriding concern was how to secure a great increase in the output of Staff College graduates. Thus Sir Ian Hamilton (not a p.s.c. himself) stated that he thought one year at Camberley would suffice for officers destined for the Adjutant-General's branch. Perhaps all the officers could go on courses and detachments after one year so that the numbers could be doubled. Four members of the Commission, including Viscount Esher, gave Maj.-Gen. Hildyard a grilling on this point, but he made a strong (and apparently convincing) case for the retention of the two-year course. It was wiser, he pointed out, to increase accommodation. He was also pressed as to why so non-professional a subject as foreign languages was taught at Camberley; and replied that the study of languages was now voluntary, and that it was surely of value for the few linguistically gifted officers to use this period of comparative leisure to learn Russian, Turkish or Arabic.[18] In these questions one senses a danger from those well-meaning critics who would have cramped the Camberley syllabus by confining it entirely to a practical apprenticeship to the craft of war.

It was appropriate that the severest critic among the witnesses of staff work in South Africa should also present the best thought-out remedy. This was L. S. Amery, a young Fellow of All Souls and the principal member of *The Times* journalists who were then writing an incisive and valuable history of the war. Amery's solution bore a close resemblance to the German General Staff. There was often a lack of cooperation between our different forces, he argued, because 'there was no *esprit de corps* of the general staff', and each General had a natural tendency to play for his own hand . . . staff officers became his own personal adherents . . .' The Staff College was useful in providing a theoretical training but that was not enough. Students 'may have had the same lecturer perhaps, but what you want is a general staff where future campaigns are worked out and discussed . . . and where you get a common sentiment and a common theory of war . . .' The current (and short lived) Army Corps scheme by no means satisfied Amery's vision. Doubtless Viscount Esher listened particularly carefully to Amery's views and drew on them in devising the outlines of the General Staff, but in one important respect the latter's Berlin-orientated scheme did not find favour. In order to inculcate *esprit de corps* and a common theory of war, Amery advocated a permanent staff corps from which officers would only be temporarily attached to fighting units.[19]

The Elgin Commission was of course concerned not simply with staff work but with pre-war preparations and the conduct of the war. Its report and the weighty supporting evidence underlined the need for radical and far-reaching reforms, not least among which was the creation of a General Staff.

Not for the last time the Staff College was gradually allowed to peter out as a war progressed. On mobilization in October 1899 some of the instructional staff and students were summoned to the Colours, and more and more disappeared until finally the College closed in April 1900. In the autumn, however, it re-opened, and Col. (by then Brig.-Gen.) Sir H. G. Miles resumed as Commandant.

Sir George Aston, who was himself a graduate of the Staff College, returned there to teach in 1904 and found an invigorating new atmosphere. Whereas previously the gap between staff and students (with Henderson a notable exception) had been 'as wide as that between the headmaster of a school and the denizens of the lowest form', the South African War changed all that: 'There seemed to be a new spirit in the place and staff and students were the most inspiring community I have ever had the good luck to come across. At a full muster at dinner in the mess four V.C.s and twenty-three D.S.O.s sat down at the table.' Another instructor, Lt-Col E. S. May, recalled that 'we lived in an atmosphere full of zeal and high ideals', and that some of the very best soldiers in the Army were to be met at Camberley.[20]

One conspicuous weakness was that the College was still grossly understaffed. Five 'professors' (a title little coveted by army officers and soon to be discarded) and one instructor were responsible for sixty-four students, many of whom were experienced men who had already learned a good deal about staff duties the hard way in South Africa. Thus the professors had to lecture at least once every day, reconnoitre training grounds, set schemes and mark a forbidding mass of paper.[21]

Among the instructors who later rose to prominence were Hubert Gough (commanded the Fifth Army), R. C. B. Haking (commanded a Corps), L. E. Kiggell (Commandant of the Staff College 1913–14 and Chief-of-Staff to Haig in 1917), and Thompson Capper (universally regarded as a brilliant officer, killed commanding a Division at Loos). Slightly later, when Henry Wilson was Commandant, there were J. P. du Cane and G. M. Harper, who both achieved command of Army Corps, and W. P. Braithwaite (Commandant of the Staff College Quetta in 1911–14 and Chief of Staff to Sir Ian Hamilton at the Dardanelles). Competition for entry had not, surprisingly, fallen off during the South African War, but thereafter the keen and ambitious sought admission in ever-increasing numbers. In 1904, for example, there were 101 candidates for 24 competitive vacancies.[22]

'The Commandant of the Staff College,' Gen. Sir Evelyn Wood emphasized to the Elgin Commission, 'ought to be one of our most gifted people, because he has the training of 40 or 50 of what are presumably the best of the officers.' Sir Herbert

Miles (ironically nicknamed '*Miles* the Soldier' by irreverent students) certainly did not come into this category though, according to one of his instructors, he 'had a positive genius for getting the most out of the day's work in the pleasantest possible way, the glow of his humour never failing to cheer up the gloomiest pessimist'. By contrast, Generals Hubert Gough and Ballard remember Miles in almost identical terms as 'a War Office type', whose idea of teaching staff duties was to urge the students to memorize Queen's Regulations, a copy of which he was believed to keep under his pillow. Lord Roberts, who lived near Camberley and kept in close touch with the College, also thought Miles insufficiently practical and that there was a falling off during his regime (1900–3).[23]

There could hardly have been a better choice as Miles's successor than Sir Henry Rawlinson. He was obsessed with the importance of improving military education and training, and he had proved himself to be an energetic and capable leader in the field as well as a first-rate staff officer.

'Blessed with an extremely attractive personality, a hand-some appearance, high social standing, and more than an average share of this world's goods, he was one to inspire his students unconsciously to follow in his footsteps. He brought a youthful debonair spirit with him, for he was only forty when he took over his duties, and he went hard with the Drag on a big seventeen-hands grey.' Perhaps, as his biographer suggests, his prowess as a sportsman was equally important for the reputation of the College: no one could accuse him of being a theoretical bookworm. If it is a slight exaggeration to claim that 'he swept away the last remnants of pedantry which clung to the College', he certainly did succeed in making the course broader in scope and more practical. When, for example, Hubert Gough returned to the College as an instructor he found the prevailing spirit refreshingly different to Miles's con-cern with routine staff duties in peacetime. Rawlinson and his staff thoroughly examined definite operations of war. 'Tommy' Capper, especially, 'inculcated a spirit of self-sacrifice and duty, instead of the idea of playing for safety and seeking only to avoid getting into trouble. This high-minded inspiration . . .

was like a silver thread which ran through every problem we discussed and studied.'[24a]

One of Rawlinson's first accomplishments was to abolish the title of professor which carried too many associations from the days when most of the teachers were civilians and the curriculum contained many subjects only remotely connected with war. The new designation was 'Directing Staff'. Rawlinson also continued Hildyard's sensible policy by further reducing the number and importance of examinations. Instead, much more emphasis was placed on close personal knowledge of the students and on continuous assessment of their work and capabilities as staff officers. Henceforth the only important examination took place at the end of the first year when students had to get a minimum of marks in order to qualify for the second year. Grading by personal assessment may have had its drawbacks but it seems to have worked very well; a concensus of opinion among all the instructors diminished the dangers of favouritism or prejudice, while the method also made full provision for the importance of physical and character traits as well as mental aptitude.

The contents of the course were also made more practical and up-to-date. Although the Continental tours to inspect the battlefields of the Franco-German War were resumed, the South African War was also scrutinized for its practical lessons, while during the Russo-Japanese War a syndicate of students used to lecture every Saturday on the events of the week. Far more attention was now being paid to administration, and such problems as the organization of a base and lines of communication were studied in detail.

The most important innovation at Camberley in the years immediately following the South African War was the belated establishment of regular connections with the Senior Service. In 1901 Gen. Miles arranged for some Naval officers from the Royal Naval College to lecture at Camberley on combined naval and military operations, and that autumn Lt-Col E. S. May (Henderson's successor as Professor of Military Art and History) visited Greenwich to lecture on the roles of the two Services in Imperial Defence. The Commandant assured May

that he could hardly pitch his note too low since the Naval
officers knew virtually nothing about strategic matters.

A few years later a much more important step was taken,
largely through the initiative of Lt-Col Aston, a Royal Marine
on the instructional staff at Camberley, and the Commandant
Sir Henry Rawlinson. They arranged a lunch party at the
Naval and Military Club for Henry Wilson, then a colonel in
the Staff Duties section of the War Office, and Admiral Slade,
Commandant of the Naval War College at Portsmouth.
Aston outlined a scheme for naval officers to go to Camberley
to see for themselves the nature of Army staff work. This was
implemented in 1906 when two naval officers took the course,
and graduates from Camberley also began to attend naval war
courses. Even more important, the quartet also instituted
annual combined staff tours for all officers at both establishments to practise amphibious operations. At last staff officers
from what had hitherto often been regarded as rival Services
began to appreciate the other's problems and different expertise. As Aston later remarked, 'The scheme was so obviously
sound that it is a wonder that it had never been tried before.'[25]

Inter-service cooperation and the institution of a General
Staff at last made possible the realistic theoretical study of
strategic problems and also of practical experiments in the
form of staff tours and amphibious operations. In 1904, for
example, the Autumn Manœuvres consisted in the landing of
a hostile invasion force (a division commanded by Sir John
French) on the Essex coast, and the defence of an area in the
neighbourhood of Clacton and Colchester. The principal strategic problem in 1904, however, still appeared to be the defence
of the North-West Frontier of India. Arthur Balfour, the Prime
Minister, adopted the 'Blue Water' school's approach that the
Royal Navy could be implicitly relied upon to prevent a large-
scale invasion of Britain, so that the main task of the Home
Army was likely to be the dispatch of reinforcements (nine
divisions was mentioned) to India.

At the Staff College each annual class was split up into small
syndicates to concentrate on one or two foreign countries and
to work out what would now be called 'scenarios' of possible

wars with Britain. This was not only a great spur to a knowledge
of imperial geography, but also established that no strategic problems could be meaningfully studied without considering the naval viewpoint. Gone were the invariable assumptions
of pre-1899 schemes that armies numbering hundreds of thousands were fighting in the south of England, the Royal Navy
being absent or non-existent; that Britain could continue to
fight with sea communications disrupted; and that Britain had
a vast Continental-style Army for home defence.

With Russia's crushing defeat by Japan and the intensifica-
tion of Anglo-German Naval rivalry, strategic priorities changed
at Camberley as at the War Office. Between 1905 and 1907 the
Staff College began to focus on the problem: what should
Britain do if Germany attacked France, violating the neutrality
of Belgium? Sir George Aston later recalled that by the time he
left the staff at Camberley in 1907 the development of German
railways in the area Aix-la-Chapelle-Malmédy made it certain
that in event of war Germany would invade Belgium. Some of
the hypothetical plans prepared by the students closely foreshadowed the real events of 1914, but Aston admits that they
did not give Germany credit for putting her reserve troops in
the field in the *Aufmarsch,* nor for concentrating in such great
force north of the river Meuse.[26]

A special college for staff instruction in India had been proposed as early as 1875 but it met with numerous objections. In
India, it was said, students would not have the benefit of meeting officers of all branches of the Service, and from all parts of
the world, as at Camberley; there was no opportunity in India
to study foreign manœuvres and recent battlefields; and, except
in the hills, the climate was unsuitable for the severe study
required at a Staff College. Another underlying suspicion was
that the War Office would not treat the certificate as equal to
that of Camberley.[27]

As a poor alternative, the War Office sanctioned a scheme in
1877 whereby six selected officers from the Indian Army were
allowed to enter Camberley. The results were disappointing
because very few officers applied. Reasons were not hard to

find. The Camberley certificate was not an essential qualification for staff employment in India and in fact very few
commanding officers favoured Staff College officers; the expense of going to Camberley was estimated at between £100
and £250 per annum over and above the officers' pay; and
there was the danger of missing the opportunities of a frontier
campaign.

It was only when Lord Kitchener became Commander-in-
Chief in India at the end of 1902 that the urgent need for far
more trained staff officers was exposed and the proposal for a
separate Staff College revived. Kitchener's major redistribution
of the Army in order to release a larger force for field service
called for a far larger staff for which there was no source of
supply. By 1903, Kitchener was devoting his legendary determination and drive to the creation of a Staff College which he
envisaged (despite his own lack of a p.s.c.) as an almost exact
replica of Camberley: the same regulations, entrance examination and syllabus, even the possibility of interchange of instructional staff and regular inspection by the Camberley
Commandant. 'I hope there will be no hitch at home,'
Kitchener wrote to Lord Roberts on 18 September 1903, 'as
I am sure the military education is lamentable, and a Staff
College instruction is much required.'[28]

The proposal was welcomed in India but encountered stiff
opposition in Britain from both the Army Council and the
Prime Minister. Although Kitchener, as usual, eventually got
his way, it is worth examining this opposition in some detail
for the light it throws on the peculiar attitudes to higher military education which still flourished in the aftermath of the
South African War.

When the Army Council discussed the establishment of a
Staff College in India early in 1904 the weight of opinion was
against it. The Quartermaster-General (Sir Herbert Plumer)
openly disapproved of there being any Staff College in India
and urged instead the enlargement of Camberley. The Chief of
the General Staff (Sir Neville Lyttleton) agreed with Plumer's
proposal on the grounds that Kitchener had reorganized the
Indian Staff on completely different lines to those adumbrated

in the Esher Report, which was ironical in view of his own procrastination in implementing that Report. The Adjutant-General (Sir Charles Douglas) was impressed by none of the three alternative schemes designed to combine preliminary staff training in a one-year course at Quetta with a second year at Camberley for selected officers. He preferred the present system, which was in fact adhered to, of a two-year course for all. The Master-General of Ordnance (Sir James Wolfe Murray) agreed with Douglas that there must be no tampering with the two-year course, and he alone came out in favour of Quetta: 'It seems to me that it is better to have another school of thought – even though it might differ from the school at home slightly – rather than no school of thought at all.'

The objections of the majority of the Army Council were unavailing for they were informed that the Secretary of State for India had sanctioned the creation of Quetta. To this the Chief of the General Staff observed unenthusiastically that while he was still against the scheme 'we must now make the best of it'. The Army Council's concern was henceforth to ensure administrative sovereignty over Quetta and to this end the Adjutant-General presented eight conditions to which Quetta must conform if she and her graduates wished to be recognized by the War Office. For example, the syllabus of both Colleges was to be drawn up at the War Office, examinations were to be set and marked by the same officers, staff duties in India were to be identical to those in Britain, and p.s.c. certificates were to be issued for both Colleges by the Chief of the General Staff.

Stalemate continued through 1904 and into the following year, for on 26 February 1905 Rawlinson (who had been in close touch with Kitchener throughout), wrote to Lord Roberts from Staff College House to ask him to intercede with Lyttleton. 'Perhaps it is not unreasonable,' Rawlinson wrote, 'that he [Kitchener] should be allowed to examine his own officers for the Quetta College – I think we can trust him not to be too lenient . . .'[29]

In March 1905 the Army Council learnt that Kitchener's reply had been moderate and accommodating on most of the main points, so his minor reservations were allowed to stand and the existence of Quetta was officially recognized. Kitchener had won a minor triumph, and all talk of one-year courses and the selection of a proportion of the officers for a second year at Camberley was dropped. Although the Army Council had some grounds for anxiety about the standard and objectives of the Quetta course, its deliberations make it clear that War Office control was the prime consideration. Another small but significant point was that the establishment of Quetta increased the annual cost of Camberley by £2,800, which was the amount India had hitherto paid as a contribution for home effective services.[30]

As the Army Council's opposition waned, the Prime Minister's increased. Arthur Balfour was concerned over a far graver issue than regulations or comparability of certificates. He feared no less than that a deep chasm would open in military thought and methods between the Home and Indian armies which would seriously handicap their cooperation in the event of a major war, presumably against Russia. In other words, the creation of a second Staff College within the Empire would foster rival 'schools of thought'. In explaining Balfour's objections to Kitchener in June 1905, Sir George Clarke (the first secretary of the Committee of Imperial Defence 1902–7) unfortunately clouded the main issue by including all the hackneyed secondary obstacles to a Staff College in India. He did not think, for example, that 'any deep study of military art or any original historical research work can be possible in India, even if climatic conditions were more instead of much less favourable'.[31]

Kitchener replied at great length, ponderously refuting the notion of a separate 'school of thought'. In the first place it would not be allowed; but in any case the Army had no military school of thought anywhere – opinions were simply moulded by a few leading officers. As a safeguard, Rawlinson could come out to ensure that the lines of instruction coincided.

Kitchener's notion of staff education was in fact severely circumscribed: indeed, Sir George Barrow, who taught at both Camberley and Quetta, concluded that 'he did not understand the real purpose of a Staff College'. For Kitchener, staff training was not a doubtful science which could admit of divergent interpretations. A Staff College is not a 'school of thought' he wrote: 'It is more like a veterinary or signalling or engineering course or class and has no resemblance whatever to the collegiate system of education in England.' The South African War had proved conclusively that we were short of trained staff officers and 'the more I read of the Japanese operations [in the war against Russia 1904–5] the more I see how vastly deficient we are in comparison to them in the number of officers of capacity to organize all those necessary staff arrangements that spell success in war'. If Balfour would make staff training compulsory he would gladly drop the Quetta scheme but in present conditions it was unrealistic to expect the best officers in India to go to Camberley. By contrast 'A Staff College here means a change of station not a change of life – horses, servants, household gods (sic), go with him to his quarters at the Staff College and he has no more expense than he would have in his regiment'. Perhaps a selection of his p.s.c.s could go to Camberley for a further year's course?[32]

Balfour was still not satisfied by Kitchener's re-assurance, for Clarke in his reply (with the Prime Minister's approval) raised the analogy of rival public schools. 'If you ran Eton and Winchester on identical curriculums, they would assert different individualities, and in this case when two Staff Colleges are in widely diverse countries the differences will be the more marked.' More important, while agreeing with Kitchener that the Army had no military school of thought anywhere, Clarke regarded this less as a matter for complacency than as a serious defect to be remedied. The British Army, he wrote, suffered more than any other in the world from discordant views on every possible subject. One result was that Ministers and intelligent civilians had learned to distrust all military opinion; another was that there were too many unthinking officers who opposed even the most necessary reforms. While of course there were routine staff duties that could be taught in a stereotyped course, the Esher Committee (of which Clarke had been a member), had more ambitious plans. 'We desired to teach the highest branches of the art of war; we wanted men who could think for themselves and were qualified to form reasoned opinions upon all great military questions. We desired to encourage original historical research which . . . appears impossible at Quetta. We hoped to get hold of our ablest young officers and to give them an intellectual equipment which would fit them for high command and which, as they spread throughout the Army, would help to create a higher standard generally.' Camberley now had the instructors to teach more demanding subjects while Quetta had not. Future generals, for example, ought to have studied Imperial Defence in all its facets but this could hardly be done in India. 'Where could you find a qualified lecturer to deal with the great lessons of naval history? Who will analyse for you the conditions of the national overseas trade and their bearing upon national defence . . .'[33]

Clarke was surely excessively pessimistic about the limitations of instruction at Quetta (why not send out experts from England?) but his letter illustrates very clearly the exciting broad vistas in staff education which were being opened as a consequence of the Esher Committee's Reports and the creation of a General Staff.

Meanwhile, Kitchener's plans had gone forward and by the end of 1905 a temporary Staff College had been opened at Deolali. It provided for twenty-four officers, approximately one-third to belong to the British Army in India and two-thirds to the Indian Army. The first Commandant, Brig.-Gen. A. W. L. Bayly, and the first three professors were all p.s.c.s and the syllabus was very similar to Camberley's, one obvious modification being the substitution of Oriental for European languages among the optional subjects. Rawlinson visited the College six months after it opened and was generally satisfied with the progress of staff and students.[34]

In March 1906 Col. Thompson Capper was appointed Commandant direct from the staff at Camberley, and in April 1907 the College moved to its permanent site at Quetta where it still functions as the Staff College of the Pakistan Army. Advantage was taken of the break in the programme to send a party of twenty students and some instructors to explore the Manchurian battlefields, while another party toured the North West Frontier. The junior division had recently spent a week in Bombay inspecting the forts, the system of electric search-lights for coast defence, submarine mining, the docks and the sewage-disposal works.

The new College was officially opened on 1 June 1907 by Lt-Gen. Sir H. L. Smith-Dorrien, commanding the 4th (Quetta) Division. The General contrasted the present high value placed on the p.s.c. qualification with its status when he graduated in 1888. After great efforts by Sir Evelyn Wood he had at last obtained a minor staff berth. In a chance meeting with the Military Secretary (to the Commander-in-Chief in India), he asked whether he had done himself any good by going to the Staff College. 'Well, I shouldn't say that you have done yourself any harm,' he replied, 'for if there were two candidates for an appointment, one with a p.s.c. and one without, and the Chief knew neither of them, it is possible, though I couldn't vouch for it, that he would select the p.s.c. man!' Now an officer is certain to be tried in staff appointments and only if found wanting relegated to regimental duty. Before 1899 commanders may have had some justification for preferring regimental officers to very theoretically-inclined p.s.c.s, but the Boers and Japanese had changed all that. 'Higher training nowadays, gentlemen, is a very serious matter. The whole education of armies is on a higher plane and therefore the brains of an army must be very highly trained indeed.' Smith-Dorrien was in advance of the majority view among senior officers in believing that staff officers must study foreign politics and contemporary history in order to put their work in proper perspective.

How far did the course at Quetta before 1914 live up to Smith-Dorrien's expectations? There was certainly plenty of emphasis on practical outdoor work. In 1909, for example, a ten-day staff ride was held in the Quetta area to practise siege operations, and there were frequent long-distance patrols of up to 160 miles. From 1909, also, two Australian captains regularly attended the course to add an Imperial flavour, among them (in 1912) T. A. Blamey who fought at Gallipoli, was Chief of Staff of the Australian Corps in 1918, and eventually became a Field-Marshal. In military history and strategy Hamley's *Operations of War* remained the standard textbook. Hamley's method of illustrating the permanent 'principles of war' from past campaigns was continued, the prescribed campaigns being the Continental Wars 1796–1815, the American Civil War 1861–4 (why the final year was omitted is a puzzle), the Prussian Wars of 1866 and 1870, and the Russo-Turkish War of 1877. The South African War seems to have been omitted (too many blunders committed by generals still serving perhaps), but at least 'special attention' was to be paid to the Russo-Japanese War in Manchuria. Among the essays written by Capt. Philip Howell in the first year of the Quetta course was a comparison between the strategic situation at the commencement of the Sikh War and the South African War in 1899, and a study of the Afridi Campaign of 1897–8: 'how far would procedures in attack, retirement and protection need to be modified should a second invasion of Tirah be necessary'.[35]

Another student officer, Richard Meinertzhagen, has left his impressions of the Quetta course on the eve of the First World War. Meinertzhagen, who had never before considered the more academic branches of the art of war, recorded in May 1913 that he had thoroughly enjoyed the first three months' work: 'All our teaching here aims at training us for the ordeal of war. The more I learn the more I appreciate the necessity of a thorough and sound training for regular officers. I realize what hopeless chaos would result from reliance on half-trained amateur citizen soldiers ... [commanders and staffs] cannot be improvised.' At the end of the year he felt that the Staff College had made him a better soldier but he was frankly disappointed at not having gained more practical knowledge. 'I expected a better groundwork in staff duties, a better insight into the art of war and more confidence in myself to conduct war and to satisfy the requirements of a staff officer ...' Despite his self-doubt, however, Meinertzhagen was to prove himself a brilliant staff officer in the Middle East during the First World War. His *Army Diary*, however, provides several instances of Staff

College instructors as well as p.s.c.s who failed in their duties either before or during the war.[36]

As Director of Staff Duties and subsequently Chief of the General Staff in India, Sir Douglas Haig took a keen interest in the development of Quetta as the source of the future Indian General Staff. Already in 1909 he envisaged a long war which the British Empire should be able to win 'by wearing the enemy out', provided the right measures were carried through at once: 'it is of vital importance,' he wrote to Kiggell, 'to have the machinery available in India trained as soon as possible to turn out staff officers who may be of use when the time comes, and the resources of that country organized for *Imperial* needs . . .'

After a visit to Quetta in October 1911 Haig wrote enthusiastically of the improvements wrought by Braithwaite: 'I must add how thoroughly Braith[waite] has justified my selection of him for the post of Commandant. T[hompson] Capper did well but he was too full of nerves and too much of a crank to get the best out of officers . . . In my opinion things are on a much more satisfactory footing than they were a year ago, and professors and students seem now a happy family party which augurs well for a *united* staff in years to come.'[37]

Haig's impression that Braithwaite had greatly improved the atmosphere at Quetta was borne out by Lt-Col George Barrow who was transferred – like Braithwaite and Capper – from the Directing Staff at Camberley at the beginning of 1911. In complete contrast to the camaraderie between staff and students at Camberley, Barrow found that friendly relations were sternly forbidden at Quetta. He recalled that when he entered the ante-room of the mess, students chatting or reading sprang to attention and stood stiffly beside their chairs until he asked them to sit down. He might have been a Prussian general entering a room full of young cadets. Social relations, moreover, were rendered intensely uncomfortable by an over-zealous concern on the Commandant's part to avoid any suspicion of favouritism. Barrow had been a close friend of Capper's when they were fellow-students at Camberley and later admired him as a brilliant colleague on the Directing Staff there. He sadly concluded that Capper possessed a streak of 'genius' but his sense of balance had suffered with his professional advancement. Despite his outstanding ability 'he failed to impart a feeling of happy and confident frankness so essential to the well-being of an institution such as the Staff College, and he carried some of his principles to an extreme stage where they became unworkable'. He maintained, for example, that it was the duty of a staff officer to be killed in battle. True to his principles he threw away his own life early in the First World War by riding his horse fully exposed between the British and German lines to encourage his men when commanding the 7th Division. Thus the Army lost, tragically, one of its ablest and most gallant officers.[38]

Although Quetta undoubtedly did suffer in its early years from some of the handicaps predicted by its opponents, such as its extremes of climate and distance from both large bodies of troops and the sea, the College had fully justified Kitchener's confidence and persistence by 1914, by when 218 officers had graduated. Formal and informal relations with Camberley remained extremely close and no more fears were voiced about the dangers of a 'separate school of thought'; indeed Quetta may have suffered from being made to walk too closely in the footsteps of its elder sister.

CHAPTER 6. NOTES

1 L. S. Amery, *The Times' History of the War in South Africa* (London, 1902), Vol. II, p. 9.
2 *Ibid.*, p. 40.
3 *Ibid.*, pp. 37–8. G. F. R. Henderson, *The Science of War*, p. 397.
4 *Royal Commission on the War in South Africa*, Cd 1789 of 1903. *Report*, para. 96.
5 Viscount Esher to the Duchess of Sutherland, 7–9–1906, in Maurice V. Brett (ed.), *Journals and Letters of Reginald Viscount Esher* (London, 1934), Vol. II, pp. 183–4.
6 Esher to *M.V.B.*, 25–9–1902, *ibid.*, Vol. I, p. 353. See also Vol. II, p. 261n.
7 *Report of Committee on Military Education* (Akers-Douglas), Cd 982 of 1902. *Report*, paras 6–7, 9, 73–86 (R.M.A. Woolwich), 90–101 (R.M.C. Sandhurst).
8 *Ibid.*, paras 111, 134–40.
9 *Ibid.*, paras 153–7. See also A. V. Tucker, *op. cit.*
10 *Report of Committee on Military Education*, paras 160–1. In a lecture, which itself goes far to explain why military history was held in low esteem by army officers, Col. Lonsdale Hale remarked that many officers found 'Study' and 'History' bad enough by themselves, 'but when in juxtaposition, forming a combination absolutely detestable'. 'The Professional Study of Military History', *R.U.S.I. Journal*, 1897, Vol. I, pp. 690–721. The ensuing discussion is worth the attention of any student of the development of military history.
11 Amery, *op. cit.*, II, pp. 27 and 288. Esher, *op. cit.*, I, p. 261. See also Lady Briggs, *The Staff Work of the Anglo-Boer War, 1899–1901* (London, 1901), pp. 135–6.
12 Amery, *op. cit.*, III, pp. 335–8, 448–50. P. Magnus, *Kitchener* (London, 1958), pp. 160–71.
13 Callwell, *op. cit.*, II, p. 100. D. S. Macdiarmid, *The Life of Lieut General Sir James Grierson* (London, 1923), p. 271.
14 Amery, *op. cit.*, II, pp. 346–7, 360–1 (Modder River); pp. 367–82 (Stormberg); III, pp. 396–400 (Waterval Drift). Maj.-Gen. Sir Frederick Maurice, *History of the War in South Africa* (London, 1907), Vol. II, pp. 74–80 (Waterval Drift). C. R. De Wet, *Three Years War* (Westminster, 1902), pp. 47–51 (Waterval Drift); W. Baring Pemberton, *Battles of the Boer War* (London, 1964) (Modder River, Magersfontein, Colenso, Spion Kop); Amery, *op. cit.*, III, pp. 298–301 (Spion Kop).
15 *Royal Commission on the War in South Africa (Elgin Report)*.
16 *Ibid., Report*, para. 95, Minutes of Evidence 10447.

17 *Ibid.*, 175–80 (Kitchener); 4327, 4311, 4335–7 (Wood); 15972, 16097 (Hildyard); 21853, 22038–40, 91195–6 (Kekewich); 16974, 172026–30 (Colvile).

18 *Ibid.*, 14088–93, 14104–13, 14122–8 (Ian Hamilton); 16041–97 (Hildyard). Sir Evelyn Wood was also pressed on the possibility of relaxing the qualifications for entry (4310–2).

19 *Ibid.*, 20493–20516.

20 Aston, *op. cit.*, pp. 239–40. May, *op. cit.*, pp. 267–8.

21 *Ibid.*, p. 267. After 1918 the instructional staff was increased to fourteen while the number of students increased by only forty per cent.

22 Maurice, *General Lord Rawlinson of Trent*, pp. 84–5.

23 *Elgin Report*, 4341 (Wood); May, *op. cit.*, p. 268. Ballard, *op. cit.*, p. 46. Gen. Sir H. Gough, *Soldiering On* (London, 1954), pp. 64, 69. Esher, *op. cit.*, II, p. 193 and see also p. 262n.

24 Godwin-Austen, *op. cit.*, p. 242. Maurice, *op. cit.*, p. 84. Gough, *op. cit.*, p. 93.

25 The Royal Naval College moved from Portsmouth to Greenwich in 1873. In ran strictly technical courses for the training of sub-lieutenants, naval constructors, etc., which had 'no relation either to the processes of fighting or the principles of war'. These latter aspects began to be studied at a 'War Course' in 1900 for commanders and captains. From 1903 the course lasted four months and included naval history, strategy, tactics and international law. In 1908 Fisher expanded its functions to include the investigation of problems sent down to it from the Naval Intelligence Department. The Course was transferred from Greenwich to Portsmouth (1906–14) and returned permanently to Greenwich in 1920. See A. J. Marder, *From Dreadnought to Scapa Flow* (London, 1961), Vol. I, pp. 32–3. May, *op. cit.*, pp. 268–9. Aston, *op. cit.*, pp. 241–2.

26 *Ibid.*, pp. 147–9. See also below Chapter 8, p. 256 *et seq.*

27 The information on Quetta in the following section, unless otherwise stated, is drawn from *Records of the Staff College, Quetta, Vol. I 1905–1914* (Army Headquarters, India 1916). See also Godwin-Austen, *op. cit.*, pp. 248–54 and Sir George Arthur, *Life of Lord Kitchener* (London, 1920), II, pp. 173–6.

28 Kitchener Papers, P.R.O. 30/57/29 (typed copies of letters to Lord Roberts).

29 Minutes of Proceedings and Précis prepared for the Army Council, 1904. W.O. 163/9. Précis No. 85, p. 215 and No 121, pp. 331–3. Sir Henry Wilson's Diary 1 July, 29 September, 8 November 1904. Roberts Papers R61/34.

30 Minutes of Proceedings and Précis prepared for the Army Council, 1905. W.O. 163/10. Précis No. 200, pp. 261–4.

31 Kitchener Papers, P.R.O. 30/57/34, Sir George Clarke to Kitchener 15–6–1905.

32 *Ibid.*, Kitchener to Clarke, 5–7–1905. See also Barrow, *op. cit.*, pp. 93–4.

33 *Ibid.*, Clarke to Kitchener, 8–8–1905.

34 Roberts Papers R61/36. Rawlinson to Roberts, 20–12–1905.
35 Howell Papers I/L/1. A copy of the Original Regulations for the Quetta Staff College can be seen in L/Mil/7, Collection 74, file 20, at the India Office Library. Unfortunately this Collection contains little of interest on the history of the Staff College.
36 Col R. Meinertzhagen, *Army Diary 1899–1926* (London, 1960), pp. 30, 53–75, 280.
37 Haig to Kiggell 27 April 1909 and 22 October 1911. Kiggell Papers 1/2, 1/27.
38 Barrow, *op. cit.*, pp. 122–4. Edmonds puts a different complexion on Capper's self-sacrifice in remarking (in his *Reminiscences*) that he died while urging forward a 'sticky' unit by his own example.

CHAPTER SEVEN

The creation and development
of the General Staff
1904-1914

The creation of a General Staff in the decade before the First World War belatedly crowned the edifice for which the Staff College had long provided a foundation. That Britain was so slow in following the example of the great Continental armies was not due primarily to that traditional fear of militarism which Campbell Bannerman so trenchantly expressed after the report of the Hartington Commission in 1890. Until the South African War and the menacing growth of the German Navy, there had been little incentive for the War Office to undertake strategic planning for military operations in Europe; indeed, the Stanhope Memorandum of 1891 had emphatically given such operations the lowest priority.[1] Secondly, the civil and military heads of the War Office had displayed very little interest in the creation of a General Staff which, as Dr Gooch has written, 'represented an alien grafting on to the War Office as well as into the Cabinet system'.[2] Rather, military reformers had grown accustomed to piecemeal adjustments to the system created by Edward Cardwell, and it was significant that the report of the Hartington Commission, which did recommend a thorough reorganization was shelved. Thirdly, the Treasury was consistently suspicious, if not positively hostile, to the institution of anything resembling a General Staff which was likely to entail increased expenditure. As the Esher Committee roundly stated in its section on Military finance:

> The entire system of War Office finance, which has been built up during many years, and had its origin in a distant past, is based upon the assumption that all military officers are

necessarily spendthrifts, and that their actions must be controlled in gross and in detail by civilians. This theory is largely responsible for the unreadiness for war which has been frequently exhibited, as well as for reckless and wasteful expenditure.[3]

Financial opposition also goes far to explain the slow development of the Intelligence Department which, before 1904, constituted an inadequate substitute for a General Staff. Between 1896 and 1899, for example, the Department was allotted £20,000; and of this £2,000 p.a. was spent on duties connected with South Africa. It was subsequently estimated that the Topographical Department alone required £17,000 p.a. to perform its duties adequately in addition to £150,000 p.a. for a topographical survey of the Empire.[4] Successive Directors of Military Intelligence in the 1890s found it difficult to break clear from the widespread political assumption that the only strategic danger which should concern them was invasion; and the other departments were unwilling to consult and accept their opinion. The inferior status accorded to the Intelligence Department was exemplified by the fact that its heads held the rank of temporary major-general, whereas the heads of the other military departments were permanent lieutenant-generals.

Despite minor improvements during the South African War, Lt-Col W. R. Robertson found a depressing situation when he became head of one of the sub-sections of what was now styled the Intelligence Division in October 1901: 'On taking over the new duties I found that, chiefly owing to an inadequate staff, imperfect organization, and the lack of clear direction, there was not, with one exception . . . a single up-to-date statement giving a comprehensive and considered estimate of the military resources of any foreign country.'[5] He and a few other enlightened officers were becoming convinced of the urgent necessity to create a proper General Staff. One of these was Maj. G. F. Ellison, who had been impressed by the German manœuvres he had attended between 1885 and 1895, and was soon to play a very important role in establishing the General

Staff, first as secretary of the Esher Committee and later as military secretary to Haldane.

It was, however, a civilian who, through his membership of the Elgin Commission in the South African War, conceived the boldest vision of War Office reform. Viscount Esher, although he held only the lowly position of Secretary of the Office of Works (1895–1902), was already politically influential through his friendship with several leading statesmen, notably Arthur Balfour, and with the Prince of Wales. In a memorandum appended to the Report of the Elgin Commission, Esher pointed out the main defects in the War Office. These were the lack of coordination between the various branches, which weakened the influence of the Secretary of State with his colleagues, and the absence of a proper system of inspection to ensure that War Office policy was actually implemented by the Army. In particular he advocated the abolition of the office of Commander-in-Chief and the establishment of a board on the lines of the Board of Admiralty. In this brief note lay the seeds of the future Army Council and a thoroughly reorganized General Staff for, unlike the Elgin Commission, Esher and his two colleagues in the War Office (Reconstitution) Committee assumed the powers to impose their main proposals upon an astonished and indignant military hierarchy.

In its celerity, boldness and comprehensiveness the work of the War Office (Reconstitution) Committee has no parallel in British military reform and few in any other branch of administration. Esher and his colleagues, Sir George Clarke (lately Governor of Victoria and subsequently Secretary of the Committee of Imperial Defence) and Admiral Sir John Fisher, only began to meet towards the end of December 1903, yet published three reports in the first quarter of 1904. Although this chapter is concerned only with one important aspect of 'the Triumvirate's' work, namely its proposals for a General Staff, it will be useful to outline their other recommendations.

The fundamental assumption was that the War Office should be reconstituted with a view to the effective training and preparation of the military forces for war, and not administered as hitherto from the point of view of peace. No measure of

TABLE 2
Distribution of Duties at the War Office

THE ARMY COUNCIL

THE SECRETARY OF STATE FOR WAR	CHIEF OF THE GENERAL STAFF	ADJUTANT-GENERAL	QUARTER-MASTER-GENERAL	MASTER GENERAL OF THE ORDNANCE	CIVIL MEMBER	FINANCE MEMBER
Responsibility to the Crown and to Parliament	Operations of War	Provision of *Personnel*	Transport, Remount, Railway, Supply and Veterinary Services	Armaments.	Barrack Construction.	Estimates
Submissions to the Crown	Intelligence	Organization	Barrack Administration	Ordnance Factories	Chaplain's Department.	Financial Policy and Advice.
	Training and Education	Mobilization of units	Maintenance of authorized reserves of Food and Material	Fortifications	Purchase of Lands	Review of Contracts
	Official publications dealing with the theory of War	Discipline and Military Law	Contracts	Barrack Maintenance	Non-effective Services	Examination of Accounts
	Mapping	Medical Services	Administration of Votes for above services	Custody of Lands and Ranges	Administration of Votes for Services	Cash Payments
	Administration of Votes for above services	Army Schools		Technical Committees		
		Administration of Votes for above services		Contracts		
				Administration of Votes for above Services		

SECRETARY OF THE WAR OFFICE.

Interior Economy of the War Office.

Secretarial Work of the Army Council.

Correspondence with other Departments of State.

reform would avail unless provision was made for providing
the Cabinet with all the information and expert advice required
for shaping national policy in war, and for determining necessary preparations in peace. For this purpose a permanent
nucleus should be created for the Committee of Imperial
Defence, which had been set up in 1902. The office of Commander-in-Chief should be abolished and War Office business
should be conducted by an Army Council consisting of the
Secretary of State, four military and two civilian members.
The first military member would be entitled Chief of the General Staff and would be responsible for all aspects of military
policy. Finally the Committee stressed the need to divorce
administration from command. There must be a great decentralization of administrative work to relieve congestion at
the War Office, and to this end eight administrative districts
should be set up under major-generals.[6]

Although the Triumvirate, then, with the backing of the Prime
Minister, was empowered to implement the heads of their
proposals, by a combination of Letters Patent and Orders in
Council, it would be completely wrong to imagine that in such
a short space of time a Committee, *with no responsibility*, could
actually institute a body of officers collectively known as 'The
General Staff' and define its responsibilities and composition
in any detail. On the contrary, the brevity and elegance of their
Report was only made possible by wisely confining themselves
to laying down general principles. The unusual aspect of the
Committee's proceedings was that in a whirlwind 'purge'
they removed from office the Commander-in-Chief (Lord
Roberts) and all the military departmental heads of the War
Office, and replaced them (excepting, of course, the office of
Commander-in-Chief) with their own nominees who were then
expected to put flesh on the bare bones of the Report. It seems
likely that only by such drastic – even high-handed – actions
could such a far reaching reorganization have been set in motion,
but inevitably the Triumvirate created many bitter enemies and
ironically several of its nominees proved lukewarm reformers,
particularly as regards the General Staff.

The very first section of the Esher Committee's First Report contained an ambiguity which was greatly to handicap the development of the General Staff, and indeed of strategic planning and advice generally before 1914. The Committee took the view that the body which should be responsible for giving expert advice to the Cabinet on military policy in its broadest aspects was the Defence Committee of the Cabinet (or C.I.D.). The latter was inadequate as then constituted because it had no permanent nucleus, and because it was composed of political and professional members distracted by administrative duties and therefore unable to devote their undivided attention to the complex problems of Imperial Defence.

> The grave danger to which we call attention remains, and demands effective remedy. The British Empire is pre-eminently a great Naval, Indian and Colonial Power. There are, nevertheless, no means for coordinating defence problems, for dealing with them as a whole, for defining the proper functions of the various elements, and for ensuring that, on the one hand, peace preparations are carried out upon a consistent plan, and, on the other hand, that in time of emergency a definite war policy, based upon solid data, can be formulated.

What was needed was something resembling the German General Staff, but this was not entirely satisfactory as a model both because Britain's defence problems were far more complex, and because the chain of political responsibility in Germany was completely different.

The solution, and what the Committee regarded as 'the corner stone of the needed edifice of Reform', lay in the addition of a permanent nucleus to the Defence Committee and the clarification of the latter's duties. The permanent nucleus would comprise a secretary appointed for five years and eligible for renewal; and under him two naval officers, two military officers and two Indian Army officers (nominated by the Viceroy), with, if possible, one or more representatives of the Colonies. These officers were not to be of high rank and their appointment should be limited to two years. The duties of

the secretariat would be: to consider all questions of Imperial
Defence from the point of view of the Navy, the Military
Forces, India and the Colonies; to obtain and collate relevant
information from all the departments of State; to prepare
documents required by the Prime Minister and Defence
Committee; and to keep adequate records for the Cabinet and
its successors. In short, the Committee proposed to allocate
to the C.I.D. Secretariat the vital role of supplying strategical
advice which was normally regarded as the role of a capital
staff. Esher's intention to bestow on the new secretariat some of
the functions of a General Staff is underlined by the title of
'The Department of Scientific or Theoretical War Problems'
which he gave to the former in his original draft.[7] The confusion
of responsibilities was also glossed over in the final paragraph
of Part III where the Triumvirate urbanely concluded:

> The Defence Committee, assisted by a small Secretariat,
> will deal with questions of National Defence, and will foresee
> Imperial requirements. The General Officers Commanding-
> in-Chief, assisted by the General Staff, will be able to
> concentrate their energies upon the training and the pre-
> paration of the Forces of the Crown for War. The Major-
> Generals in the eight Districts will be able to devote themselves
> to administration. The Inspector-General and his staff will
> watch over the working of the military system, and bring to
> light its defects. Lastly, the Army Council, freed from
> routine, will find the time and the means to direct military
> policy, to foresee military requirements, and to frame the
> measures of organization, the neglect of which in time of
> peace entails disaster or ruinously expensive improvisation
> in war.

Henry Wilson, then a Colonel in the newly-created Staff
Duties directorate of the General Staff, noted in his Diary the
Committee's curious proposal to make the C.I.D. secretariat
the nucleas of a 'Great General Staff', but nevertheless thought
it sound. Balfour, however, *did* foresee the danger of '*two*
Headquarters Staffs, who, from the very fact that they are two,
and not one, will tend to polarise into a kind of natural

TABLE 3
Duties of the Chief of the General Staff

CHIEF OF THE GENERAL STAFF

The Military Defence of the Empire. Collection of Intelligence. Supervision of the training of the Military Forces. Their use in War. War organization. Education of Officers. Selection and administration of the General Staff. Telegraphs and Signalling

Director of Military Operations			Director of Staff Duties		Director of Military Training	
Information about British Empire, and its military forces	Intelligence and Secret Service	Mapping and Topographical Section	Appointments to, and instruction of the General Staff	Preparations for publication of all works bearing on war training, war organization and the tactical instruction of the Army	Home Defence	Instruction and training of forces in United Kingdom
Strategical distribution of the Regular Army			Appointment of the higher staff of the Staff College and Cadet Colleges	Military History	Plans of concentration for war	Manœuvres in United Kingdom
Preparation of schemes of offence			Instruction at and examinations for the Staff College and Cadet Colleges	General Staff Libraries both at headquarters and in commands	Reconaissance of United Kingdom	Concentration for Manœuvres
Study of schemes of Imperial defence (other than in the United Kingdom)			Regulations governing the granting of Commissions in the Army		Study of local defence schemes in United Kingdom	Allocation of funds for manœuvres and training
			Professional education and examination of officers for promotion			Instruction in and the appointment of the higher staffs at Schools of Training (other than gymnasia, and schools of cooking and music)
			Examinations in foreign languages			Telegraphs and Signalling

opposition'. If a von Moltke were available, he enquired, would he be made First Military Member (C.G.S.) or Secretary of the C.I.D.? Esher replied that he foresaw no fundamental conflict between the collective deliberations of the C.I.D. and the separate intelligence staffs of the two services. A British von Moltke would be made Chief of Staff and like the original would take the field in war. (Ironically the C.I.G.S. did not take the field in the First World War, while the nearest Britain could approach to a von Moltke was probably Sir Maurice Hankey who was Secretary of the C.I.D.) Later, however, Esher did acknowledge Balfour's criticism to be just, for on 18 February 1906 he wrote to Clarke:

> As we have created it, the G.S. is going to be our Franken-stein. I can see that clearly. The Defence Committee should have been the G.S. for our Empire, with merely an 'Intelligence Branch' for the W.O., developed through the commands. The German model is going to be our curse.[8]

The Esher Committee dealt with the composition and duties of the General Staff in a section of its second Report. Its proposals were prefaced by a potted history of the varied fortunes of the British substitutes for a General Staff since 1815, a story of muddle and neglect which had reached its nadir in 1899 when 'the most important duties of an operations staff were not assigned to any branch of the Army, and seem to have been forgotten'.

The keynote of the Committee's proposals, as Dr Gooch has remarked, 'was the concept of specialization and division of labour', with the Directorate of Military Operations left largely free to concentrate on what would now be termed contingency planning. In theory all the work of the General Staff would be made available to the Army Council through the Chief of the General Staff. In fact the Committee omitted to discuss the relationship between the General Staff and the other departments of the War Office and this was to prove a source of considerable friction.

Logical and persuasive as were the General Staff proposals in outline, the Committee was imprecise on a number of important details, cramming their ideas on the recruitment and rewards for the General Staff into a single paragraph.

Thus they recommended that the General Staff should be recruited 'mainly from the Staff College', and all officers selected should serve a probationary period of at least three months. As a general principle continuous employment on the General Staff should be restricted to four years and should, in all cases, qualify an officer for accelerated promotion. A distinct General Staff uniform was essential. Elsewhere it was casually stated that in war time General Staff officers should be prepared to direct operations in the field. Thus the Esher Committee envisaged the General Staff as a *corps d'élite*, though not a separate corps within the Army, with an attractive incentive of accelerated promotion, and the prospect that in time the ladder to high command would virtually be confined to officers who served satisfactorily on the General Staff at the War Office.[9]

The imperfections of the Esher Committee's Reports were small indeed compared with their lucidity and cohesion, and much of the subsequent controversy and delay might have been avoided had the Triumvirate been more fortunate with their selection as Chief of the General Staff and the other military members of the Army Council.

There was one other omission which is as remarkable as any other aspect of this whole unusual episode: apart from a brief announcement by the Prime Minister, the momentous proposal to create a General Staff was never adequately debated by the House of Commons.[10]

It is natural to assume that the Esher Committee Report created the General Staff. In fact, virtually nothing was done to implement the Report under Balfour's Conservative administration which remained in office until December 1905. Explanations for the delay, which so exasperated proponents of a General Staff, such as Esher and Henry Wilson, are not hard to discover.

In the first place, the haste and discourtesy with which the Triumvirate had made a clean sweep of the military heads of the War Office antagonized many of the senior officers who were then required to organize the General Staff.

Indeed, even supporters like Wilson were unhappy about their methods:

> Our days pass like nightmares. The Triumvirate are carrying on like madmen. This morning I was in Nick's [Sir William Nicholson's] room talking over things with him, and his opinion is that all these sudden changes lead straight to chaos, when in walked Jimmy Grierson and said Esher had ordered him up from Salisbury to take over Nick's office [he was then Director General of Mobilization and Military Intelligence]. Nick himself had not been informed, nor had he been told to hand over, and he called me to witness that he gave over the keys of secret boxes, etc., to Grierson simply on the latter's word. This is most scandalous work. Gerald Ellison lunched with me and I impressed on him with all my power that this bull-headed way of proceeding will absolutely ruin the scheme, which in itself has some excellent points . . .
>
> Gerald tells me the Committee will go on their galloping career, kicking out and appointing, destroying and constructing at a pace and with a lack of knowledge which quite takes one's breath away.[11]

Secondly, there was a lack of Ministerial drive to overcome military opposition or inertia. Balfour was far more interested in the C.I.D. than the General Staff, while Arnold-Forster, though one of the best informed Secretaries of State for War on military matters, had become so deeply entangled in his unpopular re-organization scheme that he had little time to spare for other aspects of Army reform. Moreover, the Government itself was *in extremis*; public confidence was ebbing and Parliamentary majorities falling, while Joseph Chamberlain's Imperial Preference campaign threatened to disrupt the Unionist Party from within.

Political indifference would have mattered less had the Esher Committee been wiser – or more fortunate – in its choice of the Chief and heads of sections of the General Staff. Grierson, Stopford[12] and Hutchinson[13] all proved disappointing in various ways as Directors of Military Operations, Training and

9a. British infantry advancing at Magersfontein, 11 December 1899. Wire and entrenchments greatly increased the strength of the Boer defences.

9b. The loss of the British supply train at Waterval Drift, 15 February 1900. A notorious instance of faulty staff work.

10. Maj.-Gen. W. F. M. Hutchinson (Commandant 1899–1900), *above, left* and Col. H. S. G. Miles (1898–9 and 1900–3), *above, right*, made little impact at Camberley, but Brig.-Gen. Sir H. S. Rawlinson (1903–6), *left*, was the first of three outstanding Commandants who began to apply the lessons of the South African War.

Staff Duties respectively, but the worst choice was that of Sir
Neville Lyttleton as the first Chief of the General Staff.[14] He
was the third of eight sons of Viscount Cobham and was a
noted games-player. He had served in the Mobilization
Section from 1894 to 1897 and after preserving his reputation
in the South African War had become Commander-in-Chief
there. Nevertheless, Repington (*The Times'* Military Correspondent) had warned Esher that 'Lyttleton, good man as he
is, knows practically nothing of great problems of Imperial
Defence and less than that about the problems which confront
foreign strategists . . .', and Sir George Clarke also had doubts
about his suitability.[15] When every allowance has been made
for Henry Wilson's bias as a frustrated subordinate in the
Directorate of Staff Duties between 1904–1906, his numerous
tirades against 'N.G.' (Lyttleton) in his private Diaries make a
convincing case that Lyttleton was a disaster as the first Chief
of the General Staff. For example, Lyttleton would not give a
lead to the Army Council to resist Treasury opposition to
expenditure on a General Staff. In May 1904 he accepted a
demand from the Treasury that the cost of the General Staff
be reduced by £17,000 p.a. even though Arnold-Forster had
given his sanction to increased expenditure in this area. 'I am
much dissatisfied at the way things are going,' Wilson noted on
31 May, 'and I feel sure that the Treasury will beat us and that
we shall be crippled in our General Staff; and I think we deserve
it. We are a vacillating, ignorant crowd.'[16]

When all these factors have been taken into account, however,
the most serious obstacle to the creation of the General Staff
was a fundamental divergence of opinion as to its composition,
status and role. On the one hand there was the 'blue ribbon'
school who envisaged the General Staff as a specialist *élite*;
on the other the non-specialist or 'Administrative' school who
opposed the conferment of special privileges on the General
Staff and deplored its separation from the administrative staffs
of the other War Office Departments (i.e., the Adjutant-
General's and Quartermaster-General's branches). A particular
bone of contention was whether the p.s.c. qualification should
be obligatory. Inevitably the views of the two 'schools' were

TABLE 4

Distribution of Headquarters Staff Duties in the Field

GENERAL OFFICER COMMANDING-IN-CHIEF

Chief of the General Staff.	Adjutant-General.	Quartermaster-General	Director of Army Finance
Operations of war	Supply of officers and men	Supplies of all kinds except medical stores and cash	Financial advice
Intelligence	Raising forces locally	Transport of men and material	Examination of accounts
Selection of lines of communication, and advice as to their garrisons	Organization and mobilization of improvised units	Railways	Cash payments
Framing orders regarding moves of men and material	Hospital and sanitary arrangements, and the supply of medical stores	Remounts	
Selection and protection of camps and bivouacs	Accommodation and rest camps	Postal services	
Organization higher than the unit	Control of the press and of press correspondents	Embarkations and landings, if these are not operations of war	
Telegraphs and Signalling	Casualties and invaliding		
Censorship	Military, martial and international law		
	Chaplain's duties		
	Provost Marshals and police measures		

sometimes blurred and not all the proponents of each approach necessarily saw eye to eye, but the basic conflict between the rival viewpoints is clear enough.

The Esher Committee Report, as already suggested, was strongly for an élitist General Staff in that it urged the necessity of keeping the latter from routine administration so that it could concentrate on analysis of military problems and planning for war. The Adjutant-General's staff – at the War Office and in Commands – was to be quite distinct from the General Staff, though service in the one was to be no impediment to service in the other. [17]

In the months following the publication of the Esher Committee Report, Sir George Clarke, then Secretary of the C.I.D., was probably more concerned than anyone else about the role of the General Staff. He felt it vital to impress upon the Army that a General Staff appointment was a thing to strive for, the blue ribbon of the service.

> The only possible means of raising the educational standard, and the military efficiency of our Army is to have a highly trained G.S. to leaven the mass of ignorance from the top downwards. The more I study the S.A. war, the more I see that Staff incompetence, muddling and disorder lay at the very root of our humiliations. I don't think it is too much to say that a competent trained staff with defined duties which it knew how to perform would have saved us 50 millions at the very least.[18]

Repington, Ellison and Wilson were others who believed that if the General Staff were not made the blue ribbon of the service it would be stifled by the administrative staff. Wilson recorded one episode in this long struggle in his Diary on 9 October 1904:

> After lunch I went down to Charlie Douglas [Adjutant-General] and took him out for a couple of hours walk. We talked over our present army position and he is very fearsome (sic) of the way things are going. He was very down on N.G. for idleness and slackness. I wrote N.G. a long letter

tonight about the new Decentralization Scheme and how I thought the General Staff was being squeezed out. How important I thought it was to take a stand now and to make certain that the General Staff in Commands was not absorbed by the Administrative Staff, pointing out that the proposals of Douglas and others were that in every command the Administrative staff officers were to be *much* senior to the General Staff which I feared would lead to the gradual extinction of the newly formed General Staff and the glorification of the Administrative Staff into the old and pestilent form of Chief Staff Officer . . .[19]

The conflicting schools of thought were made manifest in reactions to the Report of a Committee on General Staff Appointments in 1904, of which Maj.-Gen. H. D. Hutchinson was chairman and the other members were Maj.-Gen. H. S. G. Miles, Brig.-Gen. H. M. Lawson and Col. J. S. Ewart. The Committee's main recommendations may be summarized as follows. The General Staff was not to be a separate corps and good service in the Adjutant-General's or Quartermaster-General's branch should be a distinct recommendation for employment on it. All appointments would be for four years without extension, and except in very special circumstances a p.s.c. should be obligatory. The reward for approved General Staff service would be accelerated promotion, normally by a brevet up to lieutenant-colonel and above that by selection for substantive colonel. A certain number of Staff College graduates were to be attached to Headquarters for one year immediately after leaving Camberley. The chief avenue of appointment to the General Staff was therefore the Staff College, and 'in the process of time it will result, from the preferential treatment accorded to officers of the General Staff that such officers will hold the majority of important posts in the Army'. The Committee also recommended that the General Staff should wear a distinctive uniform of crossed belts, but this was not at first adopted. Generals Miles (Director of Recruiting and Organization) and Lawson (Director of Movements and Quarterings) appended a memorandum opposing the 'blue ribbon' emphasis of the Report. In order to combine experience with ability they urged that the majority of General Staff officers should be selected from those who had served or were serving in one of the branches of the Administrative Staff.

It seems clear to us that, if the recommendation in this memorandum is not adopted, the General Staff will suffer from lack of administrative knowledge which cannot fail to be prejudicial to the Service, especially when such officers reach the higher posts, and the efficiency of the Administrative Staff will be lowered: because the better class of officer may decline appointment thereon in the hopes of being ultimately selected for the General Staff. Further we consider that, unless the General Staff be selected in this manner the Staff of the Army will lack homogeneity, and jealousy and friction may perhaps result.[20]

The details of the Hutchinson Committee's recommendations were criticized at great length in the Army Council, and in June 1905 Gen. Miles elaborated his misgivings in a memorandum. The choice, he felt, lay between two organizations: a 'staff apart', with specialized tasks and where the appointment would carry General Staff status; or a selected body of officers who were accepted as qualified for staff appointments where the man rather than the job would form the basis of a General Staff list. Miles resented the pejorative connotations that seemed to be attaching themselves to the term 'administration'. Administration was referred to as though it concerned purely indoors office work but this was far from true. 'There is no better practice,' he wrote by way of illustration, 'than drawing up large bodies of troops in ceremonial.' His two chief worries were that an over-specialized General Staff would be lacking in essential administrative experience, and that too much favouring of the General Staff would lead to feelings of jealousy and a sense of inferiority on the part of the Adjutant-General's branch. These apprehensions were shared by several senior officers at the War Office including Sir Charles Douglas and Sir James Wolfe Murray (Master-General of the Ordnance).[21]

Meanwhile, on the invitation of Arnold-Forster, Henry

Wilson had gone behind the back of his chief, Lyttleton, to present his own views on the Geneal Staff. His paper, sent to Arnold-Forster on 6 June 1905, seems to have been (in the words of Dr Gooch) 'the most incisive contribution on the question of the General Staff so far made'. Eventually it was to prove very influential. The objectives of the General Staff, argued Wilson, were to gather together the ablest men in the Army and by a system of promotional inducements to ensure that they always controlled the Army's fortunes. It should also form a school of thought in order that the well-considered advice of a collective body of experts would always be available to the Secretary of State for War. If these goals were to be achieved, Wilson believed, the C.G.S. must be relieved of all routine work and given absolute control over the General Staff so that he could act as the Secretary of State's sole adviser on strategy. (It was Lyttleton's failure to pursue even this dazzling prospect that so exasperated and depressed Wilson.) Finally, the General Staff should be an *élite* composed of the pick of each year's Staff College graduates whose incentive would be accelerated promotion.[22]

Wilson's proposals received weighty support on 28 June 1905 with the presentation, as a C.I.D. paper, of a supplementary memorandum by the Esher Committee or Triumvirate. This was much more precise and specific about the role and organization of the General Staff than the original Report and concluded:

> The experience of South Africa has proved to demonstrate that the army suffers from the want of a trained General Staff. The Japanese have created such a staff, with the result that huge forces have been handled in the field with conspicuous success. Great Britain alone of great military Powers has neglected to make this essential provision. In the earnest hope that this vital defect may be remedied before we are again called upon to conduct large military operations, we venture to urge that the measures suggested should be taken without further delay.[23]

In the autumn of 1905 Arnold-Forster, under the prompting of Clarke, Esher, Repington and Wilson made belated attempts to form a General Staff, including authorizing Wilson to leak a draft memorandum (based on Wilson's own paper) to the Press. That he was frustrated was due primarily to Lyttleton's obduracy in clinging to office and the Prime Minister's lack of interest. It was therefore left to Haldane to garner the credit for establishing the General Staff which should have been in existence before the end of 1904.[24]

Personalities were of crucial importance for the early fortunes of the General Staff. Haldane's advent to the War Office was speedily followed by a strengthening of the 'blue ribbon' school in influential positions. Although Haldane was unwilling to force a showdown with the Government over Lyttleton, he did the next best thing by promptly appointing Sir William Nicholson Quartermaster-General in succession to Plumer with the promise that he would succeed Lyttleton. Robertson, Wilson (a close friend of Nicholson's) and the War Minister's soldier cousin, Sir Aylmer Haldane, may all have had a hand in 'Nick's' appointment. Esher was chiefly responsible for getting Maj.-Gen. Sir Douglas Haig recalled from India in August 1906, first to replace Stopford as Director of Military Training, and the following year to succeed Hutchinson as Director of Staff Duties.[25] With Wilson already the driving force in the latter directorate and Esher, Clarke and Repington all maintaining indirect pressure, the prospects for action improved. Most important, Haldane himself, until in the course of 1906 he became preoccupied with Army reorganization, showed enthusiasm for the development of the General Staff along the lines sketched by the Esher Committee. His inclination towards the 'blue ribbon' school is evident in a letter to Spenser Wilkinson:

The Esher Report is far from being like Holy Writ. But for the present it does to work under. The broad object which impresses itself on my vision is the fatal confusion which arises if the General Staff get immersed or even entangled in administration . . . I am busy trying to impress the principle of division of labour on my Generals.[26]

These efforts at last bore fruit in the Special Army Order of 12 September 1906 which established the General Staff on a firm basis that only required minor readjustment before 1914.[27] At the outset, staff duties at Headquarters were differentiated from those in Commands and Districts. They were:

> . . . to advise on the strategical distribution of the Army, to supervise the education of officers, and the training and preparation of the Army for war, to study military schemes, offensive and defensive, to collect and collate military intelligence, to direct the general policy in Army matters, and to secure continuity of action in the execution of that policy.

The General Staff would consequently be drawn from officers 'considered most likely to prove capable of forming a school of military thought'. The Order skilfully combined the views of the 'blue ribbon' and 'Administrative' schools of thought in dealing with the composition of the General Staff. From the former was taken the scheme of a specific list of posts to constitute General Staff appointments, and from the latter a special list of officers considered qualified for such posts – the 'General Staff List' which would not be published. To qualify for this list it would usually be necessary to have a p.s.c. and at least eight years' service. Experience on the administrative staff, stated the Order guardedly, while not indispensable, would not be disregarded. All General Staff appointments would be for four years, the first year being probationary, followed by a return to regimental service for at least one year. General Staff officers below the rank of lieutenant-colonel who did not have the p.s.c. could automatically go to the Staff College for one year's training at the end of their staff duty without having to take the entrance examination. The role of the Staff College as the nursery of the General Staff was thus specifically recognized.[28] Approved service on the General Staff would normally be rewarded with accelerated promotion; by brevet up to lieutenant-colonel and substantive rank above it.

In Appendix A were detailed General Staff duties at the War Office and in Commands. The scope of the Staff Duties directorate, for example, was: 'Organization, formation and

instruction of the General Staff, appointments to the General
Staff, entrance to Staff and Cadet Colleges, higher training
and promotion examinations of officers, foreign language
examination, preparation of works on military operations,
military history, and General Staff libraries.' Appendix B
detailed the establishment of the General Staff. The total at
Headquarters was 57 (D.M.O. 35, D.S.D. 9, D.M.T. 13),
while the total in Commands, Districts and Overseas Stations
was 144[29] giving a grand total of 171. In the following year
the General Staff gradings were finally settled as General
Staff Officer (G.S.O.) 1, 2, and 3.

In 1907 the military members of the Army Council succeeded
in diluting the rigorous qualification for the General Staff List
laid down in Army Order 233. It was agreed that G.S.O. 3s
need not be selected from the General Staff List; that the eight
years' minimum service qualification should be dropped; and
that accelerated promotion might be awarded for meritorious
service in any staff post and not on the General Staff only.[30]

Although these modifications showed that the 'Administrative
school' was still strong in the Army Council, the issue of Army
Order 233 witnessed a considerable triumph for the 'blue
ribbon' school. All that was needed to translate a paper victory
into practical advantages was a British version of von Moltke
as Chief of the General Staff. Several individuals deserve
credit for accomplishing what only a few years previously had
appeared unthinkable, notable among them Esher, Clarke,
Repington, Nicholson, Arnold-Forster and Haldane. Not least
the practical details of the General Staff organization were the
work of Henry Wilson. As early as 24 March 1904 he had noted
with pardonable self-congratulation 'It is getting known that I
am running the General Staff'; and in this instance his biographer's eulogy only slightly exaggerates his achievement:

While some credit for this tardy consummation of an urgently
needed reform was undoubtedly due to the Esher Committee,
some to Mr Arnold Forster, and some to Sir W. Nicholson
for his helpful attitude from the time that he joined the Army
Council, the main credit belongs to Wilson, although he was

still serving in a comparatively subordinate position in Pall Mall. By his initiative, by his comprehensive and prescient understanding of the question in all its bearings, and by his indomitable resolution in the struggle to achieve his object, he had not only devised a workable and an effective scheme, but he had also in the end overcome the resistance of hostile and unwilling members of the Army Council to its provisions, and he had made it a prominent feature in the accepted military organization of the country.[31]

In January 1907 the General Staff was installed in the recently completed War Office building in Whitehall. Thus for the first time all its departments were under the same roof. There was a marked improvement in staff work at headquarters, particularly after Nicholson replaced Lyttleton as Chief of the General Staff in 1908. The General Staff did indeed become the 'blue ribbon' of the Army, not least because of the attraction of accelerated promotion, whereas the Administrative Staff tended to be avoided by the abler officers.[32]

Another manifestation of the new professional enthusiasm which accompanied the foundation of the General Staff was the importance attached to Staff Conferences and Staff Rides.

At the beginning of January 1905, a large number of officers holding General Staff appointments at Headquarters and in districts and commands assembled at the Staff College for a conference which lasted over several days. The idea of holding such a conference was entirely Wilson's; all the arrangements, as well as the programme that was to be followed, had been worked out by him, and it was acknowledged by all who took part in the proceedings that the scheme had proved a success. It thenceforward became the practice to hold these conferences each year in January, and not the least of the benefits arising from such meetings was that General Staff officers were brought together and became acquainted with each other, and that a bond of sympathy and of mutual understanding was established amongst them as a body.

The participants would have derived even more benefit from them had Lyttleton or Hutchinson shown ability to analyse mistakes and point out lessons at what Wilson facetiously referred to in his Diary as the evening 'bow-wows'.[33]

The scope of the General Staff to hold Staff Tours or Rides – simulated war exercises without troops lasting several days – was improved when Haldane made provision in each year's estimates for money to be expended on such exercises at the General Staff's discretion. Some idea of the importance attached to these exercises may be gained from the fact that Henry Wilson began working up background material (from European campaigns) as early as 23 April for the Autumn Staff Ride in the Severn Valley in 1905.

In 1908 the Staff Ride was given additional significance as a practical test of the new manual of Field Service Regulations Part II which dealt with the organization and administration of troops in the field during war. Preliminary war games were held at the War Office on 16 and 21 October to familiarize officers with the problems of the actual Ride from 26 to 30 October. The rather bizarre scenario envisaged a war between Scotland and Holland on neutral ground. Sixty-nine staff officers, including an Australian, Maj.-Gen. J. C. Hoad, were confronted with problems of disembarkation, entraining and detraining, accommodation and concentration for battle. Apart from the usual evening conferences there was a general conference on the last day when the new Chief of the General Staff, Sir William Nicholson, summed up the lessons to be learned and laid down general principles for dealing with major staff problems. The main defect revealed as far as staff work was concerned was the lack of coordination between the different branches which on several occasions resulted in the congestion of the Army.[34]

Staff Conferences and Staff Tours thus became regular General Staff exercises after 1905, testing intellectual ability and practical knowledge, providing opportunity for the rapid assimilation of problems and the issuing of orders in situations of simulated stress, and, not least, enabling officers to become familiar with colleagues with whom they would have to cooperate in war.

If the General Staff was to live up to the hopes of its champions such as Esher, Clarke and Wilson as the 'brain' of the Army which would be instrumental in forming a 'school of thought', one would naturally expect the intellectual ferment to find outlet in a first-class professional journal. In this respect progress was rather disappointing. Only towards the end of Nicholson's term of office was the *Army Review* first published with the aims of disseminating the latest professional information, inculcating the lessons of history and encouraging the study of the military art. The editor, Col. Repington, had been a brilliant staff officer but he was not ideally suited for this post. He and Henry Wilson had been bitter enemies for several years since the scandal over Repington's affair with a diplomat's wife for which he had had to leave the Army; Repington was therefore effectively excluded from Wilson's extremely important Directorate of Military Operations. He had also made some other prominent enemies as *The Times*' military correspondent. Moreover, he admitted to Northcliffe that he had accepted the editorship solely because he was short of money.[35]

At least the publication of the *Review* from 1911 to 1914 provided a forum for debate and showed that the General Staff was making a serious attempt to educate the Army for war. Unfortunately, the needs of security and the prevailing view that serving officers should steer completely clear of all topics even remotely connected with politics, prevented the *Review* from becoming a platform from which the C.I.G.S. could expound General Staff opinions. But in any case the *Review* barely had time to establish itself before its brief run was ended by the outbreak of war in 1914.

Meanwhile, the return of Henry Wilson to the War Office in 1910 as D.M.O. marked the beginning of the General Staff's preoccupation with practical planning for war in alliance with France and against Germany. Although in comparison with what had gone before enormous strides were made in the years 1910–14, most arrangements were bedevilled by the underlying assumption that the war would be short. Thus, for example, a War Office Committee considered in 1910 that in event of war the major pressure on the General Staff would be over in two months. The first edition of the *War Book* in 1912 similarly detailed arrangements for a short and limited war. The routine circulation of messages and telegrams, if adhered to, would soon have brought War Office business to a halt. There was no definite acknowledgement that military planning must continue after the mobilization phase other than in theatres where the Expeditionary Force was not operating. The General Staff section responsible for the preparation of all maps would cease to function on the outbreak of war; and the Staff College would be closed.[36]

In conclusion, while there was probably a steady improvement in practical General Staff work both at the War Office and in Commands, there was a marked decline in the higher direction. Nicholson had been a great improvement on Lyttleton but he too showed signs of tiring and of losing interest before the end of his term of office in 1912. Sir George Clarke was no longer in England, while Esher, quite apart from turning his energies to other subjects, lost much of his political influence with the death of Edward VII. Haldane's active encouragement of the General Staff, though vital in his early days in office, had been brief as he became embroiled in the controversies surrounding his Territorial Army scheme. From 1912 to 1914 the two officers chiefly responsible for the General Staff were Sir John French as C.I.G.S. and Col. J. E. B. Seely as Secretary of State for War; the former was certainly not the long-awaited von Moltke, nor the latter a Roon. The General Staff was unfortunate in having this comparatively weak team at its head during what Henry Wilson and others at the time recognized to be a crucial pre-war period.

Worse changes were to follow the Curragh Incident in March 1914 over which both Seely and French resigned. Asquith himself took over the War Office and Sir Charles Douglas, the former Adjutant-General who had espoused the 'Administrative' view of the General Staff, became C.I.G.S. Thus, when the political crisis arose at the end of July, the Prime Minister was fully occupied with Cabinet business, while Douglas had so little standing that he was not intially summoned to meetings of the C.I.D. 'The General Staff,' as Dr Gooch justly remarks, 'went into war under the direction of a novice as far as knowledge of their functioning was concerned.'[37]

The existence, from 1909 onwards, of a British officer entitled Chief of the Imperial General Staff, has sometimes led to the logical but incorrect supposition that there also existed an Imperial General Staff. Certainly the Esher Committee had entertained the hope that the General Staff would in time breed replicas in the Dominions. Two factors above all prevented the realization of this dream. Ironically, at the very time that Britain was instituting a Committee of *Imperial* Defence, and a General Staff with mainly Overseas and Colonial military problems in mind, the growth of the German Navy and closer cooperation with France were drawing British interests inexorably towards Europe. Conversely, from the Dominions' viewpoint, a closer military relationship with Britain stood little hope in an era marked by the rise of Colonial nationalism and of deep suspicion of British designs for hegemony in any scheme of Imperial Federation. Consequently, even in 1914 the grandiose initials 'C.I.G.S.' denoted British aspirations rather than existing fact; 'an impressive name masked the loosest of structures'.

It was already apparent at the Colonial Conference of 1907 that Britain was preoccupied with the possibility of a major war in Europe and was chiefly interested in discovering in advance what help she could expect from the Empire. Haldane thus concluded his address:

> Our great object must be to make the General Staff an imperial school of military thought, all the members of which are imbued with the same traditions, accustomed to look at strategical problems from the same point of view, and acquainted with the principles and theories generally accepted at headquarters.[38]

The Dominions representatives, with South Africa the most

reluctant, eventually approved a cautiously-worded resolution which emphasized that the General Staff was a purely advisory body.

Esher propagated the idea that staff education might be made the basis of greater Imperial military cooperation. Canada was just beginning to form a small General Staff of her own and the War Office was concerned lest she slip away from its influence as regards staff qualifications and training. Two Canadian officers per annum were to be admitted to Camberley provided they could pass the usual entrance examination. If a common standard of military knowledge and uniformity of thought were to be attained, a Staff College education was essential for all members of an Imperial General Staff, and for the foreseeable future only Camberley and Quetta could fulfil this role. In the meantime, British staff officers could be attached to the Dominion forces and Dominion officers sent to London. A War Office memorandum of July 1909 saw education as 'the keynote' for the creation of an Imperial General Staff: 'not only that higher education at a Staff College which is essential if the Imperial General Staff is to be composed of a body of officers trained to *think alike* on all matters of principle, but [also] the preliminary education, by which officers can be so grounded and prepared as to be able to profit by the Staff College training when their time comes to be selected to go to the course at Camberley or Quetta, or, in the future, at the local Staff Colleges.'[39]

At a Defence sub-Committee of the Imperial Conference of 1911, Sir William Nicholson pointed out that only Canada had so far been able to produce officers sufficiently well-educated to compete for Camberley; in any case the latter housed barely 100 officers and was already producing too few p.s.c.s for Britain's own needs. He proposed to expand Camberley so that twelve to fifteen officers could be taken annually from the Dominions. The Canadian and Australian representatives responded favourably to the suggestion that they might pay about £200 per student per annum. However, the former's Defence Minister, Sir Frederick Borden, criticized the paper before them on the grounds that it considered Imperial Defence solely from the Mother Country's point of view. In what circumstances could the Dominions expect the Imperial (i.e. British) Army to come to their support? Nicholson could only agree to the withdrawal of the Paper while tactfully requesting the Dominions to prepare not only local defence schemes but also for an expeditionary force in a general war – without of course specifying the enemy. 'It is much better to hold our tongues about it and not say anything, according to the old Persian proverb, "What two ears only hear, God himself does not know".'[40]

Quite apart from the Dominions' (and especially Canada's) well-founded suspicions that Britain envisaged an Imperial General Staff as a sure means of committing them in advance to assist Britain in a European War, the feeling was growing in Britain that the C.I.D. rather than the General Staff should provide the means for Imperial military cooperation and planning. Consequently, no significant developments took place after 1911 in the discussions concerning an Imperial General Staff. Between 1903 and 1911 only seven Canadian officers, four Australians, two New Zealanders and two from Natal had passed through either Camberley or Quetta. It was therefore not surprising that by 1914 the Dominions had only very small and rudimentary General Staffs and that they were forced either to appoint non-p.s.c.s or accept a large quota of British Staff officers. Canada in particular showed a strong preference for the former course and was well on the way to developing her own independent General Staff by 1914.[41]

Before the First World War, Australia alone sent senior officers to London as representatives attached to the British General Staff. The first, Col. W. T. Bridges, was kept so badly briefed from home and his responsibilities were so anomalous that he remained in a kind of limbo, and returned to Australia in November 1910 after just over a year in England. His successor in 1912, Lt-Col Legge, did at least have well-defined functions, but they were so circumscribed that he was little more than a junior observer at the War Office.[42]

Thus the splendid vision of an Imperial General Staff was

nullified by the widely differing political and strategic concerns of Britain and the Dominions, not to speak of the considerable differences between the Dominions themselves. True, the outbreak of war in 1914 revealed that all but South Africa were immediately willing to assist Britain, but the war was also to demonstrate that 'the Imperial design came in practice to nothing'.[43]

For all its shortcomings the General Staff was beginning to effect a great improvement in the British Army by the outbreak of the First World War: among other things it established definite training principles by means of the staff manuals; contributed to practical staff work through field exercises at various levels; and provided a fairly efficient 'thinking department' at the War Office. That it did not achieve even more was largely due to the failure to discover a first class Chief of the General Staff. On a wider view the equivocal relationship between the General Staff and C.I.D. Secretariat as regards the analysis of defence problems and the formulation of national strategy was never properly resolved. The General Staff in effect became the 'brain of the Army' but the Royal Navy retained a 'brain' of its own (though a highly defective one since the Naval Staff was not created until 1912 and had scarcely begun to function before the outbreak of war in 1914),[44] and neither service's staff exercised a dominant influence on the C.I.D. It was therefore hardly surprising that as Secretary of State for War, Lord Kitchener, who had little sympathy for or understanding of the General Staff, should have virtually ignored it during 1914 and 1915. Only after Sir William Robertson became C.I.G.S. in December 1915 did the General Staff begin to play a prominent part in the formulation of strategy and by then the pattern of Britain's war effort had to a great extent become the prisoner of events.

As far as the Staff College is concerned, the significance of the formation of a General Staff can scarcely be exaggerated. At last the Army had recognized the importance of preparing for war in times of peace and that the ablest and keenest officers were necessary for this work. True, the General Staff had been created in typically pragmatic British fashion without being accompanied by a systematic re-organization of the military educational institutions which were to serve it; but when Brig.-Gen. Henry Wilson became Commandant at Camberley in January 1907, the unique importance of the College as the nursery of the General Staff was at last recognized.

CHAPTER 7. NOTES

1 See J. K. Dunlop, *op. cit.*, Appendix A.
2 John Gooch, 'The Origin and Development of the British and Imperial General Staffs to 1916' (unpublished doctoral dissertation, University of London, 1969), p. 16. I am greatly indebted in this chapter to Dr Gooch's scholarship and advice.
3 *Report of the War Office (Reconstitution) Committee*, Cd 1968, Part II, Section III, para. 3 (The Esher Committee). See also Gooch, *op. cit.*, pp. 16–19, 30–34, 54 *et seq.*
4 *Royal Commission on the War in South Africa*, Minutes of Evidence 881, 888, 5126–32.
5 W. R. Robertson, *op. cit.*, p. 130.
6 See especially the Esher Committee's letter to the Prime Minister which prefaces Part II of its Report (Cd 1968). For Ellison's important contribution to the General Staff section see Dunlop, *op. cit.*, pp. 205–6.
7 *Ibid.*, Part I (Cd 1932), Section I. Gooch, *op. cit.*, p. 106.
8 Henry Wilson's *Diary*, 1 February 1904. Balfour to Esher, 14 January 1904, Balfour Papers B.M. Ad Mss 49718 quoted by Gooch, *op. cit.*, p. 128. *Esher Journals and Letters*, Vol. 2, pp. 144–5.
9 For the duties of the three sections of the General Staff see Table 3 on p. 219.
10 Esher Committee *Report*, Part II, *passim*.
10 Gooch, *op. cit.*, p. 144.
11 Callwell, *Field-Marshal Sir Henry Wilson*, Vol. I, pp. 55–6.
12 Stopford's subsequent performance at Suvla Bay in August 1915 bore out Sir John French's assessment of 1904 that he was an awful pessimist and too much given to detail. See Gooch, *op. cit.*, p. 123.
13 Henry Wilson's reason for favouring Hutchinson as his Director was that 'he would probably let me do what I chose'. *Diary*, 18 March 1904.
14 Nicholson, Director General of Mobilisation and Military Intelligence until removed by the Esher Committee, was better equipped mentally than Lyttleton to be C.G.S. but this appointment was opposed by the King on the grounds that he was unpopular in the Army and unable to command its confidence since he had never held a field command in war. Esher to Knollys, 5 May 1907, RA W40/111.
15 Repington to Esher, 9 February 1904, Esher Papers, 'Army Letters', Vol. I. Clarke to Esher, 23 March 1904. *Ibid.*, 'Sir George Clarke', Vol. I, quoted by Gooch, *op. cit.*, pp. 150–1.
16 See for example Wilson's *Diary* entries for 2, 31 May, 7–10, 13–15 June 1904 and Callwell, *op. cit.*, I, p. 57. In surveying the year 1906

Wilson wrote on 31 December: 'N. G. has been increasingly useless until he has reached an almost incredible degree of uselessness'.

17 Esher Committee Report, Part II, Section III, para 23; Part III, Section I, para. 22.

18 Clarke to Esher, 13 June 1904, Esher Papers, 'Sir George Clarke', Vol. I, quoted by Gooch, *op. cit.*, p. 153.

19 Wilson's *Diary*, 9 October 1904.

20 *Report of Committee on General Staff Appointments* (Hutchinson Committee), A 935 1904.

21 *Minutes of Proceedings and Précis prepared for the Army Council*, 1905; Memorandum by General Miles, 9 June 1905. Appendix 1 to Précis no. 249, pp. 483–96, WO 163/10.

22 Callwell, *op. cit.*, I, p. 63. Wilson's *Diary* for 1905 has a great number of references to his memorandum and Arnold-Forster's use of it, e.g. 29, 30 May, 17, 18, 23, 28 August, 21 November.

23 'The General Staff', 28 June 1905, Cab 17/14.

24 Gooch gives a detailed account of Arnold-Forster's efforts on behalf of the General Staff. *Op. cit.*, pp. 189–210.

25 *Ibid.*, pp. 215–6.

26 Haldane to Wilkinson, 6 January, 1906, Wilkinson Papers 13/32, Ogilby Trust, quoted by Gooch, *op. cit.*, p. 217. Wilson's *Diary* for 1906 contains numerous very critical references to Haldane's scheme for Army re-organization, and thus undermines the popular belief that the War Minister succeeded in mollifying the generals by a display of patience and sweet reasonableness.

27 Army Order 233, 'Organisation of the General Staff', 12 September 1906, WO 123/48.

28 The Order did not apply to the Army in India whose administration, as was seen over the establishment of Quetta, was virtually independent of the War Office.

29 This figure included 8 at the Staff College, 8 at the R.M.C. (Sandhurst), 5 at the R.M.A. (Woolwich) and 3 at R.M.C. (Kingston).

30 *Minutes of Proceedings and Précis prepared for the Army Council*, 1907, WO 163/12. Précis no. 367, p. 71.

31 Wilson's *Diary*, 24 March 1904, and Callwell, *op. cit.*, I, p. 65.

32 J. Adye, *op. cit.*, p. 226. Gooch, *op. cit.*, pp. 243–4.

33 Callwell, *op. cit.*, I, p. 61. Wilson commented on Lyttleton's summing up at the Staff Conference at Aldershot 'N. G. was worse than ever at Conference tonight. He is really too appalling . . .'; and at the Severn Valley Ride 'N. G.'s summing up at the Conference was pitiable and only equalled by Hutch's concluding remarks in the Report'. *Diary*, 7 January and 31 December 1906.

34 Gooch, *op. cit.*, pp. 250–2.

35 *Ibid.*, p. 270.

36 *Ibid.*, pp. 260–8.

37 *Ibid.*, pp. 275–6.

38 *Minutes and Proceedings of the Colonial Conference 1907*, Cd 3523, p. 98, quoted by Gooch, *op. cit.*, p. 288.

39 'Proposals for so organising the Military Forces of the Empire as to ensure their effective co-operation in the event of war.' C. G. S. 17 July 1909. Part III, 'Proposals for the development of the Imperial General Staff', WO 106/43.

40 Proceedings of a Committee of the Imperial Conference convened to discuss questions of Defence (Military) at the War Office. 14 June 1911, W.O. 106/43.

41 Progress of the Imperial General Staff and the development of its functions, 19 May 1911, Cab. 5/2/2/84c. For a full discussion of the development of General Staff organization in the Dominions up to 1914 see Gooch, *op. cit.*, pp. 319–56.

42 *Ibid.*, pp. 349–50.

43 *Ibid.*, p. 356.

44 For good, concise accounts of Admiralty resistance to the formation of a Naval Staff and Churchill's success in overcoming it, see W. S. Churchill, *The World Crisis, 1911–1914* (London, 1923), Vol. I, pp. 82–3, 90–3, 507–11 and A. J. Marder, *From Dreadnought to Scapa Flow*, Vol. I, pp. 205, 246–9, 256–7, 265–6, 400–1.

CHAPTER EIGHT

A school of thought:
Henry Wilson and the Staff College
1906-1910

Henry Wilson was one of the most flamboyant and controversial officers of his era, and certainly one of the most remarkable Commandants in the history of the Staff College. He was a tall, gangling Ulsterman who impressed everyone he met – though not always favourably – by his sharp intelligence, caustic tongue, oddities of dress and quirky sense of humour. He was incorrigibly flippant and loved to play the buffoon. Characteristically he capitalized on his irregular features – further disfigured by a war wound – by claiming the distinction of being the ugliest officer in the British Army.

Apart from an almost total lack of regimental command experience, he was admirably qualified to be head of the Staff College. A fertile imagination, a wide outlook upon public affairs, an indomitable enthusiasm and 'that magnetic power of compelling the admiration and the affection of others which can best be summed up in the expression "personality"' – these were the qualities of the ideal Commandant sketched by his friend and biographer Charles Callwell, and Wilson had them all. Also, reading his Diaries, it is easy to agree with his most recent biographer that Wilson's three-and-a-half years at Camberley were among his happiest and most rewarding times. The position gave him prestige in the Army, and with it the power to influence opinion and to create a 'School of Thought' among the ablest of the younger officers who would henceforth look to him for help and guidance as he himself looked to Lord Roberts.[1]

Although the value of the Staff College was now widely appreciated by the Army, there were two reasons why it was of crucial importance that the high standard achieved by Rawlinson should be maintained by his successor. Firstly, the years after 1906 were to witness the establishment of the General Staff, for whose members the Staff College constituted virtually the exclusive source. Secondly, it was in these years that British military planning swung powerfully – if not irreversibly – towards intervention in a future continental war on the side of France against Germany. Thus at long last staff officers could be trained with a specific and realistic contingency in mind. This was the Armageddon that Lord Esher later depicted in flowery, but essentially accurate prose:

> From the Surrey village where, as Head of the Staff College, he [Wilson] taught the principles of war, his pupils went forth imbued with a sense of its cataclysmic imminence. Below the ascending woods where he so often stood, there lay before his mind's eye, in lieu of cricket fields and polo grounds, curving reaches of the Meuse and bloodstained flats of Flanders . . . When others prattled of peace, he prepared young men's souls for war, not an indefinite war, as men barricade their doors against imaginary thieves, but for a specific struggle with the German nations, the early stages of which he foresaw in detail with a soldier's insight.[2]

His qualifications and influential supporters notwithstanding, Wilson's appointment at the Staff College was only achieved after a long and unpleasant wrangle with the Chief of the General Staff. This is worth recounting in some detail because it not only underlines how highly the post was regarded, but also reveals how unpopular Wilson had already become with some of his military superiors.

Wilson first heard in March 1905 that Rawlinson had been promoted Brigadier-General and was soon to leave the Staff College, but his hopes of succeeding his friend were temporarily frustrated because Lyttleton vetoed Rawlinson's move to Aldershot. Meanwhile Wilson, who in these years was extremely hard up, gambled on returning to Camberley by again taking the lease of a charming cottage, Grove End, two miles from College where he and his wife had lived happily thirteen years previously when he was a student.[3]

By July 1906 Rawlinson's term at Camberley was drawing to a close and the question of his successor became an interminable matter for gossip and intrigue at the War Office. Wilson was by far the strongest candidate but he was kept in suspense until the end of October.

Lyttleton's ostensible reason for opposing Wilson's promotion was that he was too friendly with Lord Roberts and had too many enemies in the Army. When Wilson discussed the subject with Sir Charles Douglas (Adjutant-General), the latter 'let fly about N.G., for whom he has the greatest contempt' and said 'he had great difficulty in not spitting in his face'. On 13 September Wilson recorded that Lyttleton was still maintaining that the former had so many enemies that if he was appointed there would be such an outcry in the Army that the War Office could not face it. Lyttleton's first choice was still the competent but unassertive gunner, Col. E. S. May, whose unfortunate soubriquet was 'Edna'. Rawlinson told Wilson that other candidates preferred to him included Robertson, Altham, Bethune, Allenby, Reade and Robb: in short, as Wilson laconically noted, 'anyone except me'.

Among Wilson's many staunch supporters, however, were Rawlinson, Hutchinson, French, Roberts and Esher. The two last named in particular pressed Wilson's claims upon Haldane at the beginning of October and it seems probable that their influence was decisive.

On 5 October Esher wrote to Roberts:

All I know about the Staff College is this, that there is some idea that Mr Haldane will appoint May to succeed Rawlinson. But I also know that he has also been very much exercised in his mind to discover an officer who exactly comes up to the standard which he has fixed for himself. The only candidate he has ever discussed *with me* is Henry Wilson, whom personally I think qualified perfectly to hold that post, by intellectual attainments and general capacity.

Mr Haldane has been told that this appointment would be very unpopular, but I have altogether been unable to discover the reason for this statement.

From all I have heard of Henry Wilson, I hope that he will be the next Commandant. I have never said a word on this subject to anyone but you, and to French, who absolutely agrees.

If you *disagree*, I wish you would tell me at once, as there is no one whose opinion would, I feel sure, carry more weight with the Secretary of State.

I am all against a worthy but stupid officer being appointed to that post. Wilson may have demerits, for all I know, but no one can say of him that he lacks intellect.

I *know* that he has one or two powerful enemies in the W.O. (sic).

and Roberts replied:

I entirely agree with you as to the fitness of Henry Wilson for the Commandantship of the Staff College, and I have written to Mr Haldane expressing my hope that he will be appointed. I know that Wilson has enemies at the W.O. and that they are trying to make out he is generally unpopular in the Army. So far from this being the case, I should say that Wilson is perhaps the best known and the most popular man in the Army. He is looked up to as a very promising officer, chiefly I believe on account of the excellent manner in which he performed his Staff duties in South Africa, and I know that the Officers now at the Staff College are looking forward with great hopefulness to his being Rawlinson's successor.

The Staff College in the past has suffered from not having had practical men at its head. Hildyard did much to improve matters. It fell off under Miles, Rawlinson has raised it up again. And now a good man – above all a man of character – is needed to keep it up to the mark.

None of the possible men I have heard mentioned can, in my opinion, and I feel sure I am expressing the opinion of the Army generally, be compared to Henry Wilson for the post.

The fact is that Wilson has too much character for some of the men with whom he is associated at the War Office.

On 24 October Wilson's selection for the Staff College was confirmed and encircled in red ink in his Diary. It was a 'red letter day' in the fullest sense, for the appointment meant that he had gone from Captain to Brigadier-General in only five years and one month.[4]

Wilson's regime did in many ways reflect the unique character to which Roberts referred. His natural flair for teaching was manifest in his periodic Commandant's lectures, and in his informal conversations with the students. His irrepressible humour, avoidance of dogmatic utterances, and strong personal opinion on most issues combined to arouse interest even in comparatively arid subjects. Col Lonsdale Hale, for many years the Professor of Military History at Sandhurst, told the Junior Division of 1908 that a lecture Wilson had just given on the topography of Bohemia and its effect on the 1866 campaign was the best he had ever heard.[5] Like Henderson before him he also possessed the gift of always persuading the student that he greatly valued his opinion, which was particularly useful in discussing points that had arisen in a lecture or staff tour. One of his staff at the College remarked that 'his influence on the students was extraordinary, which was not to be wondered at considering his remarkable personality'. 'He seemed to give out some of his personality to those he was with,' remarked another.[6]

Lt. A. P. (later Field-Marshal Earl) Wavell arrived at the Staff College in January 1909 at the very early age of twenty-five. He left this vivid impression of Henry Wilson as a teacher:

'Henry Wilson was tall and lean with a curiously shaped head and face, humorous and ugly. He liked to refer to himself as the ugliest man in the Army. He had a very quick and agile brain, a ready wit, a great fund of humour and geniality. He was a very interesting lecturer.' The themes of his occasional lectures, Wavell added, were invariably highly topical and contentious matters such as the inevitability of war with Germany and the consequent necessity for conscription. Sir

George Barrow, then on the Directing Staff, recorded a remarkably similar impression. He regarded Henry Wilson as:

the most original, imaginative and humorous man I have ever known. He riveted the attention and made the dullest subjects bright. He brought something new, something nobody else had thought of into the discussions of lectures and problems, and his summings-up at conferences and on Staff tours were models of well-balanced judgements.

Since Wilson extemporized from notes and published practically nothing, it is difficult to recapture the qualities that made him so arresting a speaker. One set of lecture notes were, however, begged from him by Lord Roberts, and from these some hint of his appeal may be glimpsed. Under the astonishing title (for an audience of staff officers) of *Psychology: the Science which classifies and analyses the phenomenon of the human mind*, one finds a down-to-earth comparison between the British Army and the German. Are we, he inquired sceptically, more religious than the Germans – for fanaticism or fatalism may be great moral assets. Again, asserting that 'By far the most important individuals in an army are the Generals and their Staff Officers', he asked whether our p.s.c. officers were as good as the Germans. 'It is undoubtedly stretching a concession almost to breaking point.' He drove home the German advantage in having a permanently organized capital staff by the sarcastic remark, 'the Berlin Staff takes the field as the Imperial Headquarters, whereas I understand no one has the temerity to suggest that the Army Council should take the field when we mobilize'. He concluded with the sober forecast: 'It cannot be contended that . . . this mass of un-Generalled, unstaffed, under-officered and ill-trained men [of the B.E.F.] will compete with any hope at all against the well-Generalled, well-staffed, well-officered and well-trained and drilled men of the German Army. Even psychology won't do that for us.'[8]

Henry Wilson's Diaries reveal that he was extremely robust and energetic and was possessed by a passion for sports and exercise. Indeed, one suspects that much of the awed respect in which the students held this often untidy and ungainly middle-aged general stemmed from his ability to out-play most of them and out-run, out-walk and out-cycle them all. He habitually, for instance, required the instructors and students to run the two miles of von Bredow's charge at Mars la Tour during the annual visit to the Franco-German battlefields. On 5 May 1909 he proudly records 'I took the extreme left, and so had much the furthest to go, and yet was easily in first, Perks [Col. Perceval, in charge of the Senior Division] coming next. Not bad on my 45th birthday; 2 miles over plough and 3 young seed (?).'[9]

Another regular feature of the course was an annual visit to North Wales to practise staff problems connected with mountain warfare. Apart from serious attention to staff work, Wilson used these Welsh forays as further trials of the physical endurance of his students, delighting as ever to prove that – like a mountain goat – he could race them to the summits. 'Today,' he records on 30 June 1909, 'we walked up Moel Siabod and although I stayed back at first talking to [Lt] Irby, I caught the others up and got on top first . . . I went from Hotel to top in 63 minutes and I could have done it in about 55 if I had not hung back.' Moel Siabod rises 2,880 feet above sea-level, and rears its crest some 2,200 feet above the Capel Curig hotel, so Wilson was clearly very fit; he frequently alludes to members of his staff who were unable to stand the pace, more particularly on his long-distance Continental cycling tours.

Despite Wilson's own unorthodoxy in dress, manners and ideas, there was still a tendency for the staff to show suspicion towards unusual students. Thus Wavell describes the most attractive of his friends at the Staff College, Everard Calthrop, who enjoyed the unique distinction of passing through both the Japanese and British Staff Colleges and who was killed in action as a lieutenant-colonel in 1915:

> He was the son of an artist and was himself artistic to the finger-tips. I always wondered why he chose the Army as a profession, but he was a good soldier. He had spent several years [1904–8] in Japan as a language student, and was a

great admirer of Japanese artistry and of their simplicity
of life. He himself reduced the baggage of life to a minimum.
I think he never had more than one suit and one pair of
boots at a time. I remember his coming to stay at Cranborne
for a week-end and arriving on a bicycle with a small
package containing his washing kit and one shirt which he
considered ample equipment. It shook my very conventional
mother to the core. He had the most original and independent mind of our term at the Staff College; but the Directing
Staff considered him too unorthodox and he did not make the
impression his abilities deserved.

According to Wavell, the instructors put little stress on the
factor of morale, or how to induce it and maintain it, apparently
taking it as axiomatic that the British soldier was naturally
brave. Nor were the students asked to consider the differences
that would occur in handling a national as distinct from a
regular army. Calthrop was the only one who had thought
about such matters, and he made the original suggestion that
a section of the Intelligence Branch at the War Office should be
created to study the reactions of the average British civilian
to war and the Army. The teachers scoffed at an idea which, in
Wavell's opinion, would have obviated many of the mistakes
made in the First World War.[10]

Henry Wilson took up his duties at Camberley convinced
that the Staff College had a crucial role to play both in implementing a new military policy and in improving operational
efficiency. As one of his students vividly put it, 'He had persuaded himself that the Juggernaut car of war was already
lumbering on its way. "The storm-clouds," he would say, "are
gathering over Europe. I do not know what will draw the
lightning, but something will and soon." He had made up his
mind that only one course was open to us, namely to join
the French and with them fight the Germans. He bent all the
resources of his fertile mind to that end. The students at the
Staff College were obvious and handy instruments, and he
got to work on us at once.'[11]

In his opening address to the students, Wilson made plain

his hostility to any scheme which threatened to bring about a separation in training for administrative as distinct from general staff duties.

During the autumn of 1906, Haldane approved the plan for a six-months course under the distinguished geographer, Halford Mackinder, at the London School of Economics designed to prepare officers for higher appointments on the administrative staff of the Army. Wilson opposed the course on the grounds that it might 'do an infinity of harm to the S.C.', and determined to fight it for all he was worth. 'Neither N. G. nor Hutch,' he wrote, 'have the slightest idea what Mackinder's school may mean, but Miles [Director of Recruiting and Organization] sees clearly enough that it may lead to a rival to the S.C. and complete separation of Administrative and General Staff.' He proposed to attend as many lectures as possible 'so as to be in the best position to fight the game if necessary'.

After attending the opening lectures in January 1907 his worst suspicions were confirmed: the course was a dangerous experiment devised by Miles to siphon administrative staff appointments away from Staff College graduates and so reduce the prestige and power of the College. Mackinder informed him that Miles had prohibited Staff College instructors from attending the lectures. Thirty-one officers took the first course, which ended in July 1907 and all were said to have done well. The subjects examined were not overtly military but included law, economics and statistics.[12] It is doubtful if Wilson's sniping was influential because the courses continued to run until the First World War, by which time 241 officers had qualified.

Wilson inherited an excellent instructional staff of seven officers, including Col. (later Maj.-Gen. Sir George) Aston and Lt-Col (later Lt-Gen. Sir Walter) Braithwaite, and he took great care to replace them with the best available officers when their term expired. In only one instance do the Diaries reveal that Wilson failed to obtain the services of the man he wanted.[13] He also went well beyond the call of duty in getting to know his staff informally, so much so that at least two, the

Hon. C. Sackville-West ('Tit Willow' in the Diaries) and
George Harper ('Uncle') became life-long friends of the family.

Not least among Wilson's achievements at the Staff College
were the substantial increases he obtained in the numbers of
both staff and students. The first increase, which was sanctioned on 31 March 1908, was the outcome of a meeting between Wilson and Haldane, the Secretary of State for War, at
Lord Roberts' home, Englemere at Ascot. Haldane visited the
College with Haig, Kiggell and Ellison and as a result sanctioned the addition of three instructing officers and twenty-two
students. In the Spring of 1910 the Treasury approved the
addition of five members of staff and five students, thus bringing
the grand total to seventeen staff and ninety-eight students,
not counting the temporarily-attached naval officers.[14] Though
still a modest number in view of the Army's needs, it was a
tribute to Wilson's persuasiveness and perseverance in face of
the current Radical Parliamentary campaign against military
expenditure.

Nor should the increases be attributed solely to the urge for
'empire building' to which Wilson was certainly not immune.
He was already evincing concern over the deficiencies of the
Expeditionary Force which would later become an obsession
when he became Director of Military Operations. In the lecture
on 'Psychology' referred to earlier, he had flippantly remarked
on the available number of p.s.c.s – 'We all fully realize ... that
if this building is closed and the officers now here are given
suitable appointments, the happy termination of the campaign
is assured!' – but went on to estimate more soberly that the
Expeditionary Force would be about 150 staff officers short on
mobilization, not considering wastage on active service.[15]

He also went to a great deal of trouble – with frequent 'wire
pulling' visits to the War Office that he clearly enjoyed enormously – both to obtain desirable billets for his p.s.c.s and staff
and also to advance the cause of the trained staff officers.
On 21 December 1908, for example, he saw Sir Charles Douglas
and clinched appointments for two members of his staff, Stopford and Sackville-West, and also for about twenty of the Senior
Division soon to graduate. In 1909 he successfully pushed the

claims of Braithwaite to succeed Capper as Commandant at the Quetta Staff College.[16]

One of the few subjects on which Wilson was critical of his friend and predecessor as Commandant, Rawlinson, was the latter's alleged neglect of the administrative side of staff duties, over which there was still continuing controversy in the establishment of the General Staff. Wilson's chief point in his opening address in January 1907 was that 'it is impossible to be a good General Staff Officer or Superior Commander unless one is possessed of administrative knowledge'. He extended the scope of staff duties taught at the College by adding officers from the Army Service Corps and the Medical Department to the Directing Staff. Despite Wilson's emphasis, however, so perceptive a student as Wavell selected this as the weak point in the instruction of that time:

> The instruction had, I fancy, greatly improved in quality in the few years before we went there and was more practical . . . But it was still to my mind too academic and theoretical and aimed too high. Its main object should surely have been to turn out good staff officers and not to train commanders of corps and armies . . . What seemed to me weak was the administrative side, especially supply and transport. It was never rubbed into us that all operations were entirely dependent on transportation, and it was not till much later in my career that I really realised this truth . . .[17]

Unfortunately, Wilson's *Diary* entries are usually too cryptic to provide more than a tantalizing hint of genuine concern with practical training for war; and of course he very properly left the bulk of such training to his staff. Nevertheless, a careful reading of the Diaries must lead to a rejection of the extreme view that he was exclusively concerned with politics and grand strategy. He was, for instance, extremely interested in combined operations – which indeed he had helped to introduce to the College – and often stayed out all night on schemes. Thus on 20 May 1909: 'We were out all night on a disembarkation scheme, the signalling going very badly – not a single message

11. 'Henri' and 'Wully'. Brig.-Gen. H. H. Wilson (Commandant 1907–10) *left*, and Maj.-Gen. W. R. Robertson (1910–13) *right*, were soldiers with very different characters and methods but both supplied drive and direction at the Staff College. In 1918 Wilson replaced Robertson as Chief of the Imperial General Staff. Both became Field Marshals.

12. Henry Wilson and his Directing Staff. Wilson is fourth from the left (*seated*) and on his left is Col. J. E. Gough V.C. The top-hatted old gentleman seated on the right is Col. Lonsdale Hale.

getting through from battalion H.Q. to the outposts or vice-versa.'

A Diary entry for April 1910 shows clearly how Wilson employed the battlefield tours of the Franco-German War to inculcate his own technical doctrine. The battle of Wörth, for instance, was valuable as illustrating:

(1) The absolute and vital necessity for having a plan. There was none at Wissembourg, none at Wörth.
(2) The importance of moving the troops on to the field in agreement with the plan, and not allowing them to dump themselves anywhere.
(3) The best way to decide on a line of defence is to choose that one which allows you to employ the three arms whilst confining the enemy to one or two.

As a Rifleman and devoted supporter of Lord Roberts, it was hardly surprising that Wilson adopted a progressive view in the cavalry versus mounted-infantry controversy. After discussing various cavalry actions in recent history he noted: 'my mind becomes clearer and clearer as to the uselessness (and worse) of the arme blanche'.[18]

Within a year of seeing his first aeroplane he had got Thompson Capper to give two lectures on the subject, lamenting 'the awful way in which we are doing nothing'. He shocked his friend Kiggell by presenting a report which criticized British troops' training compared with that of the French and Germans.[19] Other Diary entries show him to have been progressive in his views on a variety of important matters including the combination of the three arms in defence, mechanical transport and the importance of mobility. As Dr Summerton admirably sums up: 'while Wilson belonged to that category of persons who are agents rather than original thinkers, he was an intelligent and competent soldier who was conscious of significant developments and who was capable of ensuring within the limits of his substantial influence that the army kept abreast of them'.[20]

Important as Wilson's teaching on tactical matters was, however, it was on strategical-political instruction that he

K

placed by far the greater emphasis. In order to appreciate the importance which this subject came to occupy in the Camberley course under Wilson's direction it is necessary first to describe the changes that were then occuring in Britain's foreign policy and strategy.

Between 1900 and 1905 the main contingency in War Office planning remained an increasingly improbable war against France and Russia, but early in the latter year a war game examined the possibility of British military support of Belgium in event of Germany infringing her neutrality in an attack on France. Not surprisingly the game was 'woefully inaccurate' as a prediction of what was to happen in 1914, but two false assumptions are worth noting because they continued to colour War Office thinking for some time; namely that German violation of Belgium would not be the initial act in a war against France, and that the German advance would take place south of the river Meuse.

The war game was not a purely academic exercise but rather denoted the growth of strong anti-German sentiments among some of the most influential officers at the War Office, including Grierson, Robertson and Wilson.

Already, too, by the end of 1905, complete disagreement had arisen between the War Office and the Admiralty. In a war against Germany the latter persistently advocated landings on the German coast whereas the War Office was highly sceptical and did not seriously reconsider such a strategy before 1914.

Early in 1906 Haldane gave permission to the Director of Military Operations (Grierson) to carry on unofficial staff conversations with the French General Staff regarding co-operation in a war against Germany. Although other contingencies, some for war outside Europe, were still being considered the Continental plan gradually became dominant. The Admiralty, particularly as represented by Sir John Fisher as First Sea Lord, remained utterly intransigent, but the absence of a Naval War Staff (which Fisher and his successor adamantly opposed) entailed that the Admiralty did virtually nothing while the War Office went ahead with more detailed plans.

It cannot be over-emphasized, particularly in view of the erroneous picture painted by Lord Hankey in his later years, that in the period before 1914 the Committee of Imperial Defence was in no sense the centre of strategic planning.[21] The failure of the C.I.D. even to discuss the broad question of war against Germany left the two Service departments free to pursue their own utterly incompatible strategies. In consequence, improbable though it may sound, the Cabinet did not learn collectively of the Anglo-French staff talks until 1911, and several members really were in complete ignorance about it until then, by which time British military planning had fallen into rather rigid grooves.

Grierson's successor as D.M.O., Spencer Ewart (1906–10), likewise believed in principle that the British Army should fight on the side of the French, but he was very worried about the irregularity of the staff talks (i.e., that they might prove politically binding) and, like Wilson, was obsessed by the fear that the B.E.F. (of six infantry divisions and a cavalry division) was far too small.

Henry Wilson has sometimes been regarded as the 'evil genius' whose advent to the office of D.M.O. in August 1910 signalled a regrettable change in British strategy, away from reliance on maritime power to wage a limited war primarily through economic blockade, and towards an open-ended commitment to mass Continental warfare. Apart from questionable assumptions about the strategic options open to Britain before 1914, and about the strategies actually advocated by the Fisher school (which were in essence equally 'Continental'), this interpretation greatly exaggerates Wilson's scope for originality.

As shown above, Wilson inherited a military policy – of direct assistance to France if attacked by Germany – which had been hardening since January 1906. Wilson did not question the 'grand strategy' of British intervention in the main theatre of a European War; he merely undertook a rigorous examination of the feasibility of existing plans.

Strategically, Wilson rightly decided that the details of existing plans must be modified because Germany was likely to violate Belgian neutrality at the very beginning of a war. Zealous, self-confident and Francophile, Wilson believed that Britain should give uncompromising support to France. Like most senior officers in most European armies he believed that the war would be short, and – more optimistic than Ewart – he expected the B.E.F. to tilt the balance to an Allied victory, not (as actually happened) to help avert a catastrophic French defeat.

From his strategic analysis Wilson naturally grasped the crucial importance of speedy mobilization and definite military (and shipping) arrangements. These he found in most respects to be non-existent or at best utterly inadequate. Perhaps his greatest achievement as D.M.O. (1910–14) was in the innumerable practical arrangements – such as the provision of horses and transport – which made the mobilization of the B.E.F. an outstanding success, when four years earlier it would certainly have been a shambles.

Wilson's obsession with the coming struggle with Germany could hardly fail to fire the imagination of a group of keen young staff officers who could easily picture themselves rising to hold key positions in that conflict. Nevertheless, one of the more acute students, Lt A. P. Wavell, felt that 'it would have been better to keep our feet more firmly on the ground'. Many years later he reflected that a serious defect in the Staff College course at that time was that too little attention was paid to the production of clear orders and instructions under pressure. A paper requiring orders for the move of a brigade or division might be issued on a Monday and the answers not required until Saturday. True, in the second year the students took part in large-scale exercises on Salisbury Plain, the South Coast, the Midlands and North Wales, but Wavell thought there was too much emphasis on manœuvres on a grand scale, dealing with armies and corps, rather than divisions and brigades, and with command on a high level rather than the machinery of staff work.[22]

Among the small band of military and civilian reformers who had struggled to improve military education, training and organization, including Esher, Clarke, Ellison, Haig and

Nicholson, Henry Wilson was pre-eminent in urging the necessity for a coherent 'School of Thought' which would in time create a sense of uniformity and harmony in the Army as a whole. The Staff College, sending out accomplished young staff officers into every branch of the service, would seem the ideal place to create such a school – indeed Wilson and his supporters argued that that was its chief function – but others believed that its role should be more modest.

In fact the term 'School of Thought' consisted of two distinct aspects, which were nevertheless closely related. It was employed first in a purely professional sense to mean the training of a body of staff officers imbued with uniform methods of work and a common approach to staff problems. This meaning Wilson expressed in summing up after the 1909 tour of the Franco-German battlefields: 'I ran through the whole of the battles they have seen from Wissembourg to Gravelotte pointing out that the same thread of disaster and victory ran through all, and for the same cause, i.e., want of purpose on our side (*sic*) and purpose on the other side due to a *School of Thought*.'[23] His own work as Director of Military Operations from 1910 to 1914 in preparing the Expeditionary Force was to be characterized by this same professional thoroughness regulated down to the smallest detail by a pivotal strategic concept.

It was the second and wider political meaning of the phrase that was to prove so controversial. As far as Henry Wilson was concerned a 'School of Thought' in this sense embodied, first, the need for a close relationship with France against Germany and, second, the introduction of conscription. These two strands, though inextricably associated in Wilson's thought and activities, will be treated separately.

For Wilson, of course, a Francophile policy stemmed not just from a cool appraisal of British national interests, but was also inspired by his unusually strong admiration for the French people, their country and their army. Quite apart from the regular jaunts to the battlefields in 1870, Wilson habitually spent part of his summer holidays travelling by bicycle and train along the French and Belgian frontiers. In 1909, for instance, he spent ten days travelling from Valenciennes to Belfort. For organized parties of officers to have made such patently non-historical tours would have aroused too much suspicion, but Wilson and his instructors passed on their impressions to successive contingents of officers. In Callwell's words: 'He laboured unceasingly to inspire them with the force of his own convictions on the subject.'[24]

Towards the end of 1909 Henry Wilson took a step which was to have some important short-term repercussions for the Staff College, and far more important long-term repercussions for the Anglo-French Entente. He arranged, through the British Military Attaché in Paris, to visit his opposite number, General Ferdinand Foch, Commandant of the Ecole de Guerre Supérieure. Foch at first appeared unimpressed by his eccentric visitor but was gradually won over by Wilson's pertinacity and by his voluble command of French. Soon the two were great friends; so much so that the austere Frenchman was persuaded to join in Wilson's uninhibited clowning. 'Closeted together in private they would exchange hats and march about the room in them while discussing quite earnestly the fates of their respective armies and nations.'[25] They found themselves in close agreement about German strategy, while Wilson was most favourably impressed by everything he saw at the French Staff College. In the following summer, shortly before he left Camberley, Wilson was able to return Foch's hospitality, showing him not only the Staff College, but also escorting him to Aldershot, Bulford Camp, Netheravon and the artillery ranges at Larkhill. In London he introduced Foch to Haldane and to several leading generals at the War Office. This friendship was to be of enormous importance to Wilson as D.M.O. and also of advantage to the B.E.F. in the early part of the War.

In the short term Wilson doubtless considered it good for publicity that a prominent French general should pay an admiring visit to Camberley and, more specifically, his glowing report of the work done at the Ecole Supérieure helped to persuade Haldane to make another increase in the establishment of staff and students.[26]

Only one practical innovation in the Camberley course can definitely be attributed to the favourable impression Wilson brought home from the Ecole Supérieure. At the latter, tactical schemes were carried out at the double, the directing staff simulating the tension of war-time command with harrassing cries of '*Vite, vite*' and '*Allez, allez*'. This was just the sort of thing to tickle Wilson's fancy and henceforth '*Allez, allez*' schemes were frequently practised at Camberley.

Important though Foch's friendship doubtless was in confirming Wilson's Francophilia, his latest biographer – Bernard Ash – appears to go beyond the evidence in suggesting that he was so deeply influenced by Foch's strategical and tactical ideas that he can be said to have founded 'an Anglo-French School of Military Thought' at Camberley. On the strategical plane he had for several years been convinced of the necessity for Britain to give military support to France, either directly by extending the left wing of her Army or indirectly by intervention in Belgium. True, as D.M.O., Wilson was to share the erroneous French beliefs that the Germans would be weak in the centre, that their attack was unlikely to extend north of the Meuse, and that the allies would win the battle of the frontiers. But it is unjust to Wilson's considerable professional competence as a strategist to imply that he was incapable of reaching these operational conclusions for himself.[27]

On the tactical level it remains to be proved that Wilson was influenced by the French extremist doctrine of the superiority of the offensive which Foch had done much to encourage both by his teaching at the Ecole Supérieure and by his book, *The Principles of War*. To be sure, Wilson was not among the small band of prophetic military critics who fully grasped before 1914 the enormous advantages which increased fire power had given to the well-prepared defensive, and it is a valid criticism that too little attention was paid to the problems of fire and movement at the Staff College. But neither was he a convert to the suicidal dogmas of such French pundits as Grandmaison. For one thing he possessed too healthy a respect for the training and discipline of the German Army, not to speak of the comparatively puny size of the B.E.F. For another, as mentioned earlier, he was primarily interested in the highest levels of staff work where military and political considerations interacted. If he is to be criticized it is for the neglect of more mundane tactical problems rather than for inculcating an unrealistic offensive doctrine.[28]

Given Wilson's activist temperament and his convictions in the sphere of politics and strategy, it was only to be expected that he should publicize his dissatisfaction with the size of the B.E.F. and the voluntary principle on which it was recruited. One of his favourite dicta was: 'There is no military problem to which the answer is six [infantry] divisions and one cavalry division' (the then strength of the British Expeditionary Force).[29]

   Thus, although it was the policy of none of the political parties, Wilson was a fervent supporter of compulsory military service – as indeed were many other senior officers, either privately or in public. He was savagely critical of Haldane's army reorganization scheme precisely because it made no provision for massive expansion by compulsion in event of war. As early as November 1905 (that is, when the military conversations with France had barely begun) Wilson upbraided 'the Chief' (Lord Roberts) for not going 'the whole hog and by *compulsion* form[ing] a great Reserve'. In succeeding years the Diaries are crammed with references to the pressing necessity for conscription. In November 1909, for example, at the request of the Senior Division 'so as to clear the air', he delivered two lectures on the theme 'Is Conscription Necessary?' On 4 November he complacently noted 'My lecture yesterday has caused a tremendous lot of "chat", and has I think helped the Senior Division to some clear thinking. In answer to my invitation, quite a number of questions have come in.' On 26 November, in response to Lord Roberts' request, he cycled over to Englemere, gave the Chief his notes, and recorded: 'He seems to be greatly struck with the picture. He thinks of publishing the story over his name, and Milner's and Curzon's and Cromer's. Curious if my lectures should do any good.' He repeated the lectures to the whole College the following year.

When attacked in a leading article in the *Westminster Gazette* for advocating conscription, his immediate reaction was to assemble the students and discuss the topic.[30]

There had been prolonged opposition, both civil and military, to Lord Kitchener's proposal to set up a Staff College at Quetta on the grounds that this would lead to the creation of a separate 'School of Thought' in the Indian Army. It is therefore ironical that Kitchener should criticize Wilson for the same misdemeanour shortly before the latter left Camberley. Under 28 July 1910, Wilson baldly noted in his Diary: 'Lord K came over with Robertson [then a Brigadier-General and chief General Staff Officer to Sir H. Smith-Dorrien] from Aldershot. He attacked me about trying to form a "School of Thought" but he got no change out of me, and he really talked a great deal of nonsense and imputed all sorts of things to us here which simply are not so.'[31] It is unfortunate that we know nothing about the nature of Kitchener's outburst, and speculation seems pointless; it may be simply that he objected to Wilson's political intriguing and the frankly political aspects of some of the instruction at Camberley. It is also slightly ironic that his companion, 'Wully' Robertson, was to adopt a sharply critical attitude to Wilson's attempt to form a 'School of Thought', since he had more than once delivered lectures at Camberley with clear political assumptions of hostility to Germany and support of France.[32] From the 'consumer's' angle, Wavell too, though he found Wilson's lectures invariably interesting and stimulating, had thought it would have been better to keep the students' feet more firmly on the ground. More recently, Bernard Ash has criticized Wilson for his open support of Lord Roberts's National Service League, his thinly-veiled antagonism to Haldane's Territorial Army Scheme (because it involved a reduction in numbers) and his alleged enthralment with French offensive doctrine.[33]

Wilson's extra-curricular activities are difficult to justify, particularly in view of contemporary opinion that serving officers should be strictly a-political; but his injection of political-strategic issues into the teaching at Staff College is less obviously open to censure because senior Army officers were sharply divided in opinion. This emerged at a Conference of General Staff Officers held at Camberley from 7 to 10 January 1908. Col. Gleichen, himself a p.s.c., raised the issue in these terms: 'at the Staff College at Camberley senior students were given schemes at the end of their year which involved not only military questions, but very high political questions. There was a scheme which was set this last year, which entered into a number of political difficulties which might occur with reference to other countries, Belgium, France and so on. These involved discussions on very high political points; and were matters of the very highest political importance, which could only really be decided after a very long study by the higher political people . . . Instead of studying such questions at the Staff College, the time would be far better occupied in turning the officers out to be good staff officers. He did not wish to press the point, but simply to suggest that it would be better to turn the students into good Staff officers than to make excursions into the realms of politics which ought to be dealt with by higher people.'

Henry Wilson was not present but his predecessor, Rawlinson, replied that the examination of European strategic questions was already in practice when he took over, but he had extended the curriculum to cover naval problems. In studying possible campaigns of the future they were only following the course which was taken by the Staff Colleges of other nations. He took the view that at the Staff College officers should be trained not only for staff duties, but also with a view to high command in future.

He had always looked upon the Staff College as the nursery of the General Staff, and he had hoped that by inculcating broad ideas into the best of the officers there, they might become later on fitted for responsible appointments, not only on the General Staff, but subsequently for command in war. He did not mean to say that on one or two occasions, perhaps, they had not gone too far, but that was a characteristic not confined solely to the Staff College.

Robertson supported Gleichen but was unhelpful on the

crucial problem of how the soldiers were to proceed when the Government failed to provide clear political guide lines:

The writing of strategical papers, referring to military operations in which they might one day be engaged, furnished excellent instruction for the students, but they ought, in his opinion, to keep clear of political matters. In practice, the policy to be adopted in any given contingency, was assumed, but it was never discussed by the General Staff. Their duty was to consider and advise how a certain policy could best be carried out. He saw no necessity for the students to discuss questions of policy, though, of course, strategy must be in harmony with policy, and therefore the policy to be followed must be laid down, or assumed, before a useful strategical paper can be prepared.

Colonel Kiggell ended the inconclusive discussion by making a sensible distinction between

1 The need to study politics in relation to strategy and

2 the need to study one's own political problems.

In regard to the first question, he had for some time past tried to study war and had tried to teach it, and the more he had tried, the more he had become convinced that politics were at the back of all strategical problems; and he would ask officers to consider, merely as a test case, how far politics were concerned either with McClellan's failure or Jackson's success in 1862. Could Jackson have done what he did, if he had not understood the political situation? If he could, then he was prepared to agree that the study of politics was un-necessary for strategy. He thought that that point must be decided first. After that, the second part of the question could be decided – whether it was necessary or not to study their own political problems in connection with schemes set at the Staff College. It had been proposed to limit the course at that establishment to the study of staff duties, i.e., to furnish good staff officers. The latter, however, would be required to discuss with their General, questions of strategy and tactics, and consequently they must be educated in the broad fundamental principles of success and failure in war.

It was not possible to separate strategy from politics, and indeed Clausewitz based his whole theory of war on the fundamental principle that strategy must be based on policy.[34]

But Henry Wilson's trenching upon matters of high politics may also be defended in terms of military education and training. It has been a major theme in this study that until after the First World War the Staff College constituted the only institution in which experienced commissioned officers might make a broad study of their profession. The Imperial Defence College and Joint Services Staff College did not as yet exist. In these circumstances it would surely have been parochial to regard the Staff College as just another specialist School, like that of Musketry at Hythe, for the technical study of staff duties. This was certainly the view of Wilson's predecessor, Sir Henry Rawlinson who, impressed by the excellence of Japanese staff work in Manchuria, had suggested a senior course at Camberley 'for General Staff Officers aged about 40 so that they should keep themselves *au courant* with the latest ideas in military science and the Art of War'.[35] His scheme was not implemented. Haig held a similarly broad conception of the function of the Staff College and agreed with Launcelot Kiggell (Director of Staff Duties 1911–13, and subsequently Commandant of the Staff College 1913–14) that it would be a good idea to change its name to 'War School'. 'Many officers,' Haig wrote, 'look upon the Staff College as an institution for training of staff officers only, whereas, it is really a school for the training of future commanders and leaders.' Sir William Robertson, when Commandant, actually proposed the change of designation to 'War School', but without success. Wilson's first biographer, Sir Charles Callwell, also referred to the Staff College as 'the great superior war-school at Camberley'.[36]

In some respects Wilson's political activities appear as startling and indefensible as ever. He had no qualms, for example, about supplying confidential information to the opponents of the Liberal Government under which he served, and in his Diaries he sometimes revealingly referred to the Unionist Opposition as 'we'. On the other hand a longer perspective – and more evidence – on the pros and cons of British intervention at the outset of the First World War, incline one to judge Henry Wilson more charitably as a strategist. As Dr Neil Summerton has commented: 'He apprehended far better than most of his contemporaries that in the realm of strategy an understanding of the interaction between military and political matters was an extremely valuable asset for the senior staff officer.' Where he is perhaps open to criticism is that 'in a less than dispassionate manner, he tended to concentrate on this aspect to the exclusion of all others.'[37]

Although Wilson modestly noted towards the end of his term 'how poor and indifferent a Commandant I have been', the moving farewells he received from staff and students show that in their opinion he was one of the most popular and successful of all Commandants. After his final address to the Juniors he was much touched by the way in which they stood up as he left the room: a gesture he had never before seen them make. On 29 July:

> The S.C. gave me a farewell dinner, 103 of us present, much the largest dinner ever given here. Stopford, Banon and Braithwaite [former members of the Directing Staff] came down from the W.O. I made my farewell speech, which apparently took them by storm, and I got the most extravagant praise from everyone. I am so glad it is over. It was a great ordeal.

The day after the great farewell dinner one of the staff wrote to Mrs Wilson:

> . . . The most noticeable thing was how deeply attached *all* are to Henry, and can you wonder? What we all felt was that the College is parting with the greatest commandant it has ever known. When we left the dining-room there was none of the usual uproarious bear-fighting which takes place. We were, I think, too sad for that. The reception Henry got and the speech he made were indeed a fitting ending to his reign

at the College, to whose welfare he devoted all that was best
in him. Whatever the future may have in store for me, I
can at least say that I was privileged to serve under him
during his time as commandant.

Another described Wilson's departure as a personal loss to
every member of the staff, to every student, to every mess-
waiter and college employee. 'Walking up to the college the
morning after he had left I seemed to be looking at a portrait
with the head painted out.'[38]

Wilson was naturally interested in his successor, and noted
after a talk with Sir Charles Douglas 'It looks like Robertson
and I confess I am nervous. Murray doesn't want to come, and
Nick and Douglas don't think Colin Mackenzie and David
Henderson [whom Haig favoured] good enough.' On 17 June
he discovered that Nicholson was opposed to Robertson
'because of want of breeding' and preferred Joe Davies. 'Wully'
of course had risen from the ranks, and retained signs of his
origins such as a tendency to drop his 'aitches'. Wilson then
proposed Kiggell (whom Haig thought would be wasted at the
Staff College). When Robertson's appointment was confirmed,
Wilson, who presumably agreed with Nicholson, confided to
his Diary: 'This is a tremendous gamble with the chances
against him. I am very sorry . . . I am much upset at Robertson's appoint[ment] here.' The Commandant was expected to
dip into his private means in order to entertain on a scale
fitting the position, and it may be that Wilson thought Robertson even less able than himself to afford such expenses. Finally,
after Robertson had visited the College on 18 July to discuss the
change-over, Wilson wrote despondently, 'My heart sinks
when I think what it all may mean to the College and this
house'.[39]

The last three words quoted lend some credence to a story
discreditable to Henry Wilson whose source was Sir James
Edmonds, an exceptionally clever officer but one prone to
retail malicious gossip about people he disliked. Wilson was
pre-eminent in this category.

On arrival at Camberley Wully found on the hall table a

bill from Henry Wilson for £250 for various items he was leaving behind. Robertson had not £250 in the world, so he wrote to Wilson's predecessor, Rawlinson, to enquire what had happened when he handed over. 'Rawly' replied: 'That fellow Henry! My wife put in those rose trees and gave them to Lady Wilson. The furniture is a gift of past Commandants and goes with the house. You had better dig up the potato patch and see if the seed potatoes are still there.'[40]

Whether or not this story became embroidered in the telling, Wilson had evidently done something to offend Robertson and the latter took his revenge at the first opportunity. When Wilson next visited the College in December with the C.I.G.S. and other senior officers Robertson pointedly ignored him and failed to invite him into his room. Wilson was so hurt by this that three days later he rather pathetically complained to Nicholson about Robertson's 'most rude and unpardonable behaviour'.[41] This did not auger well for the personal relations of two generals whose paths were repeatedly to cross during the First World War.

'Fluent', 'bubbling', 'effervescent' are all adjectives that occur frequently in descriptions of Henry Wilson. Had Wilson not been a professional soldier one feels he would have excelled in politics, for in addition to fluency in speech and on paper he possessed great charm of manner and a genius for getting things done by what friends would term skilful manœuvre and enemies intrigue. His mind was quick and imaginative rather than original, and he was apt to deal in clichés. While he might justly be rated one of the cleverest officers of his day he was in no sense an intellectual   despite his fluent French   nor was he broadly cultured. To be sure, intellectuals and cultured types were rather rare in the pre-1914 British regular Army (who, for example, was the British equivalent of the elder von Moltke?) – but even compared with a literary and artistic soldier like Sir Ian Hamilton[42] – Wilson's non-professional interests were the circumscribed, traditional ones of his class such as hunting, horse-racing, and ski-ing. His diaries contrast sharply with those of his contemporary, Viscount Esher, in their lack of references to books or of semi-philosophical reflections on a wide variety of subjects.

Limited mental horizons combined with eccentric behaviour, however, by no means add up to professional incompetence as a senior staff officer. On the contrary, Henry Wilson was a thoroughly competent officer and few did more than he to develop the General Staff and transform the organization of the Expeditionary Force in the decade before the First World War. Furthermore, despite the limitations and blind spots which have been discussed in this chapter, his achievements in his three-and-a-half years at the Staff College were outstanding. He inspired staff and students alike by his professional zeal, greatly increased the geographical range and scope of outdoor exercises, and secured large additions to the establishment of the College. Though open to criticism in detail, his unwavering conviction that the British Army would in a few years be playing a decisive role in a war against Germany proved, after all, correct and gave a sense of urgency to all his instruction. Indeed, what he intended first and foremost by that Delphic phrase 'School of Thought' was simply – and this was an unusual state of affairs for the British Army in peacetime – preparedness for war.

CHAPTER 8. NOTES

1 Callwell, *op. cit.*, I, p. 67. Bernard Ash, *The Lost Dictator: a Biography of Field Marshal Sir Henry Wilson* (London, 1968), p. 67.
2 Reginald, Viscount Esher, *The Tragedy of Lord Kitchener* (London, 1921), pp. 84–5.
3 Wilson's *Diary*, 13, 28 March, 11, 20 April 1905. When he eventually moved to Camberley he had to borrow £350; *ibid.*, 31 December 1906. For photographs of Grove End, see Callwell, *op. cit.*, p. 64.
4 *Diary*, Prefatory note to 1906. 3, 27 July; 6 and 25 August; 13–27 September and 9–24 October 1906, *passim.* Esher to Roberts, 5 October 1906, Roberts Papers R 29/12. Roberts to Esher, 11 October 1906. Esher, *op. cit.*, II, pp. 192–3.
5 Wilson's *Diary*, 3 October 1908.
6 Callwell, *op. cit.*, I, p. 75.
7 John Connell, *Wavell: Scholar and Soldier* (London, 1964), p. 62. Barrow, *op. cit.*, p. 112.
8 Wilson to Roberts, 24 March 1908. W.O. 105/45.
9 Wilson's *Diary*, 5 May 1909 (Callwell's transcription 'young seed', p. 71, is almost certainly wrong). See also 29 April 1907.
10 Connell, *op. cit.*, pp. 63, 522. For Calthrop's distinction as a linguist, and expert on the Japanese Army see Maj.-Gen. F. S. G. Piggott, *Broken Thread* (Aldershot, 1950), pp. 25–6, 44, 57, 82 (photograph), 85–6, 90. Calthrop's Japanese sword is preserved at the Staff College.
11 Sir T. Montgomery-Cuninghame, *Dusty Measure* (London, 1939), p. 50–6.
12 Wilson's *Diary*, 7 November and Memorandum 31 December 1906. *Diary*, 10 January, 22 March, 6 April 1907. For details of the first course see *Report of the Advisory Board L.S.E.* W.O. Reports 1907, Cd 3696. See also Maj. R. B. Airey, 'The London School of Economics and the Army', *Army Review*, Jan.–April 1913, pp. 465–73.
13 Wilson's *Diary*, 2 March 1909. The officer he failed to get was 'Conk' Marker, formerly Arnold-Forster's Military Secretary. For a complete list of the Directing Staff in 1907 see Callwell, *op. cit.*, p. 68.
14 Wilson's *Diary*, 2 February, 31 March 1908, 8, 23 March, 16 May 1910.
15 WO 104/45, *op. cit.*, p. 10.
16 Wilson's *Diary*, 22 January, 21 December 1908, 17 May 1909.
17 Connell, *op. cit.*, pp. 62–3.
18 Wilson's *Diary*, 30 April to 4 May 1910.
19 *Ibid.*, 20 May 1909; 10 and 18 February 1910.
20 N. W. Summerton, *The Development of British Military Planning for a War Against Germany, 1904–1914* (unpublished doctoral dissertation, University of London, 1970), p. 369. The following account of British

strategic thought and planning before 1914 is largely based on this thesis.

21 For an exhaustive analysis of the role of the C.I.D. before 1914 see N. d'Ombrain, *The Military Departments and the Committee of Imperial Defence, 1902–1914* (unpublished doctoral dissertation, University of Oxford, 1969). Hankey's misleading account in *The Supreme Command* (London, 1961), is repeated by F. A. Johnson, *op. cit.*

22 Connell, *op. cit.*, p. 63.

23 Wilson's *Diary*, 7 May 1909.

24 Callwell, *op. cit.*, p. 73.

25 Ash, *op. cit.*, p. 74.

26 Wilson's *Diary*, 31 December 1909. Callwell, *op. cit.*, p. 80.

27 Ash, *op. cit.*, pp. 73–5. For a scholarly assessment of Wilson's professional capabilities see Summerton, *op. cit.*, pp. 368–9.

28 For a brilliant critique of Foch's theoretical works see B. H. Liddell Hart, *Foch: Man of Orleans* (London, 1937), paperback edition, Vol. 2, pp. 479–519. On the fate of French critics of the *Offensive à outrance*, see the same author's essay, 'French Military Ideas before the First World War', in Martin Gilbert (ed.), *A Century of Conflict* (London, 1966). Any notion that Wilson was an uncritical believer in every aspect of French military doctrine is dispelled by a lecture he gave before the Aldershot Military Society on 5 December 1910 on 'Initiative and the Power of Manœuvre' (War Office Library). In this he characterized the *German* creed as all-out attack (outflanking, seizing the initiative, full deployment) whereas the French favoured holding back a large reserve and waiting for information about the enemy's movements before going over to the offensive. Wilson implied that the B.E.F. was then still insufficiently well-trained and mobile to follow the French doctrine ('restricted initiative, a momentary pause and then a smashing blow') and might have to follow the German doctrine 'and trust to win by a slogging match'.

29 Connell, *op. cit.*, p. 62.

30 Wilson's *Diary*, 27 November 1905; 30 March 1907; 2, 3 March, 31 October, 4, 10, 25 and 26 November 1909; 11 July 1910. Sir George Barrow recalled that a number of M.P.s criticized Wilson's 'Belgian Scheme' on the grounds that the Staff College was 'hatching a malicious plot against the harmless, peace-loving Germans'. See Barrow, *op. cit.*, p. 115.

31 Wilson's *Diary*, 28 July 1910. Callwell, *op. cit.*, p. 84.

32 On 23 October 1907, for example, Wilson noted 'Robertson gave us a most excellent lecture on Belgium and the certainty of Germany violating her territory in a war with France, and our position when we joined in as Allies to France'.

33 Connell, *op. cit.*, p. 62. Ash, *op. cit.*, pp. 70–2.

34 *Report on a Conference of General Staff Officers at the Staff College, 7–10 January, 1908*, pp. 36–7.

35 Rawlinson to Esher, 7 July 1907. Esher Papers, 'Army Letters', Vol. II, cited by Gooch, *op. cit.*, pp. 194–5.
36 Haig to Kiggell, 27 April 1911. Kiggell Papers 1/11. Robertson, *op. cit.*, p. 170. Callwell, *op. cit.*, p. 67.
37 Summerton, *op. cit.*, pp. 367–8. The author is primarily concerned with Wilson's term as D.M.O. (1910–14), but his comments may fairly be applied to the preceding Staff College period.
38 Wilson's *Diary*, 18 April, 27, 29 July, 1 August 1910. Callwell, *op. cit.*, pp. 84–5.
39 Haig to Kiggell, 18 May 1909; 14 July 1910. Kiggell Papers 1/3, 1/7. Wilson's *Diary*, 8, 17 June, 4, 18 July 1910.
40 Edmonds Papers. This anecdote is also cited by V. Bonham-Carter, *Soldier True: the Life and Times of Field Marshal Sir William Robertson* (London, 1963), p. 74.
41 Wilson's *Diary*, 20, 23 December 1910.
42 See Ian B. M. Hamilton, *The Happy Warrior: a Life of General Sir Ian Hamilton* (London, 1966).

CHAPTER NINE

The Staff College on the eve of war
1910-1914

Maj.-Gen. W. R. 'Wully' Robertson, who was Commandant of the Staff College from August 1910 to October 1913, was a very different sort of man to his predecessor. Gen. Sir George Barrow, who was a member of the Directing Staff at Camberley from May 1908 to December 1910 and admired both his Chiefs, emphasized the contrast as follows:

> One would have to go far to find two men, with working lives passed in the same milieu and brought up in the same doctrines, belonging to the same profession in which both reached the highest post, and chosen in turn to be commandant of the Staff College, more unlike in body and mind than Henry Wilson and 'Wully' Robertson. It was the difference between the agile greyhound and the tenacious bull-dog – Wilson, expansive, giving himself out to those above him; Robertson repressive, drawing others in towards himself; Wilson's eyes searching the horizon, Robertson's closely scanning the objects at hand.[1]

The son of a village postmaster and tailor at Welbourn in Lincolnshire, William left school at thirteen and after a few years as a footman (including service with the Cardigan family at Deene Park where his interest in the Army may have been aroused), he enlisted in the 16th Lancers at Worcester on 13 November 1877. He was under the minimum age of eighteen by a few months but the recruiting sergeant cheerfully falsified his age. His enlistment horrified his mother, who wrote despairingly 'there are plenty of things Steady Young Men can do when they can write and read as you can . . . [the Army] is a refuge for all Idle people . . . I shall name it to no one for I am ashamed to think of it . . . I would rather Bury you than see you in a red coat . . .'[2]

Conditions in the ranks certainly were still very harsh, even in some respects degrading, in the 1870s, but Robertson's intelligence, industry and strength of character enabled him not merely to survive but in the end (thirty-eight years after enlisting) to reach the very top of his profession as Chief of the Imperial General Staff. The story of this remarkable career has been vividly described in his autobiography, *From Private to Field Marshal*. Robertson was a thoroughly professional officer when professionals were still comparatively rare. He had made his way with no advantages of birth, wealth or social connections, by sheer hard work and efficiency, mastering a variety of staff and command duties, and learning several languages in his spare time. Henry Wilson might disparage him for his lack of breeding, others were unimpressed by his gruff speech and dropped 'aitches' (possibly a deliberate affectation in later life),[3] but no one could take him for a fool. His appointment to Camberley showed that the War Office was determined to keep up the high standard set by Rawlinson and Wilson.

Since the College was closed for two months' summer vacation when Robertson succeeded Wilson, the former had leisure to reflect on his new duties and how to carry them out. Despite the drawback that the post was 'greatly underpaid', he gladly accepted it as a mark of favour, 'for there is no position in the army,' he wrote, 'where greater influence for good or evil can be exerted over the rising generation of officers . . .'[4]

One of Robertson's many minor triumphs as Commandant was to get an increase in pay sanctioned, but with effect from the day he vacated the appointment. Another was to get an administrative officer appointed Adjutant-Quartermaster in order to take much of the routine desk-work off the Commandant and leave him more time to get to know the staff and students. The story was that the post of adjutant had been abolished some thirty years previously because his quarters were in the Commandant's House and the Commandant, having a large family, wanted the extra rooms. Robertson

artfully avoided any repetition of domestic friction by asking
for a bachelor who would live in College. Yet another achievement was the final severing of administrative connections with
the Royal Military College, Sandhurst. In Godwin-Austen's
felicitous metaphor:

> Independent at first, the Senior Department had, so to
> speak, become affianced to the Junior; then, after a longer
> engagement than had originally been planned, wedded for
> forty years, until it seemed better that they should live
> apart, and so a legal separation had been arranged. Now
> came the divorce, happily on grounds quite creditable to
> respondent and co-respondent, who have since met as
> cordially as disunited film stars.[5]

Robertson's own summary of the syllabus gives a good idea
of the main subjects now covered at the College and shows that
the more purely academic subjects, such as mathematics and
languages, had at long last been jettisoned:

> Military history and geography, strategy and tactics, with
> special reference to modern campaigns, though older ones
> were also studied.
> Principles of Imperial Defence, defence of frontiers, plans of
> concentration, naval strategy and bases, defended ports,
> food-supplies of United Kingdom, British and principal
> foreign armies, landings on an enemy's coast, overseas
> expeditions in general.
> System of transport and supply, economic geography,
> commercial law.
> Medical and ordnance services as affecting commanders and
> Staff Officers.
> Staff tours, as time and funds permitted.

Broadly speaking, the first year was devoted to the acquisition
of knowledge and the second to its application. Thus the outdoor work of the Senior Division included not only tactical
problems, but also billeting, camping and guiding imaginary
parties of troops across roadless and unknown country by
night.[6]

As far as the course itself was concerned Robertson did his best to discourage an academic attitude (that is, study for its own sake unrelated to practical professional considerations) and to stamp out cramming; indeed, he would have liked to abolish the written examination at the end of the first year. Where the system was still open to serious criticism was the entrance examination, which lasted ten days and, as one successful competitor ruefully recalled, 'was almost as much a test of endurance as of knowledge'. Apart from the usual military subjects, it was essential for those who had hopes of obtaining a competitive vacancy (as distinct from a nomination after merely qualifying) to take voluntary papers in higher mathematics, two languages and strategy. In June 1913, for instance, no fewer than 185 candidates presented themselves in the depressing atmosphere of Croydon Town Hall to compete for 36 vacancies (there were in addition 15 places to be filled by nomination). The *United Service Magazine* published an occasional critical review of the Staff College entrance papers from which it is difficult to escape the conclusion that cramming was almost essential to succeed. Certainly a post-war essay entitled 'Notes on working for the Examination for admission to the Staff College' leaves the impression that any officer who read even a quarter of the admirable syllabus prescribed would need the brains and character of a Scharnhorst, Clausewitz or von Moltke.[7] By 1914, entry to the Staff College had evidently become a question of the 'survival of the fittest', though inevitably a few 'misfits' slipped in – mostly, one suspects, by nomination. The cynic might argue that this hectic competition merely revealed that the College was now known to constitute the royal road to personal advancement; but there is also abundant evidence that many young officers genuinely appreciated the importance of professional training.[8]

Once inside the College, however, the student was assured of continuous and scrupulously impartial assessment of his potential as a future staff officer and commander. The quality of the Directing Staff (the title 'Professor' was finally dropped in 1908) was now generally first-class and for that the main explanation is very clear. In contrast to the pre-South African

War era, when Col. Maurice had rightly feared that appointment to the Camberley Staff would brand him as an 'academic soldier' unfitted for field service, the instructors' posts were now coming to be seen as highly commendable steps in the careers of future divisional commanders and chiefs-of-staff. Jeudwine, Braithwaite, Bols, Malcolm, Hastings Anderson, Whigham, Maurice (son of Wolseley's Maurice, mentioned above), Hoskins and Burnett-Stuart all became at least major-generals. Another very promising officer, Maj. Philip Howell (Corps of Guides), was killed in the First World War, as was also one of Robertson's most brilliant instructors, Col. 'Johnny' Gough V.C. (Rifle Brigade), who was mortally wounded by a stray bullet in Flanders in 1915 when serving as Chief-of-Staff to the 1st Army. In the opinion of George Barrow, one of the most brilliant and certainly the wittiest of his colleagues on the Directing Staff was the Hon. George Morris, son of Lord Morris, a High Court judge. He had apparently inherited his father's acute legal mind, for he could take a sentence from Field Service Regulations, which had a clear meaning to everyone, dissect it and prove that it was sheer nonsense. Morris's lectures would have delighted the iconoclastic Capt. J. F. C. Fuller, had he stayed until 1914, but Lt-Col Barrow commented: 'It was all very amusing but hardly the business of a Staff College instructor to ridicule the doctrines he was being paid to teach.'[9]

The method of assessment was that introduced by Hildyard; namely, by classification by all the directing staff in conference on the ability shown in written and practical work at the end of each of the six terms. In Robertson's estimation very few of his 180 graduates failed in the First World War to come up to the expectation formed of them, while fewer still exceeded it. He had only to dismiss two students during his term as Commandant: one a Dominions officer whose education proved inadequate; and the other 'a clever and gallant officer' who contravened King's Regulations by refusing to grow a moustache.

Where Henry Wilson had delighted in stimulating the students' imagination by the discussion of broad strategic and political issues, Robertson was sternly professional and non-political. Without mentioning Wilson by name he made it clear in his memoirs that in his opinion there had been too much concern with theory. 'Details, so-called, were thought to be petty and beneath the notice of the big-minded man, and yet they are the very things which nine-hundred-and-ninety times out of a thousand make just the difference in war between success and failure. Whatever may be the case in peace there are few or no small things in war, though some are of greater importance than others...' Similarly, he was determined to crush the 'academic' tendency to employ high-sounding but imprecise phrases – such as 'pivot of manœuvre', 'interior lines' and 'offensive-defensive', since he felt that these did nothing to assist the ordinary commander to make the right decision in a crisis. Wully's simple philosophy of war was: 'There is only one road to victory, given a capable opponent, and that is the road of hard fighting, of which there is usually a great deal.'[10]

Within the limits of his orthodox and not particularly imaginative approach to war, Robertson's final addresses to the students who graduated in 1911 and 1912 are models of clarity and common sense. The following passage from the latter address epitomizes his views on the role of the Staff College:

It will further assist you to keep on the right lines if at all times you remember to study with the definite aim of obtaining guidance for future use in war, and not merely for the sake of amassing a store of information. Not one of us could compare perhaps with certain military historians who might be mentioned, as far as mere knowledge of past wars is concerned, and yet we do not admit that they would prove to be our best commanders. Why? Simply because they do not study military history, we think, in the way that we do or ought to do, namely with the object of making actual use in war of the knowledge acquired. If we conduct our investigations from this standpoint we shall not be likely to waste time in fascinating, but valueless, hair-splitting dialectics; we will not make too frequent use of stereotyped phrases which may mean one of several things or even nothing at all; we shall not burden our minds with too many historical parallels;

and will not be so apt to form conclusions which, however attractive they may appear on paper, have little or no connection with the rough and bloody work of masses of men trying to kill each other.[11]

The kind of information he expected staff officers to have at their finger-tips was forcefully expressed in his concluding address in 1912:

> Over and over again do our Regulations urge the importance of combination and unity of effort, but it is farcical to expect either one or the other unless staff officers display keen foresight, great activity, and devote the whole of their attention to their duty, and so be 'always prepared', as required by our Regulations, to give to their general concise statements showing 'not only the position, strength, and movements of all parts of his forces, but also information regarding such important matters as the quantities of supplies, ammunition, and stores available; the possibility of renewing them; the casualties that have been suffered; the fatigue and hardships that have been undergone, and the amount of remaining energy estimated to be still available'. Personally, I would not retain on my Staff for a day any officer who could not give me this information at any moment I might ask for it . . .[12]

Perhaps because he himself had risen from the ranks and had witnessed the behaviour of staff officers in war and peace from all angles, Robertson showed more concern than any other Commandant with the danger that the staff would come to consider themselves as superior beings and by their aloofness, arrogance or incompetence would earn the enmity of the rank and file and the regimental officers. It is a pity that his wise words were too often neglected in the First World War. During field operations, he remarked, he hated to see a group of staff officers collected together chatting and smoking. They were probably neglecting their duties, but even if they had time on their hands 'it is not right to take advantage of it under the eyes of the troops who may be passing you, perhaps hungry, thirsty and exhausted'. Similarly, if the baggage or food was late coming up, staff officers should not proceed to make themselves comfortable until the troops can do the same. After a cold or wet night the staff should be astir early to visit the troops, wish them a good morning and see if they can help them. He urged his departing graduates to bring home to their brother officers that the aim of the Staff was to be on the most friendly terms with them and to do all in their power to help them: this was the Staff College teaching and had been so for many years past.[13]

There exists one piece of documentary evidence at the Staff College to suggest that Robertson's severely practical attitude to the instruction of staff officers had the drawback of curbing the inquiring minds of the more brilliant students. In the summer of 1910, while Henry Wilson was still Commandant, Lt A. P. Wavell (Black Watch) had written a lengthy essay in answer to the question: 'How far are the strategical and tactical lessons drawn from the campaigns of 1815, 1862, 1866 and 1870 confirmed or modified by the experiences of the recent wars in South Africa and Manchuria?' Admittedly the future Field-Marshal set his answer in a provocatively broad context, beginning, for example, with a long and scintillating analysis of the constituents of 'The Military Spirit', and spending some time on the problems of preparation for war in time of peace; but he did go on to answer the question in practical professional terms and the modern reader, whether academic or military, would surely award him a mark of 'alpha plus' for the organization of his material, powers of critical analysis, lucidity of style and scholarly range of literary references. Although the first marker, Lt-Col Charles Ross, mentioned one or two omissions (particularly as regards the study of a theatre of war *before* the outbreak of hostilities), he nevertheless congratulated Wavell on 'this admirable piece of work'. When the essay fell into the new Commandant's hands, however, the reaction was quite different. Robertson was evidently irritated by Wavell's scholarly flourishes and even more by his academic approach to the problem.

Wavell, for example, discussed the 'moral factor' of surprise which could lead to indecision and inability to form a plan in the enemy command. 'Thus we find Napoleon III, Benedek, Bazaine, Buller, Kuropatkin all unable to make up their minds.'[14] To attain surprise on a strategic scale, however, certain political assets were desirable and these might be wanting in a democracy. 'But the necessity, where the Government is popular, of it convincing the people that preparation is necessary is the hardest task of all and precludes secrecy.' On what may be considered a perceptive point about Britain's strategic dilemma before the First World War, Robertson commented. 'I have now read nearly 14 pages, and can find nothing confirming or modifying the *strategic* and *tactical* lessons of the 4 campaigns mentioned. What on earth has the paragraph here marked got to do with either . . . ?'

When in Part III Wavell discussed the problems of a British force operating on the Continent of Europe, he hazarded the generalization that 'Voluntary armies do not tend to produce a high level of generalship. The dominance of our recruiting problem leads to too much time being absorbed in routine and office work. Also small wars are not a good school for war on the Continent, as the French found in 1870 . . . And it is a fact that the periods of our military successes since the feudal days have only synchronized with the appearance of a genius, like Cromwell, Marlborough, Wellington.' Robertson's curt comment was that 'Passages like this are out of place in a paper of this nature'. It was in his final comment, however, that the reason for Robertson's critical attitude is most clearly stated:

> You have put much good work into this and have evidently devoted to it great care and much labour. I am sorry, however, that your efforts have not been more constantly directed towards military matters, the study of which might have been of real value to you afterwards. The discussion of questions of policy and political matters generally leads to no practical result, nor benefit of any kind to the soldier, nor is it his business.

According to Wavell's biographer, the late John Connell, Robertson had Wavell 'on the mat' and addressed him as follows:

'What do you mean by writing nonsense like this? What have you to do with statesmen and their affairs? Your job is to learn the business of a staff officer, not to meddle with political matters. Never you write nonsense like that again. Do you understand?' Each sentence was punctuated by further heavy scratches at the offending passage.

Connell asserts, however, that this 'wigging' was merely the prelude to a gruff compliment.[15] This may be so but while it would be unjust to attach too much importance to a few critical remarks on a single essay, and allowing that Robertson could hardly be expected to know that the bright ex-scholar of Winchester would later become a distinguished Field-Marshal, the criticism that can be made is that he was concentrating too narrowly on the training of efficient staff officers and thereby tended to curb the originality of potential generals. This point was also made in the abrasive criticisms of another Camberley student of that era, Capt. J. F. C. Fuller.

So far as practical training methods are concerned, Robertson maintained the high standard set by his predecessor and, like Wilson, earned the respect and admiration of his students. Brig. Sir Edward Beddington was probably voicing the general opinion when he later wrote of Robertson:

He was a great Commandant, very severe yet at the same time very nice, human and encouraging. We were all frightened to death of him, yet admired him greatly and were fond of him. He taught us a lot and made of some very junior officers, like me, people who could do staff work in war well.[16]

'Wully' himself recalls that he kept the Directing Staff on their toes by visiting the lecture rooms at uncertain hours. On one occasion he arrived after twenty minutes when the instructor was just concluding what should have been a fifty-minute talk. Undismayed, he proceeded to repeat the whole lecture while the students loyally played up by simulating rapt attention to what they had already heard only a few moments before.

On staff tours, which usually lasted three or four days, Robertson was concerned above all to bring home to the students that staff employment in war was not 'all beer and skittles'. He therefore tested their tempers and physical resilience as well as their knowledge by springing new situations on them at all hours of the day and night. Sir Edward Beddington vividly recollects this happening to him on a typical 'Indian frontier' exercise in North Wales. Just as the students were wearily trudging back from the mountains at dusk after a hard day's work the Commandant called him up and said,

'Point out on the ground where you would post your outpost tonight.' After a quick look round I duly did so, and he said 'Thank you, that will do well'. We went back to the pub had a bath and dinner, did our work and went to bed. I had just gone nicely to sleep, when I was woken up by a knock on the door and told by one of the Instructors that the Commandant wanted to see me at once, and that I need not dress. I found old Wully in a dressing gown in his bedroom, and he said 'You are now in command of the outpost you posted this evening,' and handed me a message from No. 2 picket which read as follows: 'Am being heavily attacked in front and both flanks stop running short of ammo.' I said, 'What is the rest of the message, sir?' He answered, 'I don't know, I expect their signal lamp is broken. What will you do?' I answered, 'I should send a company up to help and relieve them.' He replied, 'I thought you would do that. You will find Col. Malcolm waking the rest of the students and telling them to dress. You do the same and lead them up to the relief of No. 2 picket.' We all started off in a bad temper and luckily I had marked on the map where I had put the pickets, and by the grace of God, after the devil of a climb in the dark, we arrived at the top of the right mountain half an hour before dawn. We were then told to go home independently, breakfast would be at 8 a.m., and we would start work again at 9 a.m. Very good for us but very trying, and thank God it was not raining![17]

Further evidence of the thoroughly practical nature of the

outdoor training in staff duties may be found in the elaborate notes preserved in the Papers of one of the ablest of Robertson's instructors, Maj. Philip Howell, who had been nominated to the Quetta Staff College by Kitchener and who was frequently consulted by Sir Douglas Haig. Unfortunately Howell's notes do not lend themselves to brief quotation, but they demonstrate that every general idea was clearly prepared after meticulous study of the ground, and each special idea was designed to bring out a particular lesson. Students habitually worked in pairs, alternately acting as Commander and Chief Staff Officer, the former dictating orders and the latter writing them down.[18] It would be difficult to study the schemes set in the immediate pre-war years and remain unimpressed either by the sophistication of the exercises or the practical lessons they were designed to inculcate. The wider question that inevitably arises is: what contingencies were considered realistic; were they, in short, preparing for the kind of war that actually broke out in 1914?

Even allowing that Robertson composed his autobiography after the First World War and may therefore have been tempted to exaggerate his pre-war prescience, he nevertheless deserves credit for a certain sturdy insularity in devising situations appropriate to Britain's military organisation and strength. Thus, although the well-known early battles of the Franco-Prussian War continued to be studied on the ground, Robertson also took the students to the less famous battlefields of the later, 'broken-backed', phase of the war such as Amiens, Orleans and Le Mans, reasoning that these had a special value in that they were fought by hastily-raised and partially-trained French troops and that Britain might one day face similar problems.[19]

Although preparation for a possible defence of the North West Frontier of India continued to be studied – somewhat unrealistically – in the annual North Wales staff tour, Robertson concentrated at least as much as his predecessor on the most likely strategic eventuality: full-scale war against Germany in France or Belgium. For instance, the traditional military designations 'Redland' and 'Blueland' are but transparent disguises in the Senior Division's Naval and Military Exercise of 26–29 March 1913, when the general idea was as follows:

1 Redland, an island, is at war with Blueland, a Continental Power. The former country is considerably superior in naval strength to Blueland but the latter is much stronger on land, and a Red invasion of Blueland is impracticable.
2 Eastland comprising the counties of Norfolk, Suffolk, Essex and Cambridge, is a Blue possession about 700 miles from Redland ports of embarkation. Harwich is a defended harbour, and except for its garrison and a small mobile force of all arms, there are no troops, regular or irregular, in Eastland. The capital is Cambridge . . .

In a more prophetic reconnaissance scheme of the same period the London–Reading–Aylesbury area was taken to represent Belgium between two opposing armies, 'Germany' in the West Country and 'France' east of London.[20] In theoretical terms, then, there can be no doubt that the pre-war graduates of Camberley were well-prepared for the general strategic situation that confronted the B.E.F. in August 1914.[21]

The most unorthodox and most useful training concept that Robertson introduced at Camberley was, however, the practice of staff duties connected with retreats. The training manuals displayed an obsession with the importance of the offensive, and the very idea that British troops might have to fight on the defensive was scorned. Apparently, too, it was particularly difficult to simulate conditions of a retreat in peacetime.

In his final address of 1912 Robertson wisely urged the graduating officers to study such historic retreats as Moore's to Corunna; Wellington's in 1810 and 1812; Napoleon's to Leipzig in 1813 and to Paris in 1814; and Jackson's and Lee's in the American Civil War.

Our regulations justly lay stress on the value of the offensive; but if this teaching alone is given, think what may be the effect on the troops when they are ordered to retire instead of to go forward – that is, to abandon that method of making war by which alone, according to the training they have previously received, decisive victory can be achieved. Think,

13. The Staff College at Quetta shortly after its opening in 1907. Some 5,000 feet above sea-level it has a bracing climate by Indian standards. Since Partition in 1947 it has been the Staff College of the Pakistan Army.

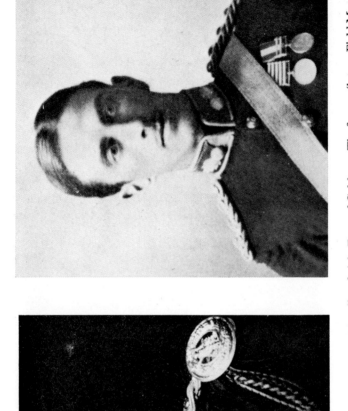

14. Two outstanding students *c.* 1910. *Left,* Lieut. A. P. Wavell and *right,* Everard Calthrop. The former (later a Field Marshal) was 'carpeted' by Robertson for introducing politics into a strategic paper. Wavell regarded Calthrop as the most original mind of his Term but the Directing Staff thought him too unorthodox. He had the unique distinction of passing through both the British and Japanese Staff Colleges, but died in action in 1915.

too, of the disintegration and demoralization which nearly always accompany retrograde movements, even when an army has not been previously defeated. It seems to me that there is practically no chance of successfully carrying out this operation in war unless we thoroughly study and practice it beforehand during peace. If we have this practice, the operation will then not come as a surprise to the troops in war; they will understand better what they are expected in do; and they will recognize it as being a form of war which may have to be adopted by any army and can be adopted, not only without failure, but with a certain measure, ultimately, of success.

This lecture was published in the official *Army Review* in 1913 by the order of the former Secretary of State for War, Lord Haldane, and its author was probably justified in concluding that it contributed indirectly to the skilful conduct of the historic retreat from Mons.[22]

Though he did not share Henry Wilson's pro-French enthusiasm, Robertson had been convinced for several years before he went to Camberley that war with Germany was inevitable sooner or later. At a hint from the War Office he refrained from mentioning the most likely enemy by name in his addresses in order 'to avoid giving offence to a friendly Power', but none of his audience at the Staff College, Aldershot or elsewhere was left in any doubt as to the enemy's identity. Thus, in his final address to the students who left at the end of 1911, he remarked:

> You do not come here for the sake of passing examinations at the end of the first year, and of obtaining a p.s.c. at the end of the second. You come here in order that you may leave the college better and more efficient members of the military community. You should endeavour to increase the knowledge you have acquired, disseminate it amongst others, and, as I have often told you, direct your studies and peace preparations in general to a special and definite end – that of fighting the most probable and most formidable adversary for the time being.

L

Finally, remember that when the day for fighting comes, the qualifications demanded of you, whether on the staff or in command, will include, in addition to a good theoretical knowledge of your professional duties, the possession of a quick eye, a good digestion, an untiring activity, a determination to close with your enemy, and a firm resolution not to take counsel of your fears.[23]

In October 1913 Robertson was succeeded as Commandant by Brig.-Gen. Launcelot Kiggell, who is now best remembered by military historians as Haig's Chief-of-Staff during 1917 and as the man who, on belatedly approaching the swamps of the Passchendaele battlefront, burst into tears and exclaimed 'Good God, did we really send men to fight in that.'[24] He was in fact a very able staff officer, but was not a strong character, being prone to overwork, worry and ill-health. Haig thought very highly of his abilities and when in India frequently consulted him about the best officers for important posts. Indeed, he had succeeded Haig in the key position of Director of Staff Duties at the War Office from 1909 until his appointment to the Staff College. One of his students, during his all-too-brief tenure of the latter post, described him as 'a scholarly type, of a retiring nature, and content to let well alone'.[25] Maj.-Gen. J. F. C. Fuller, also a student at Camberley in 1914, was more scathing in his *Memoirs* when describing Haig's General Staff (1916–18) as 'The Grand Lamasery'. Fuller characterized Haig's Staff as single-minded and honourable men, but mediocrities. Kiggell he regarded as 'a highly educated soldier, but a doctrinaire'. 'He possessed knowledge, but little vision, and at the Staff College he appeared to me to be a dyspeptic, gloomy and doleful man. I cannot imagine that his influence on his Chief was in any way decisive or beneficial.'[26] Lest Fuller's opinions be thought excessively severe – as a tank enthusiast whose ideas were repeatedly thwarted by the General Staff in France – it should be noted that John Terraine's judgement on Kiggell is substantially the same. Although Haig and Kiggell worked well together, Terraine writes, it is hard to resist the conclusion that Kiggell never was, nor aspired to be, more than a mouthpiece for Haig. He was an efficient Staff Officer, and Haig respected his opinions when offered; but in two years Kiggell made little mark on the Army, remaining always a shadowy figure in the background, signing orders, circulating papers, minding the machine . . . in truth a distinct weakness of Haig's period of command is the lack of a forceful and energetic personality at his side until the last months of the War, when Sir Herbert Lawrence joined him.[27]

The Staff College student of 1914 referred to above, who eventually became Gen. Sir Harold Franklyn, recalled that in contrast to 1939 there was no particular sense of urgency in staff training in the summer of 1914. Indeed, though he does not say so, the most likely theatre of war appeared to be Ulster almost up to the eve of mobilization against Germany.

Franklyn was favourably impressed by the meticulous training provided in Staff Duties. Errors in drafting orders and messages were relentlessly encircled in red ink until the future staff officers had mastered the form and could concentrate wholly on the substance. Another useful exercise was to write a complicated Appreciation on the back of a message form; every word had to be weighed and most of them discarded. This practice in selection and compression proved invaluable in France in 1914 when only one typewriter was allotted to each Brigade Headquarters so that almost all correspondence with units was by written messages.

On the debit side, Franklyn voiced the widespread view that there were far too many lectures; and also – a tendency that Robertson had tried to stamp out – too much teaching of military history for its own sake with no sustained effort to extract lessons applicable to modern war. Certainly the Waterloo campaign and the American Civil War continued to be studied in the most minute detail. Lastly, and rather surprisingly in view of Wilson's '*Allez, allez*' schemes and Robertson's unpredictable interventions in outdoor exercises, Franklyn recalled that the main weakness of the various schemes was that 'no attempt was made to simulate the hustle and distractions of active service; in fact they lacked realism'.

Of the more memorable personalities of his term or Division, Franklyn referred to one who 'possessed a brilliant brain, but whose critical faculty was so highly developed that it was apt to get out of control'. This could only have referred to Capt. J. F. C. Fuller, whose unfavourable impression of Kiggell has been quoted above. In the summer of 1911 Fuller decided that the freedom he had enjoyed as an Intelligence Officer in South Africa and as a Territorial Adjutant (of the 10th Middlesex), had completely spoilt him for peacetime soldiering. He describes the revelation with typical verve:

> The Second Battalion of my Regiment was then stationed at Shorncliffe, and on one exceptionally hot day I was standing not far from the Martello tower overlooking Sandgate Hill, when along marched the 52nd in full war paint. Somehow the sight of those decked-out, sweating men horrified me. Mentally I looked round for some avenue of escape, and in an instant I decided to work for the Staff College.[28]

Fuller was slow to learn that independent thought, particularly when expressed in uncompromising, caustic language, is seldom welcomed by military (or any other) officialdom. Passing into the Staff College at the second attempt he concluded bitterly that 'success does not so much depend upon what you know as upon what the examiner knows, and this can in many cases be gauged from the nature of his questions...' Again he discovered too late that the object of study (for the entrance examination) was not to fit yourself to become a staff officer, but solely in order to pass the examination.

> Abide rigidly by the manuals and regulations; do not read books which are of value, but instead crammers' productions; for the average crammer is no fool. He knows to an inch the mental measurement of the normal examiner; that is why, for practical education, their cram books are totally valueless.[29]

He goes on to describe the contents of the three surviving papers which he wrote at the Staff College between January and July 1914: all contained unorthodox views and all met with opposition from the directing staff. It is diverting to speculate whether he would have survived the course and obtained a p.s.c. had not the outbreak of war intervened.

In his first paper, called 'The Tactics of Penetration', his main contention was that tactics are based on weapon-power and not on the experiences of military history, and that since in 1914 the quick-firing field gun and the machine gun were the two most recent weapons, our tactics should be based on them. So far so good; but his deduction that the use of these weapons would 'revolutionize the present theory of war' by substituting penetration for envelopment was a heresy and was dealt with as such. Fuller's emphasis on the primacy of fire power was unexceptionable but his tactical deductions were not. Liddell Hart, for example, noted in the margins of his copy of Fuller's *Memoirs*: 'Seems the same as the French theory of 1914 which didn't work', and 'Over-emphasizes the offensive value of the m.g. (machine-gun) and overlooks its defensive value'.

The second paper dealt with the employment of artillery and was inspired by a visit to the Larkhill range on Salisbury Plain where the artillery of the 4th Division were holding a practice camp. It is revealing of the separateness of the three arms in those days that Fuller, though a regular officer and in his thirty-sixth year, had never before seen a battery of guns in action. This experience confirmed him in the view, already suggested by wide reading, that the artillery was now the superior arm; consequently battles would become more static, that is, entrenched:

> . . . to put the whole matter in a nutshell, since the introduction of quick-firing artillery, it is as much the duty of the infantry to cooperate with the artillery as it is for the artillery to cooperate with the infantry. It is no longer a question of the infantry moving from A to B and the guns covering their advance; but that, as B is tactically and topographically

suited to the maximum development of artillery fire, therefore the infantry will attack it . . . Further, to obtain full
value from the aeroplane reconnaissance, the observer must
be a highly trained artillerist. So much so, that it appears
to me that special aeroplanists will have to be trained for
artillery observation, and that these and their aeroplanes
will have to be allotted to those guns detailed to carry out
the decisive artillery attack.

This essay was not well received either, because, in addition
to the penetration heresy, it stressed the superiority of the
artillery over the infantry and the need for entrenchment in
attack as well as in defence.

One cannot repress a twinge of sympathy for the Directing
Staff in their stony reaction to Fuller's third offering, which was
a comparison of the battles of Salamanca and Chancellorsville.
Fuller, with the naïve boldness of the child who noticed that the
King was wearing no clothes, dared to point out that *Field
Service Regulations* (1909 edition), while sententiously pro-
claiming that 'The fundamental principles of war are neither
very numerous nor in themselves very abstruse, but the application of them is difficult, and cannot be made subject to rules',
nowhere deigned to mention what the principles were. Fuller
therefore derived his own principles from Napoleon's correspondence and applied them to the two set battles entirely to
his own satisfaction. He was bluntly told that it was not
the business of the student to amend the Book, but to study
it.[30]

It is difficult to believe that any directing staff drawn from
regular British officers at that period would have won the
approval of so fierce an iconoclastic a critic as Fuller, who did
not acquire the nick-name of 'Boney' for nothing. But recollect-
ing Robertson's strictures on Wavell's essay, he was surely
right to conclude that it was a defect of Staff College instruction
that it too closely resembled a machine created to produce
standardized thinking. Elsewhere he echoed Franklyn's criticism that military history was too often studied in an anti-
quarian way. Fuller, almost certainly correctly, attributed this

tendency to the pervasive influence of Col. Sir Lonsdale Hale, who had been Professor of Fortification and Artillery from 1878 to 1883. This venerable Royal Engineer officer subsequently retired and settled in Camberley so as to be near the College, busying himself in the Library and frequently appearing in photographs of the Directing Staff as an honorary member. A voluminous writer, he had served as a military correspondent for *The Times* between 1890 and 1905. As a military historian he was distinctly pre-Henderson in his obsession with minutiae. It was alleged that he had studied the Franco-German War so minutely that he could inform an inquirer of the exact position of all the German and French units down to companies at any given time in any battle during 1870 and 1871. As Fuller writes, 'He possessed what may be called a typical Bradshaw mind, and, being an enthusiast, this type of mind was cultivated by his students.'[31]

The Staff College did not entirely escape from the political backwash that followed the Curragh Incident of March 1914, when a number of British officers were put into the false position of having to choose either to be parties to the future coercion of Ulster or to resign their commissions. The published *Diaries* of Sir Henry Wilson, an Ulsterman himself and at that time Director of Military Operations at the War Office, provide abundant evidence that he actively fostered military opposition to the Liberal Government on this question and also conveyed this information to the Leader of the Opposition, Bonar Law. In Wilson's view it was essential that the C.I.G.S., Sir John French, should resign, as a symbolic gesture that the Army was unanimous in its determination not to fight Ulster. When French wavered, Wilson volunteered to consult the officers of the Staff College, 'a place which represented the opinion of the whole army'. In his Diary for 28 March 1914 he noted:

To this he agreed so I drove down to Arborfield, where the Staff College were having their point-to-point. I consulted the following: Sir Charles Knowles (a great friend of Ewart's),

Robb, Perceval, Archie Montgomery, Hugo Montgomery, Kiggell, Anderson, Cory, Harper, Gillman, Stopford, Sillem, Vic Couper. These again consulted with their friends and then reported. The result was a practically unanimous opinion that he must resign.[32]

According to Fuller, the students were divided on the Irish question. Fuller said he would probably have resigned, not because he was a friend of Northern Ireland, but on the somewhat frivolous grounds that he had spent a miserable year at Mullingar and could not imagine anything worse than being ruled by Southern Irishmen![33] The affair rumbled on subterraneously in the British Army through the summer and was only silenced, temporarily, by the outbreak of a greater conflict in August.

Three days after the assassination of Archduke Ferdinand at Sarajevo on 28 June 1914, the Staff College gave its annual garden party. Godwin-Austen has poignantly described the idyllic scene: present and past students strolling beneath the huge beeches and by the lake, watching the tennis and cricket and listening to the band. How many of them realized that Britain was near the brink of war? As July wore on there were hints of an approaching crisis: horses were to be sold, and officers going on leave were ordered to keep within distance for instant recall. As the international situation grew more tense, the Directing Staff found it impossible to focus the students' attention on abstract problems. Lt-Col W. H. (later Sir Hastings) Anderson, then on the Directing Staff and Commandant immediately after the war, recalled the last exercise of the term on a hot summer's day near Marlow, where the Junior Department of the Royal Military College had first been situated over a hundred years ago:

his syndicate lying on the grass, their unsettled minds wandering from contemplation of a picnic party on a launch to the price they had been offered for their horses, and back again to the all-absorbing questions of what the next few days should bring, till he, equally distrait, abandoned the hopeless contest and joined in the profitless speculation.[34]

Term ended on 31 July without any special orders, and most of the officers lingered on anxiously at Camberley. On 4 August the tension was at last broken and, flinging unwanted gear into boxes, they dashed off eagerly to take up junior staff appointments. More than 150 p.s.c.s were never to return.

CHAPTER 9. NOTES

1 Barrow, *op. cit.*, p. 120.
2 Quoted by V. Bonham-Carter, *op. cit.*, p. 5.
3 When Robertson was Quartermaster-General and later Chief of
  the General Staff at G.H.Q. in France, the G.S.O. 1. (Operations)
  was Col. G. M. 'Uncle' Harper. The military abbreviation for
  Harper's post was O(a). When asked what O(a) stood for, Wully at
  once replied 'Old 'Arper''. Philip Howell to his wife 11 February 1915
  (Howell Papers IV/C/3111). Was this an example of Wully's humour?
  Robertson did himself an injustice in saying he had only made one
  good joke in his life as he related this joke to Sir George Barrow: 'I was
  crossing the Channel during the war, together with Lord Rhondda,
  the Food Controller. It was very rough and, seeing my companion
  violently seasick over the ship's side, I went over to him and said, "I
  say, Rhondda, I don't think you are much of a food controller!"''
  Barrow, *op. cit.*, p. 120.
4 Robertson, *op. cit.*, pp. 168–9.
5 Godwin-Austen, *op. cit.*, p. 258.
6 Robertson, *op. cit.*, pp. 171–2.
7 Gen. Sir Harold. E. Franklyn in Lt-Col F. W. Young (ed.), *op.
  cit.*, pp. 22–5. For criticisms of the Staff College examination papers see
  United Service Magazine, Vols XXXVIII (1909), pp. 179–83 and
  XLIII (1911), pp. 261–72. See also Bt-Maj. A. V. T. Wakely,
  'Notes on working for the Examination for admission to the Staff
  College', *Royal Engineers' Journal*, June 1922, pp. 328–44.
8 Although they were critical of the British Army's comparative lack
  of professionalism, and also of many products of the Staff College,
  both Meinertzhagen and Fuller show that there was some improvement after the South African War. See Col. R. Meinertzhagen, *op. cit.*,
  and Maj.-Gen. J. F. C. Fuller, *The Army in My Time* (London,
  1935).
9 Godwin-Austen, *op. cit.*, p. 257. Barrow, *op. cit.*, p. 119. The complete
  list of Staff College instructors can be obtained from the Army List
  or from the panels in the Henderson Room at the Staff College.
10 Robertson, *op. cit.*, p. 175.
11 *Ibid.* See also *The Army Review*, Vol. II, January–April 1912, pp.
  291–8, and Vol. IV, January–April 1913, pp. 333–42.
12 *Ibid.*, 1913, p. 337.
13 *Ibid.*, 1912, pp. 294–6; 1913, p. 336.
14 Surprisingly, Robertson took exception to Wavell's criticism of Buller,
  remarking 'Steady. You do not quite realize the difficulties facing some
  of these commanders . . . I would not pillory Buller as you do.'

Wavell's original essay is in a locked display cabinet at the Staff College. All quotations are from a typed copy.

15 J. Connell, *op. cit.*, pp. 64–5. Though both took their profession seriously, Ross and Robertson were alike in their insensitivity to works of art. The former resisted all enticements to look at Amiens cathedral and finally remarked 'No, old chap, I saw the cathedral at Strasbourg, and when you've seen one cathedral, you've seen all!' Robertson reluctantly agreed to look at Salisbury cathedral but the whole expedition was over in five minutes and his only comment was: 'It's a nice, clean-looking place.' See Barrow, *op. cit.*, pp. 116–17. Connell has unfortunately omitted to give his source and has further confused the issue by writing as though there were two different essays whereas in fact all his comments and his single quotation refer to the one discussed above.

16 Quoted by V. Bonham-Carter, *op. cit.*, p. 73.

17 *Ibid.* See also Robertson, *op. cit.*, pp. 172–3.

18 See the *Howell Papers*, I/L/2.

19 Robertson, *op. cit.*, p. 180.

20 *Howell Paper*, I/L/2/6 and I/L/3/9.

21 But it should be noted that Robertson was no more accurate than Wilson in predicting Germany's actual strategical plan of 1914, i.e., neither foresaw a concentration on the German right wing for a massive drive through Belgium *north* of the river Meuse.

22 Robertson, *op. cit.*, pp. 176–8 and *Army Review* 1913.

23 *Ibid.*, pp. 178–9 and *Army Review* 1912, p. 298. For the various versions of Robertson's lecture, 'On War', see the *Robertson Papers* 1/3, *passim*.

24 On Kiggell's outburst at Passchendaele see the *Liddell Hart Papers*, letter from Sir Ernest Swinton 27 February 1930, and notes on talks with Swinton and Edmonds, B 3/2, B 3/3. The witness was Lt-Col C. F. Aspinall-Oglander, later Official Historian of the Gallipoli campaign.

25 For Haig's relationship with Kiggell see the *Kiggell Papers* 1909–14, *passim*. See also Franklyn, *The Story of the Staff College*, p. 23.

26 Maj.-Gen. J. F. C. Fuller, *Memoirs of an Unconventional Soldier* (London, 1936), pp. 140–2.

27 J. Terraine, *Haig: the Educated Soldier* (London, 1963), p. 176.

28 Fuller, *Memoirs*, pp. 20–1.

29 *Ibid.*

30 *Ibid.*, pp. 23–9.

31 Fuller, *The Army in My Time*, pp. 122–3. There is a photo of Lonsdale Hale in the Staff College Library giving details of his appointments. Godwin-Austen and J. Luvaas (*The Education of an Army*) both erroneously state that Lonsdale Hale was sometime Professor of Military History at the Staff College.

32 Wilson's *Diary*, 28 March 1914. Callwell's transcription (*Field Marshal Sir Henry Wilson*, I, p. 144) is imperfect, and on the following

day when Wilson discussed the likely effects of French's resignation with Bonar Law and Carson, Callwell omits the revealing opinion that 'this would break the Cabinet as it would carry with it the loss of Seely, Morley and Haldane'.

33 Fuller, *Memoirs*, p. 29.
34 Godwin-Austen, *op. cit.*, p. 262.

CHAPTER TEN

The Staff College,
the General Staff and the test of war
1914-1915

On the outbreak of war in August 1914 the General Staff was just as deluded as the British public in its conviction that the struggle would be short and decisive.[1] There was consequently little attempt to restrain the instinctive impulse of every senior officer fit for active service – and many who were not – to dash off to France with the Expeditionary Force. Col. J. E. Edmonds, for example, thought that at fifty-two he was too old to be the chief staff officer to a division, bearing in mind that reinforcements and replacements would be necessary, but he went out nevertheless and suffered a nervous and physical collapse after the ordeal of the retreat from Mons. Col. F. S. Maude actually noted in his diary that he ought really to remain at his important post in the Training Directorate but, like other lucky officers, he was delighted to be offered a staff appointment in the field.[2]

As a result of this miscalculation and short-sightedness, the General Staff at the War Office was seriously weakened, not only in regard to the enormous strategic problems with which it ought to have wrestled, but also in its corporate sense of experience and responsibility in dealing with the formidable new Secretary of State for War, Field-Marshal Lord Kitchener. Taking as a sample the Chief of the Imperial General Staff, the heads of his three Directorates (Military Operations, Staff Duties and Training) and their senior officers (G.S.O.s 1 and 2), only ten out of thirty-two still held their appointments in October 1914. But even these figures fail to convey the real loss of experience. In the first place the C.I.G.S., Sir Charles Douglas, was not an experienced General Staff officer (indeed he lacked a p.s.c.), and was only a stand-in for Sir John French who had resigned in April 1914 over the Curragh incident. Lord Esher described Douglas as follows in his Journal on 13 August:

> The orderly-room has left a deep aura round such imagination as it is fitting for a Scottish soldier to possess. Honest, incapable of subterfuge or of misplaced enthusiasm, he tries with conscientious and honest labour to solve insoluble problems. Everyone admires and trusts him. It is difficult to find a more typical soldier-administrator. What, however, is he doing at the head of the General Staff, where even Moltke might be overburdened?

and a week later added:

> No soldier left at the War Office or in England, except Spencer Ewart, now Commander-in-Chief at Edinburgh but erstwhile Director of Military Operations, will look beyond a few square miles on the Meuse.
> That strategical will-o'-the wisp is the attraction that draws away our forces from their true vocation. We shall rue our folly if the Germans occupy the Channel ports.[3]

Instead of encouraging the C.I.G.S. and his War Office colleagues to stand up to Kitchener on strategic issues, Esher did his best to induce them to accept his decisions, right or wrong, after explaining their views. 'He [Kitchener] has been given by the Government absolute authority, and there is really nothing more to be said.' Douglas certainly failed to make any distinctive impression before he died from overwork in October 1914. Kitchener ignored Haldane's recommendation of Nicholson (the former C.I.G.S.), Spencer Ewart or Ian Hamilton as Douglas's successor and selected Sir James Wolfe Murray who was totally unfitted for the post either by temperament or experience. Sir Philip Magnus described him as 'notoriously incompetent', and Churchill rather cruelly nicknamed him 'Sheep' Murray on account of his failure to speak up for the General Staff in the War Council.[4]

Secondly, there was an expensive failure to take physical fitness into account in selecting the senior commanders and staff of the Expeditionary Force, an error that Kitchener repeated even more flagrantly in the choice of commanders for the Suvla operation in the Dardanelles campaign in August 1915. Gen. Sir James Grierson was one of the most intelligent and experienced General Staff officers on the outbreak of war; even Col Charteris – a devout admirer of Haig – admitted that Grierson was more clever if less capable as a commander than Haig. He was also very fond of good living and very corpulent, yet he was given the command of II Corps, only to die of a heart attack on 17 August on the train journey to Mons. Charteris dismissed as 'utter nonsense' the inevitable rumour that the Germans had poisoned him and remarked 'poor Grierson was of too full a habit to stand even the comparatively comfortable strain of soldiering at Corps H.Q.'[5] Apart from his other deficiencies, which will be considered later, Sir Archibald Murray was insufficiently robust to be Sir John French's Chief-of-Staff and was apt to faint in a crisis. Also, Sir William Robertson would have been more valuable at the War Office in the opening months of the war than as Quartermaster-General of the B.E.F. These and other appointments bear witness to Sir James Edmonds's later reflection that 'Staffs for war require as careful selection as a Test cricket team. But no one except the elder Moltke has ever carried this out.'[6]

As a political appointment designed to unite the nation in support of the war – and of the Government – Asquith's selection of Lord Kitchener to replace himself (and, briefly, Haldane) at the War Office proved fully justified. Moreover, though his rejection of the Territorial organization as the foundation on which to build up reserve divisions in favour of the improvised 'Kitchener Armies', is open to serious criticism, Kitchener's uncompromising, minority view that Britain must prepare for a long and all-out struggle was perceptive and wise. But in the higher direction of the war Kitchener was to prove

a great disappointment; his chronic and even pathetic in-
decisiveness over the Dardanelles campaign in 1915 was to
convince even his warmest supporters that in the role of strategist he was as bewildered as the politicians. Indeed, had
Asquith examined his career more closely, or taken the opinion
of those who had worked with him, such as Sir Ian Hamilton,
he would have discovered that Kitchener was almost totally
lacking in experience – and even interest – in the strategic
aspects of his profession.[7]

Kitchener would have found ample outlet for his ferocious
energy and industry had he confined himself to the normal
duties of a civilian Secretary of State for War, notably the
recruitment and administration of by far the largest army
Britain had ever put in the field. But of course he was in no
sense a politician and – as the earlier quotation from Viscount
Esher correctly hinted – had been appointed by a trusting
Cabinet as a sort of *generalissimo* to direct the whole war effort.
It is only fair to Kitchener to emphasize that no single individual,
however experienced, wise and robust could have performed
these Protean duties efficiently in the circumstances in which
Britain found herself in 1914 and 1915.

From the outset Kitchener treated the General Staff with
an aloofness approaching contempt. For example, he impeded
the execution of Henry Wilson's detailed pre-war plans by
insisting that two out of the six divisions of the B.E.F. be
initially retained in Britain as a precaution against invasion. He
also reversed the General Staff policy on invasion, which was to
concentrate inland, and made preparations instead to meet the
assault on the beaches.

To Kitchener's inability to accept the need for a strong and
independent General Staff to advise him on strategic issues
were added an unwillingness to delegate and an exaggerated
concern for secrecy. Thus he virtually acted as his own private
secretary, entangling himself in a mass of trivia to the neglect
of strategic planning. It was difficult to gain access to him at all
and he insisted on seeing members of the Army Council
individually and alone so that he was never confronted with a
collective professional opinion. His brusque and un-confiding

treatment of Sir Ian Hamilton (his own choice) before dis-
patching him to the Dardanelles Command is a good example
of the short shrift that he habitually gave to senior soldiers. On
the other hand he habitually by-passed the General Staff by
directly asking the opinion of the commander on the spot.[8]

In these circumstances it is no exaggeration to say that the
General Staff at the War Office, considered as the centre of
strategic planning, was allowed to slide into limbo during the
first two years of the war, until the advent of a strong and
experienced staff officer, Sir William Robertson, as C.I.G.S. in
December 1915.

It is barely credible that, despite the experience of the South
African War, the Staff College was once again allowed to close
shortly after the outbreak of the First World War. On the
assumption that the war would be 'over by Christmas', the
Staff College was speedily denuded of its instructing staff and
students, the majority of the former, such as Lt-Cols F. B. Maurice,
J. T. Burnett-Stuart, H. M. de F. Montgomery, A. A. Montgomery (later Field-Marshal Montgomery-Massingberd) and
W. H. Anderson to take up senior staff appointments with the
B.E.F.,[9] while many of the students, including Captain J. F. C.
Fuller, suddenly found themselves serving as Assistant Embarkation and Railway Transport Officers. Thus the Staff College
deserves a good deal of the credit for the remarkably smooth
dispatch of the first six divisions.[10]

From the autumn of 1914 until April 1916 the Staff College's
humble function was to provide accommodation for officers of
the New Armies taking one-month courses at Sandhurst. For a
time, the College then served as the home of No. 11 Officers'
Cadet Battalion until this became too large and moved to
Pirbright. From September 1917 the College was used as one of
the centres for four-monthly Staff courses designed to prepare
officers who had held grade 2 appointments in war for first
grade appointments. Lastly, from September 1918 to January
1919 the College housed a School of Tactics for senior officers.
It resumed its proper functions in March 1919.

Within a few weeks of the outbreak of war the existing pool

of p.s.c. and qualified staff (q.s.) officers had dried up, and thereafter commanders had to make the best of untrained regimental officers. At first commanders in France replaced their staff casualties (and there were many) by attaching 'learners' to their headquarters. Later a comprehensive attempt was made to train Senior and Junior staff officers in France by setting up schools at Hesdin under Brig.-Gen. C. Bonham-Carter and Col. R. A. M. Currie. Not until April 1916 did the War Office attempt to introduce a uniform system: Staff Schools were set up in Britain, and the Army Council attempted to lay down minimum qualifications even for temporary staff appointments. These included a month's attachment to the Staff and completion of a six-weeks' course. Even this ten- to twelve-week training qualification proved too long to satisfy the urgent demand for staff officers in 1916 so that for home appointments only the attachment was obligatory. By September 1917 pressure had relaxed to the extent that conditions could again be imposed: apart from satisfactory Staff service G.S.O. 3s must have served an attachment to a Headquarters, while G.S.O.s 1 and 2 must have a pass certificate from a Senior or Junior Staff Course, the former for G.S.O.s 1 and the latter for G.S.O.s 2. These courses were held at Camberley, Cambridge and elsewhere; successful students at a Senior Course were designated by the letters *Sc*, and at a junior course by *sc*. These expedients were better than nothing in an emergency, but they merely served to enlarge upon the lesson of the South African War that first-class staff officers cannot be trained in a few weeks. Considering the number of p.s.c.s who were wounded or too old for field service, and who could have run six-month or even four-month courses at the Staff College, there was a deplorable waste of both facilities and expertise.[11]

Historians of the B.E.F. have been rather unrevealing about its staff work, and for obvious reasons description and judgements must be extremely impressionistic. For one thing, efficient staff work in such matters as intelligence gathering and analysis, the formulation and transmission of operational

orders, and troop movements is apt to be taken for granted so
that routine good work passes unrecorded while errors and
costly omissions receive the glare of publicity. For another, the
B.E.F. was in practice operationally subordinate to and dependent on the French so that in many matters, such as choice
of ground and the timing of offensives, its commanders had all
too little initiative. Thirdly, the B.E.F. was notoriously handicapped by shortage of *matériel* throughout 1914 and 1915;
not merely heavy artillery and high explosive shells – though
that was the most-publicized deficiency, but there were also
only two machine guns per battalion, no trench mortars, hand
grenades, or anti-aircraft guns and inadequate trench-building
materials. Indeed, there was a shortage of virtually every kind
of equipment necessary for waging a siege war such as developed
in the winter of 1914. When all these factors have been taken
into account, it needs also to be said that Sir John French
proved a poor Commander-in-Chief, and it would have required an elder von Moltke as Chief-of-Staff to have offset his
personal limitations.

In considering the influence of the Staff College on the
commanders and chiefs-of-staff in the First World War there is
little point in going beyond the Spring of 1915. By that time
the small band of p.s.c.s had suffered very heavy losses so that
the survivors had to be spread thinly throughout the home and
overseas commands. The original B.E.F., officers as well as men,
had been for all practical purposes annihilated. A new form of
static trench warfare with the huge New Armies – officered
largely by amateurs – had set in, and for these conditions the
Staff College had provided scarcely any preparation.

The salient point about the intellectual training of the British
Army leaders of 1914 is that nearly all were p.s.c.s, and most of
them, including Haig (I Corps), Murray (C.G.S.), Henry
Wilson (Maj.-Gen. General Staff), Snow and Edmonds (G.O.
C-in-C and C.G.S. 4th Division) and Macdonogh (G.S.O.
1 Intelligence, G.H.Q.) had been at Camberley in the mid-
1890s. They had thus received their higher education for
war at a time when the quality of the Staff College instruction
was improving under Hildyard and Henderson, but still

remained in many respects ante-diluvian. The campaigns they
had studied in great detail were those of the Shenandoah
Valley (1861–2) and eastern France (1870), so that the lessons
of the more recent wars in South Africa and Manchuria had
been denied to them; that is, as students: all the future Army
Commanders of the First World War were column commanders
in South Africa.[12] Nor at that time was Germany seen as the
most likely enemy, and Henry Wilson's obsession with France's
eastern frontiers still lay a decade ahead. In some respects, then,
though obviously the more professional and industrious among
them had tried to keep up-to-date with military developments
after 1900, it makes sense to think of the 1914 generation of
generals as *late Victorian* soldiers, and this is particularly true of
the Commander-in-Chief (who did not have a p.s.c.), Sir John
French.

That the Army – or at least its leaders – had at last come to
accept that a Staff College training was virtually obligatory for
high command as well as for the senior staff appointments in
war is evident in the selection of the B.E.F. Taking into account
the senior staff officers at G.H.Q., the Corps Commanders and
their Brigadier-Generals General Staff, the Divisional commanders and their chief staff officers (G.S.O.s 1) and the
Commanding Officer of the Royal Flying Corps and his G.S.O.
1, no less than 40 out of the 45 officers who held these appointments in the first three months of the war were p.s.c.s. The only
exceptions were Sir John French, Sir Nevil Macready (the very
able Adjutant-General at G.H.Q.), Sir Charles Fergusson (5th
Division), H. F. M. Wilson (4th Division succeeding Snow in
September) and Pulteney (III Corps). At least fourteen of the
p.s.c.s had also been on the Directing Staff and four (not
counting Braithwaite or Kiggell who were still at the War
Office) had been Commandants at Camberley or Quetta.[13]
The proportion of p.s.c.s in junior staff posts was equally
impressive.

The problems of the chief staff officer of one of the six
divisions of the B.E.F. were vividly described by Sir James
Edmonds, who held that appointment in the 4th Division

(Eastern Command) from 1910 to 1914.[14] In peacetime, only
two staff officers were allowed to a division – 'one of the most
short-sighted pieces of Treasury petty economy' – while in war
the establishment was six. The two officers were absurdly
overworked in peacetime, and on mobilization were joined by
four newcomers who were probably untrained and unknown to
them. Edmonds found that no divisional system existed in the
Army; no instructions on the duties of a divisional staff had
been drawn up and his predecessors had not even troubled to
record their experience. The only divisional standing orders
for war which he and the commander (Maj.-Gen. T. D'O
Snow) could discover were those of Craufurd in the Peninsular
War. This they gradually remedied and also devised
training methods as original and testing as a limited budget,
the absence of large bodies of troops and ultra-cautious
naval cooperation would permit. Snow, a fanatically keen
commander, held advanced ideas on the use of camouflage, and
by its use frequently outwitted his opponent in manœuvres.
The artillery, for example, used their waterproof sheets and
branches to hide the guns; the troops always marched and
bivouacked along the edges of fields, never in the open; and if
an aeroplane came over they changed over from the left-hand
side to the right with the result that on at least one occasion
they were reported as marching in the opposite direction.
These practices, later commonplace, were regarded as daring
innovations before 1914. Moreover, Snow fully shared Robertson's conviction as to the importance of practising retreats. A
scheme set by the latter for the 4th Division in 1913 almost
precisely foreshadowed the Division's predicament a year later
at the close of the battle of Le Cateau. As in the real battle, the
4th Division out-marched its pursuers and turned in good order
to meet them. 'It may have been a sham fight," reported the
Morning Post, 'but there was no sham rain, nor sham marching,
nor sham hunger.' Edmonds added caustically that practising
retirements had been forbidden by Sir Charles Douglas, then
Inspector-General of the Forces – 'a man with the talents of an
orderly-room clerk'. Not content with the lessons learnt in these
large-scale manœuvres, Snow devoted the winter divisional

exercise to the study of the practical problems of a retreat, deciding, for example, that the Chief Engineer was the best officer to take care of traffic control. Edmonds embodied the lessons in a booklet for the benefit of the whole Army. It was this kind of intensive pre-war study of staff problems that helped to make the orderly retreat and rapid recovery of the B.E.F. in the opening month of the war such a brilliant achievement.

On mobilization, the four additional staff officers posted to the 4th Division were strangers to it and only one of them was known to Edmonds – as his former cadet student at Woolwich. According to Edmonds, this officer, though he came straight from the Camberley Directing Staff, could not write a practical operation order, had never heard of a time sliding scale for marches, and knew nothing of the routine of preparing simultaneously sufficient copies of an order and of a march table. The senior administrative officer had no p.s.c. and could not write an operational order at all. The third was an excellent young officer but was temporarily sick; while the fourth was Capt. Hugh Elles, then a Staff College student and later first commandant of the Tank Corps. He was untrained and wild, but full of enthusiasm to see the fighting at close range, so that headquarters rarely saw him.

Edmonds may have been slightly unlucky with this quartet and perhaps over-censorious in retrospective old age, but the disadvantages of hastily improvised staffs were evident in all the formations of the B.E.F. Allenby, for example, as Inspector-General of Cavalry in peacetime and commander of the 1st Cavalry Division on the outbreak of war, had not a single permanent staff officer attached to him. As Wavell remarked in his biography of Allenby, limitation of staffs is an even more dangerous economy than limitation of peace establishments: 'the starved body can more quickly and easily be recuperated than the starved brain'. Allenby's Chief Staff Officer, Col. John Vaughan, who came straight from the Cavalry School, was 'a well-known horseman, who had perhaps been more occupied with equitation than with staff work in the years immediately preceding the war'. His most valuable acquisition was probably Col. George Barrow, 'whom he met in the passages of the War Office and annexed as his principal Intelligence Officer'. As the Cavalry Division advanced to the Franco-Belgian border with the purpose of discovering the extent of the German right wing and its strength, Barrow displayed a piece of initiative worthy of a Staff College instructor. He and another staff officer took over the railway telephone at Mons and spent all day and half the night ringing every place in Belgium not known for certain to be in German hands. Replies were usually helpful in pin-pointing the enemy's progress, while a German voice or failure to make contact showed that the enemy had already arrived. This information, which Allenby at once forwarded to G.H.Q. showed that the German right wing extended much farther west than had been suspected. But G.H.Q. refused to accept this unorthodox method of intelligence gathering and sent a pompous reply to the effect that 'only mounted troops supported by Jägers are in your immediate neighbourhood'.[15] Allenby suffered more than the infantry division commanders from the improvisation of his headquarters staff because his four brigades had been widely-scattered in peacetime. They had developed strong individual *esprit de corps* but had little sense of allegience to the division.

After being detained in England to guard against a possible German invasion, the 4th Division disembarked at Le Havre early on 23 August and the next day detrained about fifty miles south-west of Mons, just in time to provide a rearguard for II Corps in its retreat to Le Cateau. Their maps were of poor quality, Henry Wilson's characteristically flippant description of the general situation proved inaccurate, and worst of all, the 'Division' consisted only of infantry and artillery: the cavalry squadron, engineers, cyclists, medical units and signal company were mysteriously detained. Since the last-named unit comprised dispatch riders (motor-cycle, bicycle and horse), the telephone cable and instruments, the divisional flag and lanterns, message register, etc., the Division was virtually crippled, yet Sir John French asked Snow if he could cover about seven miles of frontage. French and Murray

struck Edmonds as vague not only as to the enemy's where-
abouts but also as to their own Corps boundaries and reinforcements.[16]

The staff work that lay behind the smooth mobilization of the
Expeditionary Force, its shipment to France and rapid advance
to Mons, where it fought on 23 August to the surprise and
discomfiture of the German right wing, was little short of
brilliant. G.H.Q., however, where the Sub Chief of Staff,
Henry Wilson's, views were dominant, was slow to shed its
preconceptions and grasp the true situation. Wilson was so
reluctant to discard his pre-war assumption that the Germans
would not advance in strength north of the river Meuse, that he
persuaded French and Murray to prepare for an attack north-
eastwards from Mons on 24 August. This would almost certainly have led to the annihilation of II Corps and supporting
units by von Kluck's greatly superior First Army. Fortunately,
Joffre informed French that he (French) was opposed by
two and a half German corps (and even that was a considerable
underestimation), and also that Lanrezac's Fifth Army on the
British right was retreating. The B.E.F. therefore fell back on 24
and 25 August and in doing so I and II Corps became separated
by the Forest of Mormal. G.H.Q. continued to misread the
situation in believing that II Corps had suffered much heavier
losses than it actually had and also that I Corps was being
seriously attacked at Landrécies. Smith-Dorrien, commanding
II Corps, was being so closely harassed by his pursuers that he
determined, contrary to G.H.Q.'s orders, to stand at bay at Le
Cateau on 26 August. There was a panic at G.H.Q. on receipt
of this information, and Murray, already suffering from
exhaustion, fainted. Henry Wilson, normally the embodiment
of the most optimistic view at G.H.Q., gloomily noted in his
Diary 'This will lead to disaster, or ought to'. He spoke to Smith-
Dorrien on the telephone at about 6.30 a.m. on the 26th and
the latter said he was fully confident and hopeful of giving the
enemy a smashing blow and slipping away before he could
recover. Wilson commented 'Good luck to you. Yours is the
first cheerful voice I have heard these three days.'[17]

For Lt B. L. Montgomery, of the Royal Warwickshire

Regiment (part of the 10th Brigade, 4th Division), Le Cateau was his first experience of war. In the early morning of 26 August his battalion was bivouacked in cornfields near the village of Haucourt after a long night march.

> One battalion was forward on a hill, covering the remainder of the brigade in the valley behind; we could see the soldiers having breakfast, their rifles being piled. That battalion was suddenly surprised by the Germans and fire opened on it at short range; it withdrew rapidly down the hill towards us, in great disorder.
> Our battalion was deployed in two lines; my company and one other were forward, with the remaining two companies out of sight some hundred yards to the rear. The C.O. galloped up to us forward companies and shouted to us to attack the enemy on the forward hill at once. This was the only order; there was no reconnaissance, no plan, no covering fire. We rushed up the hill, came under heavy fire, my Company Commander was wounded and there were many casualties. Nobody knew what to do, so we returned to the original position from which we had begun to attack. If this was real war it struck me as most curious and did not seem to make any sense against the background of what I had been reading.
> The subsequent days were very unpleasant ... the two forward companies which had made the attack I have just mentioned received no further orders; we were left behind when the retreat began and for three days we marched between the German cavalry screen and their main columns following behind, moving mostly by night and hiding by day.[18]

Montgomery later learned that his Commanding Officer had been cashiered for his conduct during the retreat. He joined the French Foreign Legion and recovered his honour.

Despite having both flanks more or less in the air and being outnumbered by more than two-to-one II Corps, aided by the 4th Division and the Cavalry Division, superbly justified Smith-Dorrien's confidence. After fighting all day the British withdrew practically without interference, and though the casualties were heavy they enabled the whole B.E.F. to continue its retreat through the remaining days of August. When 4th Division began its retreat at dusk and in drizzle on 26 August, Col. Edmonds rode forward to gather stragglers and found such an uncanny silence over the battlefield that he thought for a moment that his men must all have been killed or captured. In fact both sides had fought themselves to a standstill and the British columns were retiring quietly but in good heart. The Division halted from midnight until 4.0 a.m. and then continued its retreat; not until 1 September did a small force of German Cavalry catch up with their rearguard.

G.H.Q.s contribution to the fighting on 26 August seems to have been confined to issuing a number of pessimistic orders checking the advance of reinforcements to II Corps. It also fled twenty-five miles from St Quentin to Noyon without leaving cable communication with II Corps or notifying Smith-Dorrien of the change of address. Consequently, on the evening of 26 August he had to motor back in search of them to report the outcome of the action.

On the evening of 1 September G.H.Q. departed in such unseemly haste from Dammartin that the Adjutant-General was inadvertently left behind in his office. Col. Seely arrived later in the evening 'to find a deserted chateau with dinner laid, and the only human representatives of G.H.Q. a few imperturbable lorry drivers trying to start some over-loaded lorries. Seely asked them where was G.H.Q. and got the sardonic reply, "Bunked! Grind her up again, Bill!" '[19]

When every allowance has been made for the muddle and confusion which enveloped the British retreat from Mons, the flood of contradictory information and the disheartening sight of utterly exhausted troops, and the strained relations with the French, it can nevertheless hardly be disputed that Sir John French and some of the senior members of his staff were guilty of taking counsel of their fears and of exaggerating their own predicament while underestimating the enemy's difficulties. As John Terraine has aptly written: 'It has to be said that G.H.Q. was, at this stage, in the agonies of a mental defeat that far surpassed anything suffered by the Army itself.'[20] Le Cateau continued to be regarded as a heavy defeat; it was falsely believed, for example, that the 5th Division had lost nearly all its guns, and that the Cavalry Division had been virtually destroyed. Col. Huguet, the temperamentally pessimistic French liaison officer at G.H.Q., made matters worse by his incredibly despairing reports to Joffre. Thus he described the 3rd and 5th Divisions as 'nothing more than disorganized bands, incapable of offering the smallest resistance', and went so far as to state that 'Conditions are such that for the moment the British Army no longer exists'.[21] Sir John French came close to sharing this widely exaggerated view, for at the end of August he proposed to pull the B.E.F. right out of the battle to rest and reorganize, an impossible suggestion on political grounds, which was quashed by a personal visit from Kitchener on 1 September.

According to Edmonds, Robertson had warned French at a war game in 1913 that if he went to war with his present Operations Staff he was as good as beaten. French ignored the advice and G.H.Q. certainly appears to have been an unhappy institution – due to a mixture of incompetence and personal squabbles – during the opening months of the war. French, very like Buller in South Africa, got his chance to command too late in life. He was essentially a brave fighting general who proved to be out of his professional depths in the conditions of 1914. Under the strain of retreat his volatile Irish temperament fluctuated wildly between excessive optimism and blank despair. He could not speak or understand French and early on got at cross-purposes with his sarcastic neighbour, Lanrezac. His limitations might have been offset by a physically robust and professionally competent Chief-of-Staff but instead he was saddled with Sir Archibald Murray whose intellectual qualifications were dubious and whose health was certainly not up to the inevitable nervous strain of active service. French made Murray's unhappy position intolerable by relying increasingly on the Sub-Chief-of-Staff, Henry Wilson, who at least had the advantage of enjoying cordial relations with the French. Wilson was in fact the key figure at G.H.Q. during 1914, and since this period of his career, like many others, is enveloped in controversy, it is worth examining his performance from different angles.

As mentioned earlier, Henry Wilson had an incurably eccentric and facetious manner of speech and he even adopted this style in some of his written orders. To his friends and admirers – who were numerous – this was just 'Henri's' way of keeping a sense of proportion or of jollying up less ebullient natures. To his critics such infuriating levity in serious matters was inexcusable. Among the latter was Col. (later Brig.-Gen. Sir James) Edmonds who in 1914 viewed Wilson's activities first from the 4th Division and – after his nervous breakdown early in September – from G.H.Q. Edmonds instances the alarmist pencilled note which Snow received on 28 August when 4th Division had reached the Somme: 'Dear Snowball, Throw overboard all your impedimenta and trot along as fast as you can. Henry.' This unnecessarily panicky instruction was later repeated in more official language and was drastically modified in practice by both Corps Commanders.

On the other hand, several witnesses confirm that Wilson was the one senior officer at G.H.Q. who always kept a cheerful manner, no matter how depressing the circumstances. Sir Nevil Macready, at the time Adjutant-General at G.H.Q., describes an incident at Noyon during the retreat:

A long, dark room – a school I think – had been commandeered as the Headquarters office, each of us having a table or two round the walls. Murray, who for the last five days had been severely taxed day and night with a crushing weight of anxiety and practically no sleep, was sitting at a table looking over messages from the front when he suddenly dropped forward in a dead faint. Our Headquarter medical officer, Maj. Cummins, with some Staff officers, carried him to a bench and applied restoratives, while Henry Wilson walked slowly up and down the long room with that comical, whimsical expression on his face habitual to him, clapping his hands softly together to keep time as he chanted in a low tone, 'We shall never get there; we shall never get there.' As he passed me, I said: 'Where, Henri?' and he chanted on:

'To the sea, to the sea, to the sea.' It was just his way to keep up everybody's spirits, some of the younger members of the Staff not always remembering the golden rule of appearing cheerful under any and every turn of circumstance.[22]

It is easy to imagine how such behaviour, however well-intentioned, would grate on the nerves of someone not disposed to admire him.

From the vantage point of I Corps headquarters where he was appointed G.S.O. (Intelligence), Col John Charteris was increasingly critical of Wilson's handling of information at G.H.Q. Charteris at first found his job – of divining the strength and intention of the Germans opposite him – 'rather like making bricks without straw, for there is no organization or system for collecting and collating the few scraps of information we can get ourselves, and we are not told much by G.H.Q.'. In Haig's opinion, French relied entirely upon Wilson and the latter was full of preconceived and incorrect ideas; Macdonogh, the Chief of the Intelligence section at G.H.Q., was first class but could not make himself felt against Wilson. Col Seely, M.P. (until March 1914 Secretary of State for War and now attached to G.H.Q.), confirmed Charteris's suspicions that 'there is a good deal of friction at G.H.Q. and that French will not listen to his Intelligence people'. On 1 November Charteris noted in his Diary that French had at last lost faith in Wilson and begun to listen to his Intelligence. This was not entirely true, for French very much wanted Wilson to succeed Murray as Chief of the General Staff at the end of 1914. In any case, Wilson's own Diary provides ample evidence that he did indeed cling to his illusions – such as believing that the war would be speedily decided in favour of the Allies. On 13 September, for example, Wilson recorded after a meeting with the French Chief of Staff, 'Berthelot asked me when I thought we should cross into Germany, and I replied that, unless we made some serious blunder we ought to be at Elsenborn in 4 weeks. He thought 3 weeks . . .'

The flow of information from G.H.Q. to I Corps continued to be meagre so when, in mid-December, French told Haig he proposed to ask for Wilson as Murray's successor, Haig strongly opposed on the grounds that Wilson 'seemed always to have subordinated the interests of the British Army to those of the French Army'. Haig declined the post of C.G.S. for himself and pressed for Robertson, who enjoyed, he felt, the complete confidence of the Army. French actually promised Wilson that he would resign if the latter did not get the appointment but Kitchener and Asquith remained adamantly opposed, the latter on the grounds of Wilson's political intriguing over the Ulster question. In January 1915 Robertson became Chief of the General Staff at G.H.Q. and Wilson was relegated to the congenial duty of liaison with the French. All but one of the Operations Section at G.H.Q. were also removed but Sir John French survived for another year, thanks largely to the intercession of Joffre who told the British Government that he was satisfied with Sir John's cooperation and was content to work with him.[23]

Robertson's first step as Chief of the General Staff was to open up the bottleneck in staff work that had occurred under Wilson. Of the two branches of the General Staff, Operations and Intelligence, the former had come to regard the latter as its own particular handmaid. The whole range of staff responsibility, including intelligence, had tended to filter through the Operations Branch to the Chief-of-Staff and finally to the Commander-in-Chief. Robertson decided to form three branches: Operations, Intelligence and General Staff duties (i.e., training and all other duties not included in the other two branches). The head of each branch was made personally responsible to Robertson but was also expected to keep in close touch with his two colleagues. Col. E. Perceval, who had served on the Directing Staff under Robertson at Camberley, was put in charge of Staff Duties, and when he left to command a division in July 1915, was replaced by another of Robertson's trusted Camberley instructors, Col. R. Whigham. Yet another of Robertson's Staff College assistants, Col. F. B. Maurice, became head of the Operations branch, Macdonogh remaining head of Intelligence. Maurice, like his father (an outstanding member of the 'Wolseley Ring'), was exceptionally talented:

He was particularly well read in military history, had a thorough grasp of the principles of strategy and tactics, and, what was more to the point, held sound views regarding their practical application. He could express himself temperately and clearly both verbally and on paper, and he devoted every spare minute of the day and night to thinking out how best to beat the formidable enemy in front of us.[24]

Most of the junior officers in the three branches were also selected from the ablest Staff College students of Robertson's period as Commandant, and in his autobiography he paid tribute to their efficiency and loyalty.

Writing in 1921, Robertson challenged the popular view that life at G.H.Q. was one of ease and indolence. As a rule, he pointed out, the staff were kept hard at work, either in their offices or at the front from early morning till ten o'clock or later at night. They also bore heavy responsibilities and had to be prepared to initiate orders in an emergency, orders which could set off a chain of events involving perhaps the loss of thousands of lives. Staff Officers who overworked at their desks until they collapsed were of little use; Robertson set an example to his staff in taking daily exercise.[25] He also did his best to ensure that G.H.Q. staff officers should maintain friendly relations with commanders and staffs at the front.[26] In the long run these hopes were disappointed and 'the staff' acquired an unenviable reputation for arrogant behaviour, luxurious living and ignorance of front-line conditions.

As the trench lines became stronger and deeper and the Armies grew into vast communities resembling modern conurbations, it became increasingly difficult for the senior commanders to keep in touch with conditions at the front. But in the autumn of 1914 this reason – or excuse – could not be made and it was common knowledge that some senior officers were guilty of keeping well to the rear. Haig and others were very critical of the French on this score; practically no French general and very few staff officers were ever seen to go forward to visit the troops in the front line. Ironically, Charteris, who was later to be criticized for this very failing, thought that

G.H.Q. was little better: few of their staff officers came forward even as far as Corps H.Q. But it is interesting to note that, as a Corps Commander, Haig appeared to Charteris to court danger too much by constantly going to exposed positions on horseback. He also confirmed Barrow's view that the most reckless of the generals was the commander of 7th Division:

> The most active of the divisional G.O.C.s in the way of going forward and sending his Staff forward is my old Staff College Commandant at Quetta, Tommy Capper. I saw him this week, and he said – and I think he meant it – 'No good officer has a right to be alive during a fight like this.' Certainly he takes as much – and more – risk as any of his own men, and his Staff follow his example. There is a story (probably quite untrue) that he came into the Staff Mess one day and said, 'What! nobody on the Staff wounded today; that won't do!' and forthwith sent everyone available up to the first-line trenches on some mission or other. It sounds rather brutal – but it's not unwise. It heartens the men and regimental officers enormously to see Staff officers, though the Staff officers can do very little to help them.[27]

So many staff officers were killed or wounded in the opening months of the war, including Colonel 'Johnny' Gough V.C. (who was killed while saying goodbye to his battalion before leaving to command a division), that it is patently erroneous to think that staff appointments were particularly safe billets at that period.

When plans badly miscarry in war or the fighting troops' living conditions are particularly primitive, angry and envious aspersions are likely to be cast at the Staff. The First World War offered ample scope for criticism on both grounds, and because the war remained static for nearly four years the contrast between the misery of front-line conditions and the comparatively civilized ones a few miles to the rear was uniquely sharp.

Some criticisms of the Staff were evidently based on an emotional need to find a scapegoat for such terrible losses as occurred on the first day of the Somme campaign – nearly

15. Commander and Chief of Staff.

Left: Field Marshal Earl Haig, Commander-in-Chief of the British Armies in France 1915–18. As a Staff College student (1896–7) Haig was dour and industrious, but Colonel Henderson allegedly predicted that he would one day be Commander-in-Chief.

Right: Brig.-Gen. L. E. Kiggell (Commandant 1913–14). A highly educated soldier but a doctrinaire; described by an irreverent student as 'a dyspeptic, gloomy and doleful man'. Haig's Chief of Staff during the Passchendaele offensive of 1917.

16. 'The First V.C. of the European War'. Capt. Francis Grenfell (*right foreground*), 9th Lancers, leading a charge on the German guns at Audregnies on 24 August 1914, the first of two gallant actions on that day for which he was awarded the V.C.

60,000 British casualties – but others were based on objective, professional observation. Thus the sternly professional Gen. Jack of the Scottish Rifles noted in his diary on 12 June 1916:

> While the battle storm blows up in front we have to ride out a gale of paper at our backs. There are sheaves of orders, amendments, counter-orders, returns and reports to be dealt with. But, by the Grace of God, we may be able to overcome all our enemies, the Germans in front, the Staff in rear. If writing can win a campaign our foes may soon be at our mercy.[28]

Godwin-Austen cites an anonymous trench versifier who encapsulates the popular critical view, though far less savagely than the war poets such as Siegfried Sassoon:

> (If I were fierce and bald and short of breath,
> I'd live with scarlet Majors at the Base,
> And speed glum heroes up the line to death . . .)

> 'Good gracious uncle, what is That
> With red and gold upon his hat?
> Such lofty brow and haughty face,
> Such easy, condescending grace,
> Surely belong to no one save
> The very, very, very Brave!'

> 'Ah! well, my boy, they cannot show
> Their courage, for they seldom go
> To places that are dangerous
> – They stay behind and think for us.

> Theirs are the brains that guide the sword,
> Plan and control – and, 'pon my word,
> I think, when all is said and done,
> Their life's a very pleasant one!

> They drive about in handsome cars,
> And sit for simply hours and hours
> In chateaux round by St Omer
> Evolving little Ruses de Guerre.

M

> Now and again, if things are slack,
> They organize a large attack,
> And watch the battle from a hill,
> Some miles away – or farther still;
> They see what fighting there has been
> Quite clearly – on the tape machine.'[29]

Field-Marshal Montgomery is a valuable witness both because of his varied first-hand experience – he began the war as a platoon commander and ended it (aged thirty-one) as the chief staff officer of a Division – and because later he was conspicuously successful himself in bridging the gulf between the higher commanders and the troops. He notes that there was very little contact between the generals and the soldiers in the First World War:

> I went through the whole war on the Western Front, except during the period I was in England after being wounded; I never once saw the British Commander-in-Chief, neither French nor Haig, and only twice did I see an Army Commander.
>
> The higher staffs were out of touch with the regimental officers and with the troops. The former lived in comfort, which became greater as the distance of their headquarters behind the lines increased. There was no harm in this provided there was touch and sympathy between the staff and the troops. This was often lacking. At most large headquarters in back areas the doctrine seemed to me to be that the troops existed for the benefit of the staff. My war experience led me to believe that the staff must be the servants of the troops, and that a good staff officer must serve his commander and the troops but himself be anonymous.
>
> The frightful casualties appalled me. The so-called 'good fighting generals' of the war appeared to me to be those who had a complete disregard for human life . . . I remember a leave period spent in London. I went to a music hall one night and the big joke of the evening was when a comedian asked the question: 'If bread is the staff of life, what is the life of the staff?'

He then gave the answer: 'One big loaf'.

There was tremendous applause, in which I joined. In fact, the staff worked very hard. But the incident made me think seriously, and from my own experiences I knew something was wrong.[30]

Two comments may be made on this quotation: Montgomery's experiences on the Staff relates to the latter half of the war by when the pre-war band of p.s.c.s had suffered heavy losses, and many of the survivors had been posted to other theatres; and his immediate decision after the war was to get to the Staff College where, by study and reflection, he hoped to find the remedy for this and other shortcomings.

The severest critic of the Staff was not a soldier at all but a knowledgeable and respected newspaper correspondent, Sir Philip Gibbs. Gibbs's rather bitter strictures are significant because not only was he a best-selling author, who captured the atmosphere of the war and delineated the generals as well as any observer, but also because his most scathing passages have frequently been borrowed by other critics. In *Realities of War*, first published in 1920, he denounces not just the Staff but the influence of the Staff College in particular:

> Our Staff College has been hopelessly inefficient in its system of training, if I am justified in forming such an opinion from specimens produced by it, who had the brains of canaries and the manners of Potsdam. There was also a close corporation among the officers of the Regular Army, so that they took the lion's share of Staff appointments, thus keeping out brilliant young men of the New Armies, whose brain power, to say the least of it, was on a higher level than that of the Sandhurst standard.

A few pages later he shows a little more generosity but is still sweeping in his indictment:

> ... I find extenuating circumstances even in remembrance of the high stupidities, the narrow imagination, the deep impregnable, intolerant ignorance of Staff College men who, with their red tape and their general orders, were the

inquisitors and torturers of the New Armies. *Tout comprendre c'est tout pardonner.* They were moulded in an old system, and could not change their *cliché.*[31]

Viewed in the perspective of his penetrating chapter entitled 'Observers and Commanders', Gibbs's tirade against the Staff College is hard to understand. His pen-portrait of the British high command could hardly be bettered and its accuracy, as to physical appearances, can easily be verified from photographs:

> Physically, many of our generals were curiously alike. They were men turned fifty, with square jaws, tanned ruddy faces, searching rather stern grey eyes, closely cropped hair growing white, with a little white moustache neatly trimmed on the upper lip.
> Mentally they had similar qualities. They had unfailing physical courage – though courage is not put to the test much in modern generalship, which, above the rank of brigadier, works far from the actual line of battle, unless it 'slips' in the wrong direction. They were stern disciplinarians, and tested the quality of troops by their smartness in saluting and on parade, which did not account for the fighting merit of the Australians. Most of them were Conservative by political tradition and hereditary instinct, and conservative also in military ideas and methods. They distrusted the 'brilliant' fellow, and were inclined to think him unsafe; and they were not quick to allow young men to gain high command at the expense of their grey hair and experience. They were industrious, able, conscientious men, never sparing themselves long hours of work for a life of ease, and because they were willing to sacrifice their own lives, if need be, for their country's sake, they demanded equal willingness of sacrifice from every officer and man under their authority, having no mercy whatever for the slacker or the weakling.

He goes on to argue that, with the possible exception of Foch, there was not one general with charisma: the ability to inspire huge bodies of men with exalted enthusiasm, devotion and faith. In the British Army the lack of a commander with a real gift of speech (except perhaps for Sir Ian Hamilton who never served on the Western Front) was also a serious drawback. Haig possessed many fine qualities as Commander-in-Chief but was too shy and reserved to make any dramatic gesture to troops before his officers. Moreover, as Gibbs justly points out, the conditions during the greater part of his period of command virtually ruled out daring strategy on the Western Front.

In a siege war of flesh and blood against fortress positions where immense casualties could hardly be justified in terms of tiny gains of ground, it was not surprising that there should occur a passionate revolt against the generalship and staff work which directed these 'sacrificial actions'.

> This sense of bitterness became intense, to the point of fury, so that a young staff officer, in his red tabs, with a jaunty manner, was like a red flag to a bull among battalion officers and men, and they desired his death exceedingly . . .

He admitted, however, that some of this hatred for the Staff was unjust; that even the jaunty young staff officer with red tabs and polished boots was often an efficient soldier who had proved his courage in the early days of the war and was now only doing his duty, albeit with an exaggerated sense of his own importance. Sir John Burnett-Stuart and Sir Nevil Macready both make the point that many officers at G.H.Q. persistently volunteered for active service, but were often too valuable to be spared. Gibbs went on to pay a high tribute to the industry, efficiency and devotion to duty of many of the staff officers at Divisional, Corps and Army Headquarters.[32]

Three additional points need to be made about Gibbs's strictures on the evil influence of the Staff College, apart from the obvious caveat that a few of the leading generals, including Sir John French and Sir Ian Hamilton, had never been to Camberley. His strongest point – and it applies to the Regular Army as a whole and not just to p.s.c.s – is that the senior generals displayed a 'trade union mentality' and fairly successfully resisted the promotion of able young amateur officers from the New Armies to important staff and command appointments. The evidence that these 'unprofessional' officers possessed a superior quality – what Gibbs calls 'the business mind' – is drawn almost entirely from the Dominions' forces: Sir John Monash, the brilliant commander of the Australian Corps, had been a civil engineer, while Sir Arthur Currie, the Canadian Corps Commander (the youngest on the Western Front at forty-three), had been an estate agent. There is almost certainly some truth in Gibbs's assertion, that the regular officer corps was too cliquish and that the ablest officers from civil professions would have introduced a spirit of freshness and greater willingness to experiment. There are at least two grounds for scepticism however: we cannot be sure that Currie, Monash and their juniors would have done any better than the regular officers had they been given Haig's position,[33] or Army commands; and it is far from clear why the New Army officers should receive all the credit for improvements in some aspects of staff work which, according to Gibbs, occurred towards the end of the war.

Gibbs undermines his own case as to the alleged influence of the Staff College when he admits that by the time static, trench warfare set in 'the British Regular Army had withered away'. In March 1915 a lieutenant-colonel told him that he was 1 out of 150 regular officers still serving with their battalions, 'That is to say, there are 150 of us left in the fighting lines out of 1,500'. These figures were not necessarily precise but the Staff College casualties are. Excluding Quetta p.s.c.s, many of whom served in France, the Camberley list shows that 51 were killed in 1914 alone and a further 34 in 1915. Out of 447 officers in the Army List of August 1914 who were p.s.c.s of Camberley or Quetta, 219 or 49·2 per cent were killed or died of wounds during the war.[34] As with the regimental officers, these losses included a high proportion of the bravest and ablest men such as Lt-Col E. F. Calthrop, Maj.-Gen. Sir Thompson Capper, Brig.-Gen. John Gough, Lt-Col A. Grant-Duff, Lt-Col B. P. Lefroy (who was a distant relative of Sir J. H. Lefroy, and to whose pre-war guidance Field-Marshal Montgomery pays tribute in his *Memoirs*), and Maj.-Gen. S. H. Lomax (whom Charteris regarded as the best divisional commander in 1914). The consequence, as Edmonds pointed out, was that many officers not recommended for commands or staff employment, some even passed over for promotion, received appointments – and failed to make good.

> Without any training, or after a short course in one branch, young officers were posted to the staff and their generals had to make the best of them. Several divisional commanders told me in 1918 that they had to do their own staff work, and then go round to the infantry brigadiers to tell them what to do – and Haig told me that he had sent home more than a hundred brigadiers, but that he was forced to leave certain corps and divisional commanders in their appointments because he could not be sure of securing better ones.[35]

Thirdly, Gibbs exempts from criticism and indeed takes as a model the staff work of the Second Army in the last years of the war. He thus describes the Second Army's Chief-of-Staff (whose name he mis-spells):

> A thin, nervous, highly-strung man, with extreme simplicity of manner and a clarity of intelligence, he impressed me as a brain of the highest temper and quality in Staff work. His memory for detail was like a card-index system, yet his mind was not clogged with detail, but saw the wood as well as the trees, and the whole broad sweep of the problem which confronted him. There was something fascinating as well as terrible in his exposition of a battle that he was planning. For the first time, in his presence and over his maps, I saw that, after all, there was such a thing as the science of war, and that it was not always a fetish of elementary ideas raised to the nth degree of pomposity, as I had been led to believe by contact with other generals and staff officers. Here at least was a man who dealt with it as a scientific business, according to the methods of science . . .[36]

But the Chief-of-Staff, Sir C. H. 'Tim' Harington, was a p.s.c., as was also his G.S.O. 1 (Operations) Lt-Col W. Robertson R.E., and of course the Army Commander, Sir Herbert Plumer. If Camberley is to be blamed for its failures it is only

fair to give it some of the credit for the widely-praised efficiency of the Second Army.

Previous chapters have shown how the education provided
by the Staff College gradually became less pedantic and more
practical, particularly after the salutary experience of the
South African War. Moreover, as the College gained in prestige,
a greater proportion of the ablest officers competed for entry
and the standard of the directing staff similarly improved.
With the formation of a General Staff and the shift in British
foreign policy towards hostility to Germany and friendship
with France, the Staff College acquired a distinct sense of
purpose. Under the direction of Henry Wilson and his successors
Camberley became the main supplier of General Staff Officers
and a centre for the promulgation of a Continental Strategy.
For these reasons it may be called, with little exaggeration, 'the
Brain of the Army'.

Apart from a tendency to undervalue brilliant but eccentric
or unorthodox young officers, the Staff College's greatest
defect was simply that it was too small to produce more than a
fraction of the trained staff officers required when the Army
expanded beyond its original six divisions.

In these circumstances, and particularly considering the
serious losses of trained staff officers in 1914, it is difficult to
arrive at an overall judgement on the quality of staff work even
in the first year of the war. Miscalculation as to the likely
duration of the war, coupled with injudicious appointments
for some of the most important posts resulted in serious weaknesses in the opening phase of operations. The General Staff
at the War Office lacked the personalities and prestige to
impress any collective strategic policy on Lord Kitchener,
while G.H.Q. in France was handicapped by a vacillating
Commander-in-Chief, an unsuitable Chief-of-Staff and a clever
Sub-Chief who did not command general respect. The Adjutant-General's and Quartermaster-General's branches seem
to have performed more efficiently than the General Staff,
but then the latter had the disadvantage of being more directly
dependent on the decisions and cooperation of a more

powerful ally, desperately defending his own soil and disinclined to worry about the tender susceptibilities of his very junior partner.

It would be all too easy, by describing in detail the British offensives of 1915, namely the failure at Neuve Chapelle and the disasters at Aubers Ridge and Loos, to suggest that staff work in corps, divisions and brigades was criminally incompetent.[37] It was certainly the case that the senior commanders – down to corps level – were deplorably slow in adapting tactical doctrine and the cumbersome chain of command to the novel problems of trench warfare in which the machine gun was dominant. At Loos especially two New Army divisions were sacrificed by a series of errors reminiscent of the Charge of the Light Brigade or Colenso. Allowing, however, for the acute shortage of high-explosive shells, the inexperience of commanders and staffs in handling such large forces and – above all – the total unpreparedness for static trench warfare, a case can still be made that British staff work in the field during 1914 and 1915 was comparatively good; good in comparison, that is, with British staff work in South Africa and with that of some other armies in the First World War. Gen. Sir George Barrow, for example, relates that when, as chief staff officer of a Corps in 1915, he called upon his French opposite number to arrange to take over part of the French line, the latter explained that he was far too busy to visit the trenches and delegated the task to a junior, who told Barrow that the Chief-of-Staff had never once seen the trenches and did not consider it part of his job. In fact, the French divisional and corps staffs devoted their whole time to paperwork, leaving control of the fighting front entirely in the hands of commanding officers.[38] Moreover, the British Official History, in its 'Retrospect' on the fighting of 1914, and with particular reference to Ypres, remarks that 'Whilst on the Allied side the generalship and staff work largely contributed to the victory, on the enemy side it was generalship and staff work that failed'.[39]

By the severe standards of the elder von Moltke, the efforts of the Staff College to educate the 'brains' of the British Army and to create a 'School of Thought' might be accounted a failure. Its annual output of p.s.c.s was barely sufficient for the Army's needs in peacetime; the conservatism and overt hostility of some of the regiments had taken a long time to break down; and the General Staff itself was a young and tender plant lacking prestige (compared with the German General Staff) and self-confidence. Whether its ablest products, such as Henry Wilson, Robertson, Macdonogh and Harington, were quite in the same class as their French and German counterparts depends to a large extent, no doubt, on the nationality of the critic. But viewed in the longer British perspective of staff education and staff work in the era of the Crimean or even the South African War, then the history of the first sixty years of the Staff College can surely be regarded as the gradual triumph of a professional attitude to the higher education of military leaders, both in command and staff positions. If it is conceded that the B.E.F. of 1914 was better organized, better trained and better led than its predecessors of 1854 and 1899, a good deal of the credit must go to the influence of Camberley and Quetta.

In January 1919 Field-Marshal Sir Douglas Haig set up a Committee under the Presidency of Lt-Gen. Sir Walter Braithwaite to report on staff organization during the war. Even allowing that its brief was staff organization rather than staff work in the field, and that its members were all senior staff officers, the Committee's complacent conclusion should not be entirely discounted. After examining eighty-four officers in all the Armies it reported:

The outstanding feature of the evidence brought before us has been the success of the work of the Staff throughout the war. This points indubitably to the soundness of the general principles on which the Staff is organized and was trained before the war. The key-note of our system of staff organization is the unity of the Staff although its work is divided into three main branches [i.e., General, Adjutant-General and Quartermaster-General] . . . This spirit not only governed the teaching at both Staff Colleges for some years before the

war but animated the Staff of every formation in the original
Expeditionary Force . . .

The Committee recommended that even more attention should
be paid to administrative staff duties at the Staff College.
It also pointed out that some of the irritation of regimental
officers towards the Staff was due to the distinctive uniform
being worn by officers not entitled to do so, such as
aides-de-camp. Its shortest paragraph was probably the most
important; namely that 'The Staff Colleges should in future be
kept open during war'.[40]

Possibly the Staff College's greatest contribution to efficient
leadership in the First World War – so often emphasized in this
study – was simply that it provided a meeting place – enhanced
by tradition and by the realization that they were the *élite* – for
generations of able and dedicated officers. Sir William Robertson, ex-ranker, p.s.c., Commandant of Camberley and Chief of
the Imperial General Staff, certainly endorsed this view, for he
wrote that, 'in his humble belief it was beyond contradiction
that the mutual agreement and excellent comradeship established between Staff College graduates during the twenty years
previous to 1914 were of inestimable value to the Empire
throughout the Great War'.[41]

Tam Marte quam Minerva

CHAPTER 10. NOTES

1 On 12 August 1914, for example, Lt.-Gen. Sir A. Murray told Esher he thought the war would last three months if everything went well and perhaps eight if it did not. Beyond that it would be impossible to feed the armies in the field and the financial strain would be more than Europe could bear. Esher, *Journals and Letters*, III, p. 177. Haig was an exception among the generals in believing the war would be protracted.

2 Edmond's unpublished Memoirs, 'August 1914', pp. 1–2. C. E. Callwell, *The Life of Sir Stanley Maude* (London, 1920), pp. 115–16.

3 Esher, *op. cit.*, III, pp. 178–9. *Cf.* Sir Nevil Macready, *Annals of an Active Life* (London, 1924), I, p. 135. Macready wrote that Douglas 'probably knew more about the organization of the Army than any living soldier', but this hardly qualified him for the post of C.I.G.S.

4 Sir P. Magnus, *Kitchener: Portrait of an Imperialist* (London, 1958), p. 288. Hankey was 'much amused at K.'s method of working the General Staff: He sits at the head of the table and talks a lot, and bludgeons everyone into agreeing with him . . . Then K. proceeds to dictate, and it is dished up next day as a Memo. by the General Staff.' Stephen Roskill, *Hankey: Man of Secrets* (London, 1970), Vol. I, p. 219.

5 Brig.-Gen. J. Charteris, *At G.H.Q.* (London, 1931), pp. 11–12. For Grierson's rotund appearance before the war see the frontispiece in D. S. MacDiarmid's, *Life of Lieut-General Sir James Grierson*.

6 File on 'Divisional Training before 1914', *Edmonds Papers*.

7 On Kitchener's personality and working habits see Sir Ian Hamilton's frank appraisal in *The Commander* (London, 1957), pp. 98–132.

8 Sir Ian Hamilton, *Gallipoli Diary* (London, 1920), *passim*. Esher, *op. cit.*, III, p. 180.

9 Godwin-Austen, *op. cit.*, p. 263, erroneously implies that Kiggell at once went to France as Chief of the General Staff. In fact he became Director of Military Training at the War Office, and was only Haig's second choice as Chief-of-Staff in December 1916.

10 For Fuller's amusing account of his experience at Southampton see his *Memoirs of an Unconventional Soldier*, pp. 31–44.

11 Godwin-Austen, *op. cit.*, pp. 263–5, 270.

12 Sir Archibald Wavell, *Allenby: a Study in Greatness* (London 1940), p. 109.

13 For details see Appendix V.

14 The following paragraphs are based largely on the unpublished memoirs of Sir James Edmonds.

15 Wavell, *op. cit.*, pp. 118–19, 128–30. Barrow, *op. cit.*, pp. 143–4.

16 As an illustration of the incompetence of French and Murray, Edmonds relates that when Smith-Dorrien took over command of II Corps on Grierson's death he received an order beginning 'The B.E.F.

will give battle on the line of the Condé (Mons) Canal'. When he inquired whether this meant he was to attack or remain on the defensive, French, after a whispered conference with Murray, said, 'You do as you are ordered, and don't ask questions!' Edmonds, 'August 1914', p. 15.

17 *Ibid.* See also Callwell, *Sir Henry Wilson*, I, pp. 168–9 and J. Terraine, *Mons* (London, 1960), pp. 73–4, 106–7.
18 Field-Marshal the Viscount Montgomery of Alamein, *Memoirs* (London [Fontana paperback edition], 1960), pp. 32–3.
19 Macready, *op. cit.*, I, p. 207; Charteris, *op. cit.*, p. 28.
20 J. Terraine, *op. cit.*, p. 164.
21 Huguet, quoted by J. Terraine, *op. cit.*, p. 163.
22 Macready, *op. cit.*, pp. 205–6. For Esher's somewhat idealized description of Wilson's bearing during the retreat see Callwell, *Sir Henry Wilson*, I, p. 170.
23 *Ibid.*, I, p. 177. Charteris, *op. cit.*, pp. 28, 50, 55, 64–5. Sir T. Montgomery-Cunninghame, *Dusty Measure* (London, 1939), p. 187. Wilson, *Diary*, December 1914, *passim*. Edmonds, 'August 1914', p. 4.
24 Robertson, *op. cit.*, pp. 220–1.
25 For Charteris's fairly exacting routine see *At G.H.Q.*, p. 74. Charteris noted as early as February 1915 that 'In many ways D.H. [Haig] is his own Chief-of-Staff. He knows so much more about fighting than any of the Staff, and he goes round the divisions and brigades so constantly that his Chief-of-Staff has little to do, except to see that things go smoothly.'
26 Robertson, *op. cit.*, pp. 225–6.
27 Charteris, *op. cit.*, p. 58.
28 J. Terraine (ed.), *General Jack's Diary 1914–1918* (London, 1964), p. 139. John Terraine has drawn my attention to the fact that identical sentiments were expressed about the German Staff; see Capt. Rudolf Binding, *A Fatalist at War* (London, 1929), p. 233.
29 Sassoon is quoted in *General Jack's Diary*, p. 131. Godwin-Austen, *op. cit.*, pp. 266–7, quoting from *Owl Pie*, the Staff College magazine.
30 Montgomery, *op. cit.*, pp. 35–6.
31 P. Gibbs, *Realities of War* (London, 1920), pp. 46–7, 57.
32 *Ibid.*, pp. 33–5. Sir John Burnett-Stuart, unpublished *Memoirs*, p. 77. Macready, *op. cit.*, I, pp. 215–16.
33 It is worth pointing out that Monash was not a critic of G.H.Q. and never thought of himself as a possible alternative to Haig. See John Terraine, 'Monash: Australian Commander', *History Today*, January 1966.
34 *R.U.S.I. Journal*, 'Army Notes', p. 884, November 1938. I am indebted to John Terraine for this reference.
35 Edmonds to Brig. C. N. Barclay, 7 April 1950 (copy) concerning the latter's article 'British Generalship' in the *Army Quarterly*, January 1950; *Edmonds Papers*. It is too seldom remembered that for the greater part of the First World War G.H.Q. was responsible for every aspect of the welfare – quite apart from the operational side – of a population

larger than any single unit of control in England except London. For
a good brief description see Charteris, *At G.H.Q.*, pp. 208–10.

36 Gibbs, *op. cit.*, pp. 47–50. For a reasoned defence of the Staff College
see 'The Staff College after the War' by R. H. B. in *The Army Quarterly*,
October 1923.

37 For a brilliant indictment of British tactics in the First World War see
G. C. Wynne, *If Germany Attacks* (London, 1940), especially pp. 19–79.

38 Barrow, *op. cit.*, p. 158. The author, however, thought the French were
sensible on two issues; namely their willingness to yield tactically
unimportant ground and their more calculating attitude towards
raids.

39 J. E. Edmonds, *Military Operations, France and Belgium, 1914* (London,
1925), Vol. II, p. 464. However, the Germans adapted their defensive
tactics more quickly to the prevailing conditions on the Western
Front; see Capt. G. C. Wynne's careful analysis in *If Germany
Attacks, passim.*

40 Committee on Staff Organisation, 1919. W.O. 32/5153.

41 Robertson, *op. cit.*, p. 90.

Principal events affecting army organisation and the Staff College

1852   Death of the Duke of Wellington.

1854–6   Crimean War.

1855   Duties of Secretary at War and Secretary of State for War and the Colonies combined in one official to whom the military head of the Army is responsible.

1856–95   Duke of Cambridge (cousin of Queen Victoria) Commander-in-Chief.

1858   Creation of a Staff College to supersede the old Senior Department of the Royal Military College approved.

1862   Staff College at Camberley opened.

1868–74   Edward Cardwell Secretary of State for War.
            War Office Act (1870), Horse Guards transferred to the War Office building and Commander-in-Chief's subordination to Secretary of State for War confirmed.
            Army Enlistment Act (1870) introduced 'short service' system of six years in the Colours and six in the reserve.
            Council of Military Education replaced by a Director-General (1870).
            Purchase of Commissions abolished by Royal Warrant (1871).
            Linking of Infantry battalions (to provide for the garrisoning of India and the Colonies), and Home units localized in brigade districts (1872–3).

1881–2   Hugh Childers completes 'Cardwell system' by abolishing old regimental numbers and forming double-battalion regiments.

1887–8   Edward Stanhope carries out first major War Office reorganization since 1870. Office of Surveyor-General abolished and all principal departments of Army business, except finance and manufacture, united under authority of Commander-in-Chief.

1891   Stanhope Memorandum lays down requirements from the Army.
Expeditionary Force for the Continent of two Corps and a Cavalry division given fifth and lowest priority.

1895   Duke of Cambridge succeeded as Commander-in-Chief by Viscount Wolseley, but the former's responsibilities (since 1887) were henceforth to be shared among five officers all directly responsible to the Secretary of State; namely, Commander-in-Chief, Adjutant-General, Quartermaster-General, Inspector-General of Fortifications and Inspector-General of Ordnance.

1899–1902 South African War.

1900   Lord Roberts succeeded Wolseley as Commander-in-Chief.

1902   Committee of Imperial Defence established.

1904   Following Reports of the Esher Committee: Office of Commander-in-Chief abolished; Army Council established; General Staff established.

1904–7   Staff College for the Indian Army established, temporarily at Deolali and then permanently at Quetta.

1905–12   Viscount Haldane Secretary of State for War. Expeditionary Force formed of six infantry divisions and a cavalry division.
Auxiliary forces reformed into the Territorial Force.

Principal official inquiries concerning officer education and the Staff College 1854-1914

1 Select Committee on the Royal Military College Sandhurst, P.P. 317, 1855.

2 Committee on the Training of Officers for the Scientific Corps, 1857.

3 Report of the Commissioners on the Purchase and Sale of Commissions in the Army, 1857.

4 Royal Commission on Military Education, c47, 1868–70.

5 Committee on the Working of the Staff College, C.P.0774, 1880.

6 Committee on Military Educational Establishments, A117, 1888.

7 Royal Commission on the Professional Administration of the Naval and Military Departments (Hartington), c5979, 1890.

8 Committee on Military Education (Akers-Douglas), Cd 982, 1902.

9 Royal Commission on the War in South Africa (Elgin), c1789, 1903.

10 War Office (Reconstitution) Committee (Esher), Cd 1932, 1968, 1904.

11 Committee on General Staff Appointments (Hutchinson), A935, 1904.

Manuscript Sources

A. *Army Museums Ogilby Trust*
   1. Roberts Papers
   2. Spenser Wilkinson Papers

B. *British Museum*
   Napier Mss

C. Burnett-Stuart Memoirs (Mrs Evelyn Arthur)

D. *Centre for Military Archives, King's College, London*
   1. Edmond Papers
   2. Howell Papers
   3. Kiggell Papers
   4. Robertson Papers

E. Ellison Papers (Mrs J. Spencer-Ellison)

F. Esher Papers (Lionel Brett, Viscount Esher)

G *Public Record Office*
   1. Kitchener Papers
   2. Roberts Papers
   3. Cabinet Papers
   4. War Office Papers

H. *National Army Museum*
   Hunter-Weston Papers

I. *National Library of Scotland*
   1. Blackwood Papers
   2. Haig Papers

J. *Staff College*
   Wavell's Staff College Essay

K. *Scottish Record Office*
   Dalhousie Muniments

L. Wilson Diaries (Maj. Cyril Wilson)

M. *Windsor Castle*
   Royal Archives

Commandants of the Staff College
1858-1914

Lt-Col P. L. MacDougall	5 Feb. 1858 – 27 Sept. 61
Col. W. C. E. Napier	28 Sept. 61 – 31 Dec. 64
Col. T. E. Lacy	1 Jan. 65 – 30 June 70
Col. E. B. Hamley C.B.	1 July 70 – 31 Dec. 77
Maj.-Gen. Sir A. Alison, Bart K.C.B.	1 Jan. 78 – 30 April 78
Col. C. O. Creagh-Osborne C.B.	11 May 78 – 20 Dec. 85
Col. E. H. Clive	21 Dec. 85 – 11 Aug. 88
Brig.-Gen. C. F. Clery C.B.	12 Aug. 88 – 11 Aug. 93
Col. H. J. Hildyard	18 Aug. 93 – 24 Feb. 98
Col. H. S. G. Miles M.V.O.	1 Mar. 98 – 8 Oct. 99 10 Nov. 1900 – 4 Dec. 03
Maj.-Gen. W. F. M. Hutchinson	9 Oct. 1899 – 19 April 1900
Brig.-Gen. Sir H. S. Rawlinson, Bart	5 Dec. 1903 – 31 Dec. 06
Brig.-Gen. H. H. Wilson C.B. D.S.O.	1 Jan. 07 – 31 July 10
Maj.-Gen. W. R. Robertson C.V.O., C.B., D.S.O.	1 Aug. 10 – 8 Oct. 13
Brig.-Gen. L. E. Kiggell C.B.	9 Oct. 13 – 5 Aug 14

The Staff College connections of the Commanders and Chief Staff Officers of the B.E.F. August-November 1914

G.H.Q.   Commander-in-Chief – Field-Marshal Sir John French
Chief of the General Staff – Lt-Gen. Sir A. Murray, p.s.c.
Sub-Chief – Maj.-Gen. Sir H. H. Wilson, p.s.c. and C.C.
G.S.O.1 (Operations) – Col. G. M. Harper, p.s.c. and D.S.-C
G.S.O.1 (Intelligence)–Col. G. M. W. Macdonogh, p.s.c.
Adjutant-General–Maj.-Gen. Sir C. F. N. Macready
Quartermaster-General – Maj.-Gen. Sir W. R. Robertson, p.s.c. and C.C.

I CORPS   C-in-C Lt-Gen. Sir D. Haig, p.s.c.
Brigadier-General G.S. – Brig.-Gen. J. E. Gough, p.s.c., D.S.-C.

1st Division
Maj.-Gen. S. H. Lomax, p.s.c.
G.S.O.1. – Colonel R. Fanshawe, p.s.c.

2nd Division
Maj.-Gen. C. C. Monro, p.s.c.
G.S.O.1. – Col. The Hon. F. Gordon, p.s.c.

II CORPS   C-in-C Lt.-Gen. Sir J. M. Grierson, p.s.c. (died 17 August)
Gen. Sir H. L. Smith-Dorrien, p.s.c.
Brigadier-General G.S. – Brig.-Gen. G. T. Forestier-Walker, p.s.c.

3rd Division
Maj.-Gen. H. I. W. Hamilton, p.s.c. (killed 14 October)
Maj.-Gen. C. J. Mackenzie, p.s.c.
G.S.O.1. – Col. F. R. R. Boileau, p.s.c. and D.S.-Q (died of wounds 26 August)

5th Division
Maj.-Gen. Sir C. Fergusson
Maj.-Gen. T. L. N. Morland, p.s.c. (succeeded to command 18 October)
G.S.O.1. – Lt-Col C. F. Romer, p.s.c.

III CORPS   Maj.-Gen. W. P. Pulteney.
Brigadier-General G.S. – Brig.-Gen. J. P. Du Cane, p.s.c. and D.S.-C.

4th Division
Maj.-Gen. T. D'O Snow, p.s.c.
Maj.-Gen. H. F. M. Wilson (succeeded to command in September)
G.S.O.1. – Col. J. E. Edmonds, p.s.c. and D.S.-.C.

6th Division
Maj.-Gen. J L. Keir, p.s.c.
G.S.O.1. – Col. W. T. Furse, p.s.c. and D.S.-C.

IV CORPS   C-in-C Lt-Gen. Sir H. S. Rawlinson, p.s.c. and C.C.
Brigadier-General G. S. – Brig-Gen. R. A. K. Montgomery, p.s.c. and D.S.-Q.

7th Division
Maj.-Gen. T. Capper, p.s.c., D.S.-C., C.Q.
G.S.O.1. – Col. H. M. de F. Montgomery, p.s.c. and D.S.-C.

8th Division
Maj.-Gen. F. J. Davies, p.s.c.
G.S.O.1. – Col. W. H. Anderson, p.s.c. and D.S.-C.

340 *The Victorian Army and the Staff College*

CAVALRY   C-in-C Lt-Gen. E. H. H. Allenby, p.s.c.
CORPS
           Colonel G.S. – Brig.-Gen. G. de S. Barrow, p.s.c.
           and D.S.-C.
           1st Cavalry Division
           Maj.-Gen. H. de Lisle, p.s.c.
           G.S.O.1. – Lt-Col A. F. Home, p.s.c. and D.S.-C.
           2nd Cavalry Division
           Maj.-Gen. H. de la P. Gough, p.s.c. and D.S.-C.
           G.S.O.1. – Lt-Col W. H. Greenly, p.s.c. and D.S.-C.

           3rd Cavalry Division
           Maj.-Gen. The Hon. J. H. G. Byng, p.s.c.
           G.S.O.1. – Lt-Col M. F. Gage, p.s.c.

ROYAL   Commander-Brig.-Gen. Sir D. Henderson, p.s.c.
FLYING   G.S.O.1. – Lt-Col F. H. Sykes, p.s.c.
CORPS

Index